ACCESS UNLOCKED

Designing and Deploying Standalone Database Programs

By

Dr. Hesham Mohamed Elsherif

ABOUT THE AUTHOR

Dr. Hesham Mohamed Elsherif stands at the forefront of library management and research, boasting an impressive 22-year tenure in the field. Holding dual doctoral degrees, one in Management and Organizational Leadership and the other in Information Systems and Technology, Dr. Elsherif brings a unique blend of knowledge to any intellectual endeavor. An expert in Empirical research methodology, Dr. Elsherif specializes particularly in the Qualitative approach and Action research. This specialization has not only strengthened his research endeavors but has also allowed him to contribute invaluable insights and advancements in these areas.

Over the years, Dr. Elsherif has made significant contributions to the academic world not only as a professional researcher but also as an Adjunct Professor. This multifaceted role in the educational landscape has further solidified his reputation as a thought leader and pioneer. Furthermore, Dr. Elsherif's expertise isn't confined to one region. He has served as a consultant to numerous educational institutions on an international scale, sharing best practices, innovative strategies, and his deep insights into the ever-evolving realms of management and technology.

Combining a passion for education with an unparalleled depth of knowledge, Dr. Elsherif continues to inspire, educate, and lead in both the library and academic communities.

PREFACE

Welcome to **Access Unlocked: Designing and Deploying Standalone Database Programs**. This book is crafted for individuals who aspire to harness the robust capabilities of Microsoft Access to create effective, efficient, and powerful database applications. Whether you are a student, a business professional, an educator, or a hobbyist with a keen interest in database management, this guide is designed to take you from the basics of database theory to the advanced skills needed to build and deploy standalone database programs.

Why Microsoft Access? Despite the plethora of database technologies available today, Microsoft Access remains a preferred choice for developing desktop database applications quickly and with considerable ease. Its integration with other Microsoft products, combined with its powerful data handling capabilities, makes it an indispensable tool for many small to medium-sized businesses and individuals.

This book begins by introducing you to the fundamental concepts of databases. You will learn not just how to use Microsoft Access, but why and when to use it. Our journey will start with the basics of creating tables, queries, forms, and reports—each a crucial component in any database system.

As we advance, you will discover the power of automation in Access through Macros and the versatility offered by Visual Basic for Applications (VBA). These tools not only streamline operations but also open up a world of customization and enhanced functionality.

One of the unique aspects of this book is its focus on turning an Access database into a standalone executable. This is a critical skill for anyone looking to distribute their software professionally. We cover the entire process from the initial design and development stages to the final steps of compiling, packaging, and deploying the application as a fully functional, independent software product.

We believe in learning by doing, which is why **Access Unlocked** is packed with step-by-step tutorials, practical examples, and real-world case studies. These elements are aimed at providing a hands-on experience, enhancing your learning, and giving you the confidence to apply your knowledge to real-world scenarios.

Lastly, no book on software is complete without addressing maintenance and troubleshooting. Maintaining an application is as crucial as building it. Thus, we provide you with strategies to update, troubleshoot, and refine your database applications post-deployment.

We are excited to guide you through this comprehensive journey into the world of Microsoft Access. By the end of this book, you will not only be adept at using Access to its full potential but also be capable of creating an independent database application ready for real-world deployment.

Enjoy your journey with Access, and may this book unlock the door to many successful database projects.

Happy learning!

Dr. Hesham Mohamed Elsherif

WHO SHOULD READ THIS BOOK?

Access Unlocked: Designing and Deploying Standalone Database Programs is designed for a diverse audience with varying levels of experience and expertise in database management. Whether you are looking to deepen your understanding of database applications or aiming to develop professional-grade standalone database programs using Microsoft Access, this book has something to offer. Here are some of the groups who will find this book particularly beneficial:

Students and Educators: If you are a student learning about databases or an educator teaching database concepts, this book provides a solid foundation in database theory with practical applications using Microsoft Access. It's an excellent resource for coursework, self-study, or supplemental teaching material.

Business Professionals: For professionals in small to medium-sized businesses, this book demonstrates how to leverage Microsoft Access to create customized database solutions that streamline operations, from managing inventory to tracking customer interactions. The sections on automating tasks and compiling databases into executable programs are particularly useful for businesses looking to enhance efficiency and data security.

IT Professionals and Developers: IT experts who need to develop quick, scalable, and powerful database applications will find the advanced topics covered, such as using VBA for enhanced functionality and compiling Access databases into standalone applications, invaluable for expanding their skill set and delivering robust database solutions.

Hobbyists and DIY Enthusiasts: If you have an interest in database management or are a DIY enthusiast who likes to tackle projects that require organizing large amounts of data efficiently, this book will guide you through creating sophisticated databases and even show you how to package them for use by others.

Freelancers and Consultants: Freelance database developers or consultants who provide tailored database solutions for clients will benefit from the detailed explanations on custom database creation, automation, and deployment as standalone applications. This book helps in refining your skills to deliver more professional and polished products.

Non-Profit Organizations: Staff members or volunteers in non-profits who manage donor databases, event registrations, and other data-driven tasks will find the step-by-step guides to database design, report generation, and data analysis extremely helpful. The ability to create a standalone application means that even those without extensive IT support can maintain and operate their databases with ease.

Entrepreneurs: Entrepreneurs in the early stages of setting up their business will discover that custom databases can be a low-cost solution for managing business data effectively. This book covers how to start from scratch and build up to a fully functional application that can support the growing needs of a new business.

In summary, **Access Unlocked** serves as a comprehensive guide for anyone interested in mastering Microsoft Access to create and manage powerful databases and develop them into independent applications. Whether you are a novice looking to get started or a seasoned professional aiming to enhance your database skills, this book provides the knowledge and tools necessary to succeed in your endeavors.

WHY THIS BOOK IS ESSENTIAL READING?

Access Unlocked: Designing and Deploying Standalone Database Programs is an indispensable resource for anyone looking to master Microsoft Access and leverage its full potential to create robust, standalone database applications. Here's why this book stands out as essential reading:

1. **Comprehensive Coverage**: From the basics of database concepts and Access fundamentals to advanced features like VBA programming and executable compilation, this book covers every aspect of Microsoft Access. It is structured to provide a step-by-step guide to building and deploying complete database applications, making it a one-stop resource for all your Access needs.

2. **Practical, Hands-On Approach**: Unlike many other texts that focus on theoretical aspects of database management, this book emphasizes practical application. It is filled with real-world examples, detailed tutorials, and step-by-step projects that not only teach you how to use the various features of Access but also how to apply them effectively to solve real problems.

3. **Focus on Standalone Applications**: One of the unique aspects of this book is its detailed guidance on turning Access databases into standalone programs. This is a critical skill for anyone looking to distribute their application commercially or within an organization as it allows for easier deployment and a more professional presentation of your work.

4. **Tools for Professional Development**: For IT professionals and developers, this book serves as an invaluable tool to enhance your skills in database management, application development, and software deployment. It provides you with the knowledge to create scalable, efficient, and secure database solutions that can significantly impact your professional capabilities and career.

5. **Accessibility for Beginners**: Even if you are new to Microsoft Access or database management, this book starts with the foundational concepts and gradually builds up to more complex topics. The clear explanations and logical progression make it accessible to beginners while still being valuable to more experienced users.

6. **Resource for Educators and Students**: This book is an excellent academic resource, offering a structured way to learn or teach database management.

The comprehensive coverage from theory to practical application makes it ideal for use in classroom settings, providing students with the skills they need to succeed in the workforce.

7. **Latest Features and Best Practices**: It incorporates the latest features of Microsoft Access and current best practices in database design and development. This ensures that readers are learning the most up-to-date information and can apply the latest technologies and methodologies in their projects.

8. **Problem-Solving Guide**: The inclusion of troubleshooting tips, common pitfalls, and maintenance strategies makes this book not just about building database systems but also about maintaining and improving them over time.

In essence, **Access Unlocked: Designing and Deploying Standalone Database Programs** is more than just a textbook; it is a comprehensive guide that prepares you to use Microsoft Access professionally and efficiently. Whether you aim to improve your productivity, enhance your career opportunities, or simply gain a new skill, this book provides the guidance, tools, and insights necessary to achieve those goals.

Happy Reading and Learning

Dr. Hesham Mohamed Elsherif

Table of Contents

Part I: Introduction to Microsoft Access

Chapter 1 - Getting Started with Microsoft Access

Microsoft Access is a powerful database management system (DBMS) from Microsoft that combines the relational Microsoft Jet Database Engine with a graphical user interface and software-development tools. It is part of the Microsoft Office suite of applications, included in the Professional and higher editions or sold separately. Access is fundamentally designed to be user-friendly and accessible to both novice users and professional developers alike.

Key Features of Microsoft Access

<u>User-Friendly Interface:</u>

Access is renowned for its intuitive interface that helps users navigate through complex database functions without needing extensive database knowledge. The interface includes easy-to-use menus, forms, and templates.

Components of the User-Friendly Interface

- **Ribbon Toolbar**: Microsoft Access employs the Ribbon, a panel at the top of the window where almost all the tools needed to manage database elements are grouped into tabs. Each tab on the Ribbon relates to specific types of activities, such as creating tables, designing forms, writing queries, or setting up reports. This organization helps users quickly find the commands necessary to perform their tasks without digging through complex menus.

- **Navigation Pane**: The Navigation Pane on the left side of the Access window provides a hierarchical view of all database objects, such as tables, queries, forms, and reports. Users can easily view, open, and organize these objects, facilitating quick access and management of their database components.

- **Database Document Tab**: Each open object, like a table or form, appears in its tab within the main Access window. This tabbed document interface allows users to easily switch between multiple database objects, making multitasking more straightforward and less cluttered.

- **Property Sheet**: Access provides a Property Sheet for detailed settings of database objects, which is crucial when designing forms or reports. It allows users to fine-tune properties like size, format, and behavior, offering a high degree of control in a user-friendly manner.

- **Wizards and Templates**: For users who are new to database design or those who want to speed up development, Access offers various wizards and pre-designed templates. These tools guide users through the steps necessary to create tables, queries, forms, and reports, ensuring that even the least experienced users can produce functional database components efficiently.

Benefits of the User-Friendly Interface

- **Ease of Use**: The intuitive layout reduces the learning curve for new users while providing powerful tools that are readily accessible for advanced tasks. This balance between simplicity and power is a cornerstone of Access's design philosophy.

- **Efficiency**: With tools like the Ribbon and Property Sheet, users can perform tasks more quickly than if they had to navigate complex menus or memorize command line instructions. This efficiency is critical for users who need to manage large amounts of data or develop databases under tight deadlines.

- **Customizability**: Despite its simplicity, the interface of Access is highly customizable. Users can rearrange the Ribbon, customize the Navigation Pane, and modify the workspace to suit their workflow, enhancing personal productivity and comfort.

- **Error Reduction**: The guided processes provided by wizards and the structured approach of the Ribbon help prevent common errors that might occur in database design and data entry. This is especially beneficial for those new to databases, reducing frustrations and the need for frequent corrections.

The user-friendly interface of Microsoft Access is not just about ease of use; it is about making powerful database management tools accessible and manageable. By demystifying complex database tasks, Access enables users across a broad spectrum of backgrounds to create, manage, and deploy effective database solutions with confidence and precision. This foundation of user-friendly design is what sets Access apart and empowers users to leverage database technology effectively, irrespective of their technical expertise.

Database Structures:

It supports various types of database structures including tables, relationships, queries, forms, and reports. Each component plays a crucial role in database management and manipulation.

Core Database Structures in Microsoft Access

- **Tables**: Tables are the foundation of any database. In Access, tables are where data is stored. Each table is organized into rows and columns, with each row representing a unique record and each column representing a field in the record. Access allows for detailed data type specifications for each field, ensuring data integrity and proper organization.

- **Relationships**: Effective database design often involves more than one table, with relationships between tables defining how data in one table relates to data in another. Access supports various types of relationships, including one-to-one, one-to-many, and many-to-many. Setting up these relationships correctly is vital for accurate data analysis and integrity, and Access provides a graphical interface for defining and managing these relationships.

- **Queries**: Queries are tools that allow users to retrieve specific data from tables based on defined criteria. They can be simple, pulling data from a single table, or complex, involving multiple tables and advanced logic. Queries not only serve to extract data but also to perform calculations, create summaries, and update or delete data based on specific conditions.

- **Forms**: Forms in Access are designed for data entry and data display. They provide a user-friendly interface that guides users in adding new records, modifying existing data, or browsing through data. Forms can be highly customized and can include features such as drop-down lists, checkboxes, and command buttons, enhancing the data entry process and reducing errors.

- **Reports**: Reports are used to organize and present data in a format suitable for printing or sharing. Like forms, reports in Access can be highly customized to include various layouts, calculated fields, graphics, and charts. They are essential for summarizing data insights and making informed decisions based on the data stored in the database.

Benefits of Robust Database Structures

- **Data Integrity**: Properly designed tables and relationships help maintain data accuracy and consistency, which is critical for reliable databases. Access's tools ensure that data is entered correctly and relationships are maintained, which reduces redundancy and errors.

- **Efficiency in Data Handling**: Efficient queries can drastically reduce the time required to find and manipulate data. Access allows users to design queries that optimize these tasks, improving the overall performance of the database.

- **User Interaction and Accessibility**: Forms and reports enhance the accessibility of the database, allowing users to interact with the data without needing to understand complex database queries or table structures. This makes Access databases particularly useful in environments where users may not be technically skilled but need to work with data regularly.

- **Scalability and Flexibility**: Access databases are designed to grow with your needs. You can start with simple structures and gradually add more tables, complex relationships, and sophisticated queries as your database requirements expand.

The database structures provided by Microsoft Access form the backbone of efficient and effective database management. Whether you are managing small datasets for personal projects or larger databases for business applications, understanding and utilizing these structures correctly is key to leveraging the full potential of Access. By mastering these elements, users can ensure that their databases are not only functional but also powerful tools for data analysis and decision-making.

Data Management:

Data management is a core function of any database system, and Microsoft Access excels at providing comprehensive tools and features to manage data efficiently. In Access, data management involves organizing, storing, securing, and retrieving data as needed. These capabilities are critical for ensuring that data is accessible, accurate, and up-to-date. Access provides powerful tools for data entry, data search, and data retrieval. Users can sort and filter data, while queries allow for specific data operations and analytics.

Data Entry and Storage

- **Data Entry Interfaces**: Microsoft Access allows users to input data directly into tables or more commonly through forms. Forms can be designed to ensure that data is entered correctly, applying validation rules and formats that reduce errors. For example, a form could be set up to reject entries that do not meet specific criteria or to guide users through the data entry process in a step-by-step manner.

- **Table Design**: The design of tables in Access is fundamental to efficient data storage. Users can define data types for each field, such as text, number, date/time, and more, which helps maintain data integrity. Additionally, users can set primary keys to uniquely identify each record, and index fields to improve search and retrieval speeds.

Querying and Retrieving Data

- **Powerful Querying Tools**: Access provides a robust query design tool that allows users to construct queries visually or through SQL directly. These queries enable users to filter, sort, and aggregate data according to specific needs. For instance, a user could create a query to find all clients in a particular region with sales above a certain threshold.

- **Custom Queries**: Beyond basic queries, Access supports the creation of parameter queries, crosstab queries, and action queries, which allow for a broad range of data manipulation tasks. These include updating records in bulk, deleting records based on specific conditions, and transforming rows into columns for complex data summaries.

Data Integrity and Security

- **Data Integrity Features**: Access supports data integrity through features like validation rules, integrity constraints (such as foreign keys), and required fields. These features ensure that the data entered into the database is accurate and consistent, preventing errors that could occur from incorrect data entries.

- **Security Measures**: Microsoft Access includes security measures to protect sensitive data. Users can set database passwords, encrypt database files, and manage user-level security in older versions or through server-based configurations when Access databases are linked to more robust SQL Server instances. This ensures that sensitive information remains protected from unauthorized access.

Data Analysis and Reporting

- **Integrated Reporting Tools**: Access excels at turning data into actionable insights through its integrated reporting tools. Users can easily create comprehensive reports to visualize data through charts, tables, and other graphical elements. Reports can be customized extensively to suit the needs of different users, providing a powerful tool for data analysis.

- **Data Export**: For further analysis or sharing outside of Access, data can be exported to a variety of formats including Excel, PDF, XML, and others. This flexibility allows data from Access to be used across different platforms and applications, enhancing its utility.

Data management in Microsoft Access is both deep and broad, providing users with a variety of tools to input, store, query, and analyze data efficiently. The system's design caters to both novice users and advanced developers, making it an ideal choice for a wide range of applications. By leveraging the data management features of Access, users can ensure their databases are not only functional but also robust and secure, capable of supporting complex data-driven decisions in business and organizational contexts.

Reporting Tools:

Reporting is a crucial aspect of database management, providing the ability to analyze, summarize, and present data in a structured and understandable format. Microsoft Access excels in its reporting capabilities, offering a variety of tools and features that enable users to create detailed and visually appealing reports. These reports can help in decision-making processes, showcasing trends, and communicating information clearly and efficiently to stakeholders. One of Access's strengths is its comprehensive reporting features that allow users to create meaningful reports and dashboards that can include calculations, graphics, and other sophisticated formatting.

Core Reporting Features in Microsoft Access

- **Report Wizard**: For users who are new to creating reports or who prefer guided assistance, the Report Wizard in Access is an invaluable tool. It walks users through the process of selecting data, defining groupings, choosing layouts, and selecting styles. This wizard is particularly helpful for creating straightforward reports quickly and efficiently.

- **Report Design View**: More advanced users can opt for the Report Design View, which provides granular control over every aspect of the report's appearance and functionality. Here, users can manually place and format text boxes, labels, controls, and other elements. This view is ideal for creating customized reports that require specific layouts or interactive elements.

- **Sorting and Grouping**: Access reports can be configured to sort and group data based on various fields. This feature is crucial for organizing information in a way that enhances readability and insight, such as grouping sales data by region or summarizing expenses by department within a specific time frame.

- **Expression Builder**: This tool allows users to create complex expressions that calculate and display data dynamically within reports. For example, a report could include calculated fields that display total sales, average prices, or percentage changes. Expression Builder supports creating formulas similar to those used in spreadsheet applications, providing a powerful way to manipulate data directly in reports.

Enhanced Reporting Functionality

- **Charts and Graphs**: To make reports more visually engaging, Access allows the integration of charts and graphs directly into reports. Users can select from bar charts, pie charts, line graphs, and more to represent data graphically, which is essential for illustrating trends and comparisons at a glance.

- **Conditional Formatting**: Access reports support conditional formatting, which changes the appearance of report items based on specific conditions. This feature can highlight critical values, such as sales numbers that fall below a certain threshold or exceed expectations, making it easier to identify outliers and important trends.

- **Interactive Reports**: Access provides features for creating interactive reports where users can expand or collapse groupings, click through to detailed records, and sort columns interactively. These interactive elements make reports not just documents to view but tools to explore and analyze data further.

Reporting Integration and Sharing

- **Export Capabilities**: Reports created in Access can be exported to various formats including PDF, Excel, Word, and others, facilitating easy sharing and further analysis. This flexibility ensures that reports can be used beyond the Access environment, reaching wider audiences and being incorporated into presentations or shared as email attachments.

- **Integration with Mail Merge**: Access reports can be integrated with Microsoft Word for mail merge operations, allowing users to generate personalized letters, labels, and emails based on data stored in the database. This is particularly useful for marketing campaigns, customer communications, and any scenario requiring bulk personalized messages.

The reporting tools in Microsoft Access are designed to meet a wide range of needs, from simple summaries to complex, interactive analytical reports. By leveraging these tools, users can transform raw data into actionable insights, presenting information in a clear, professional, and meaningful manner. Whether for internal review, client presentations, or strategic planning, the reporting capabilities of Access are an essential component of effective data management and communication.

Scalability and Integration:

While Microsoft Access is often perceived as a tool suitable for small-scale applications, it is actually equipped with robust features that support both scalability and integration with other technologies. This adaptability makes it an excellent choice not only for small businesses but also as a prototyping tool for larger organizations. While Access is ideal for smaller, localized database solutions, it can also connect to larger SQL databases. Its integration with other Microsoft products, such as Excel and Outlook, allows for a seamless data management experience.

Scalability in Microsoft Access

- **Handling Large Datasets**: Access databases can support up to 2 GB of data, which includes a substantial amount of records for small to medium-sized enterprises. For databases approaching this limit, Access provides tools such as table indexing and query optimization to enhance performance and manage larger datasets efficiently.

- **Split Database Architecture**: To further improve scalability and performance, Access allows the database to be split into two separate files:

one for data (back end) and one for user interface elements (front end). This structure enables multiple users to access and work on the data simultaneously without performance degradation, which is crucial for medium-sized teams.

- **Upsizing to SQL Server**: When the data needs exceed what Access can efficiently manage, the database can be upsized to a more robust system like Microsoft SQL Server. Access includes an Upsizing Wizard that simplifies the migration of data from an Access database to SQL Server, maintaining data integrity and structure while allowing for significantly larger data capacities and improved security features.

Integration with Other Technologies

- **Data Import/Export Capabilities**: Access supports extensive data import and export capabilities, making it easy to exchange data with other applications. Users can import data from or export data to a variety of formats, including Excel, CSV, XML, and ODBC-compliant databases, which allows Access to function seamlessly within a larger ecosystem of business tools.

- **Linking External Data Sources**: Access can link to external data sources such as SQL Server, SharePoint lists, and other databases. This capability allows Access applications to integrate real-time data from various sources, enabling more comprehensive data analysis and reporting without duplicating data within the Access database itself.

- **Integration with Microsoft Office Suite**: Access integrates flawlessly with other Microsoft Office applications. For instance, data from Access can be directly used in Excel for further analysis or integrated into Word through Mail Merge to generate personalized documents. This interoperability is a significant advantage for users who rely heavily on Office tools for their daily operations.

- **Automation via VBA**: Visual Basic for Applications (VBA) provides a powerful way to automate repetitive tasks and enhance functionality in Access databases. VBA can interact not only with Access but also with other Office applications, enabling complex workflows that can automate tasks across multiple programs, such as gathering data, processing it in Access, and then preparing a presentation in PowerPoint.

The scalability and integration features of Microsoft Access make it a versatile tool that fits a wide range of business needs, from small local databases to large-scale applications that require robust data handling and multi-user access. By understanding and utilizing these features, users can maximize the effectiveness of Access as a central tool in their data management and business operations. Access's ability to start small and scale up or integrate with larger systems provides a flexible pathway for growth and adaptation, making it an invaluable asset in any data-driven environment.

Customization Through VBA:

Customization is a critical aspect of software use, allowing users to tailor applications to meet specific needs and streamline workflows. Microsoft Access provides extensive customization capabilities through Visual Basic for Applications (VBA), a powerful programming environment that enhances the functionality and usability of Access databases. Access can be customized and automated using Visual Basic for Applications (VBA), a programming language that enhances functionality with custom scripts and complex expressions.

Overview of VBA in Microsoft Access

- **What is VBA?**: Visual Basic for Applications (VBA) is an event-driven programming language provided by Microsoft that is used primarily to extend the capabilities of MS Office applications, including Access. VBA allows developers to write scripts and routines to automate repetitive tasks, perform complex calculations, and manage database interactions more efficiently.

- **Integration with Access**: In Access, VBA can be directly embedded into forms, reports, and modules. It interacts with the database through the DAO (Data Access Objects) or ADO (ActiveX Data Objects) libraries, which provide methods and properties for manipulating data and database structures.

Key Customization Capabilities of VBA

- **Event-Driven Programming**: VBA operates on an event-driven basis, meaning that code can be executed in response to specific actions or events within the database, such as clicking a button, opening a form, or updating a field. This makes it possible to create highly responsive and interactive database applications.

- **Automation of Tasks**: VBA can automate tasks such as data entry, data updates, and report generation. For example, a VBA script could automatically import data from external sources at scheduled intervals, or generate and distribute reports via email based on database queries.

- **Enhanced User Interfaces**: With VBA, developers can create custom forms and control elements that go beyond the standard designs provided by Access. This includes creating custom dialog boxes, integrating third-party controls, or modifying the user interface's behavior in sophisticated ways.

- **Complex Data Validation and Business Logic**: VBA allows for advanced data validation that is not possible through standard field properties in Access. Developers can use VBA to implement complex business logic for validating user input, calculating values dynamically, and enforcing business rules during data entry and processing.

Benefits of Using VBA in Microsoft Access

- **Increased Productivity**: By automating repetitive tasks and streamlining complex processes, VBA can significantly increase productivity. Users spend less time on routine tasks and more time on analysis and decision-making.

- **Tailored Functionality**: VBA enables the creation of customized solutions that are tailored to the specific needs of a business or project. This bespoke approach ensures that the database performs exactly as needed, enhancing efficiency and effectiveness.

- **Scalability and Flexibility**: VBA scripts can be modified and extended as business requirements change. This flexibility allows databases to evolve over time without the need for major redesigns or migrations to other platforms.

- **Integration with Other Systems**: VBA in Access can communicate with other applications via COM (Component Object Model) interfaces. This allows Access databases to integrate with other systems, pull data from or push data to other applications, and even control other Office applications like Excel and Outlook.

Customization through VBA is a powerful feature of Microsoft Access that unlocks a higher level of database functionality and responsiveness. By leveraging VBA, users can develop customized, automated, and highly efficient database solutions that are closely aligned with individual business processes and needs. Whether enhancing user interfaces, automating data management tasks, or implementing complex business rules, VBA stands as an indispensable tool in the Access user's arsenal, providing the means to achieve a more productive and tailored database environment.

Why Choose Microsoft Access?

<u>Cost-Effective</u>:

In the realm of database management systems, cost-effectiveness is a critical consideration, particularly for small to medium-sized enterprises (SMEs) and individual users. Microsoft Access stands out as a particularly cost-effective solution for several reasons, ranging from its integration within the Microsoft Office suite to its low barrier to entry in terms of both cost and learning curve. Access is a cost-effective solution for small businesses or departments within larger organizations that do not require the overhead of larger, more complex database systems.

Key Aspects of Cost-Effectiveness in Microsoft Access

- **Affordability of Licensing**: Microsoft Access is available as part of the Microsoft Office Professional suite or as a standalone application. This makes it more affordable compared to more complex database systems like SQL Server or Oracle, which can have high licensing fees and often require additional server hardware and software investments. For many small businesses and departments within larger organizations, Access provides sufficient functionality at a fraction of the cost.

- **Reduced Development Costs**: The user-friendly interface and comprehensive set of built-in tools allow users to design, implement, and manage databases without extensive programming knowledge. This reduces the need for specialized staff or costly external consultants. Businesses can leverage in-house talent to build and maintain their databases, significantly cutting down on development and maintenance costs.

- **Integration with Other Microsoft Products**: For organizations already using Microsoft products, Access seamlessly integrates with tools like Excel, Outlook, and Word. This integration facilitates a smooth workflow across applications, reducing the need for additional software purchases and allowing users to work with familiar tools, thus saving on training costs and increasing productivity.

- **No Additional Hardware Required**: Unlike more robust database systems that may require dedicated servers, Access can run efficiently on most standard business computers that support the Office suite. This eliminates the need for significant hardware investments, making Access a more accessible option for smaller businesses or those just starting out.

Benefits of Choosing Access for Cost-Effective Database Management

- **Quick Deployment**: Access allows for rapid development and deployment of database applications. Pre-built templates and intuitive design tools enable users to get databases up and running quickly, which is crucial for meeting tight deadlines and reducing time-to-market for new projects.

- **Scalability Options**: While Access is often chosen for its low initial cost and ease of use, it also offers scalability options. Databases can start small and grow in complexity as needed, and if the database needs outgrow Access, migration tools are available to upscale to more powerful systems like Microsoft SQL Server.

- **Low Total Cost of Ownership (TCO)**: The total cost of owning and operating an Access database remains low over its lifecycle. The ease of maintenance, the availability of widespread skills, and the integration with existing systems contribute to a lower TCO compared to other database platforms.

Choosing Microsoft Access for database management is a cost-effective decision that does not compromise on functionality for small to medium-sized project needs. It provides a robust set of tools that can handle complex data management tasks at a fraction of the cost of larger database systems. For businesses looking to maximize their technology budget while still gaining powerful data management capabilities, Microsoft Access proves to be an excellent choice. This balance of cost, ease of use, and integration with familiar tools makes it an attractive option for many organizations aiming to streamline their data management practices efficiently and economically.

<u>**Rapid Development**</u>:

In the fast-paced world of business and technology, the ability to develop applications quickly and efficiently is a significant advantage. Microsoft Access is designed to facilitate rapid development, making it an ideal choice for users who need to create robust database applications in a short amount of time. This capability is especially beneficial for small to medium-sized businesses, departments within larger organizations, and individual users who require database solutions without the lengthy development timelines associated with more complex systems. The ease of use and integrated development tools allow for rapid application development. This makes Access an excellent choice for developing prototype systems that can be later upscaled to more robust environments if necessary.

Features Supporting Rapid Development in Microsoft Access

- **Intuitive User Interface**: Access is equipped with a user-friendly interface that simplifies the process of database design and management. Tools like the Ribbon, Layout View, and Design View allow users to add and modify database components quickly. This ease of use reduces the time needed to train users and allows both novice and experienced users to begin creating databases immediately.

- **Templates and Wizards**: Access provides a variety of pre-built templates that cater to different business needs, such as contact management, inventory tracking, and project management. These templates include ready-made tables, forms, queries, and reports that can be used as-is or customized as needed. Additionally, wizards guide users through the steps of creating complex database elements like queries, forms, and reports, significantly speeding up the development process.

- **Drag-and-Drop Functionality**: The drag-and-drop functionality in Access enables users to build queries, forms, and reports by simply dragging fields onto the workspace. This feature not only speeds up the development process but also makes it more intuitive, as users can visually construct the components of their database without deep technical knowledge.

- **Built-In Macros and VBA**: For automation and advanced data manipulation, Access includes built-in macros that can be easily configured to automate repetitive tasks and streamline workflows. For more complex functionalities, Visual Basic for Applications (VBA) allows for the addition of custom scripts directly within the database. These tools enable rapid customization and functionality enhancement without extensive coding.

Benefits of Rapid Development with Microsoft Access

- **Faster Time-to-Market**: The rapid development capabilities of Access help organizations bring their database applications to market or into operational use much quicker. This speed can be a critical factor in project success, especially in environments where business needs are continually changing.

- **Reduced Costs**: Faster development times translate into lower project costs. By minimizing the amount of time spent on design and development, organizations can allocate resources more effectively and avoid the expenses associated with long-term development projects.

- **Agility and Flexibility**: The ability to develop applications quickly allows businesses to respond more effectively to new opportunities or changes in the market. Access supports agile development practices by making it easy to modify and adapt databases as requirements evolve.

- **Enhanced Productivity**: With Access, users can automate data entry, report generation, and other routine tasks. This automation reduces the workload on staff and frees them up to focus on more strategic activities, thereby enhancing overall productivity.

Choosing Microsoft Access for database development offers significant advantages in terms of speed and efficiency. Its tools and features support rapid application development, making it possible to meet urgent business needs without the delays associated with more complex database systems. Whether for creating quick prototypes or developing fully functional database applications, Microsoft Access provides the tools necessary to achieve results quickly, ensuring that businesses remain dynamic and competitive.

Versatile Data Handling:

Versatility in data handling is a crucial aspect for any database management system, and Microsoft Access excels in this area. It is equipped to manage a wide variety of data types and complex data structures effectively. This flexibility makes Access a valuable tool for users across different industries and with various data management needs, from simple data entry tasks to complex data analysis and reporting. Access handles a wide range of data types and comes with sufficient querying and reporting tools for various business needs, making it versatile enough for different types of data handling applications.

Features Supporting Versatile Data Handling in Microsoft Access

- **Broad Range of Data Types**: Access supports a wide array of data types, including text, numbers, dates, and binary data, among others. This allows users to tailor database fields to precisely match the nature of the data they need to store, whether it's quantitative information, descriptive text, or dates and times.

- **Complex Data Structures**: Access can efficiently manage complex data structures through its robust table design, which supports primary and foreign keys, indexes, and relationships between tables. These features ensure that data is structured in a way that supports both integrity and complex querying, which are essential for advanced data management.

- **Advanced Query Capabilities**: With its powerful query design tools, Access allows users to create both simple and complex queries to manipulate and retrieve data. Users can perform selections, aggregations, joins, and unions, as well as more sophisticated SQL operations. These queries can be designed visually or written directly in SQL, offering flexibility to both novice users and experienced developers.

- **Data Import and Export**: Access provides extensive capabilities for importing and exporting data to and from various formats, such as Excel, CSV, XML, and ODBC databases. This makes it easy to integrate Access with other systems and to migrate data between different platforms, enhancing its utility as a versatile data handling tool.

- **Linking External Data Sources**: Users can link to external data sources directly from Access, allowing them to manage data that resides in other databases or formats without duplicating it within Access. This capability is crucial for creating centralized views of data that are distributed across multiple systems.

Benefits of Versatile Data Handling with Microsoft Access

- **Adaptability**: Access's support for various data types and complex data structures means it can be adapted to the specific needs of any business or project. Whether managing customer information, financial records, or complex inventory data, Access can be configured to handle these data types effectively.

- **Efficient Data Integration**: The ability to import, export, and link data makes Access an efficient tool for integrating with other business systems. This integration capability ensures that data remains cohesive and consistent across the organization, reducing errors and enhancing decision-making.

- **Customization and Scalability**: The flexibility in query design and the ability to handle complex data structures allow Access databases to be highly customized and scaled as business needs grow. This scalability ensures that the database remains useful and effective over time, adapting to new requirements without the need for significant retooling.

- **Enhanced Data Analysis and Reporting**: The versatile data handling capabilities of Access support robust data analysis and reporting. Users can generate meaningful insights and comprehensive reports from complex data sets, which are essential for strategic planning and operational management.

The versatile data handling capabilities of Microsoft Access make it a compelling choice for a wide range of data management needs. Its ability to handle different data types and complex structures, combined with powerful querying, importing, and exporting features, provides users with the flexibility to manage data effectively in a variety of scenarios. Whether for simple database tasks or complex analytical projects, Microsoft Access offers the tools and features necessary to perform efficient and effective data management, making it a valuable asset for any user or organization.

Access as a Learning Tool:

Microsoft Access serves not only as a powerful tool for database management but also as an excellent educational resource for those new to databases or seeking to enhance their understanding of database concepts. Its intuitive design, combined with powerful features, makes it an ideal platform for learning and teaching database management, SQL, and application development. For students and newcomers to database technology, Access provides a gentle introduction to the concepts of database management, including the development of logical thinking skills related to data structure and manipulation.

Features That Enhance Learning in Microsoft Access

- **Intuitive Graphical User Interface**: Access's user-friendly interface includes drag-and-drop capabilities, wizards, and templates that help demystify database design and management. This environment makes it easier for beginners to understand database fundamentals by visually constructing tables, queries, forms, and reports.

- **Comprehensive Online Help and Tutorials**: Microsoft provides extensive documentation, online help, and tutorials specifically for Access. These resources are invaluable for learners, offering guided instructions, examples, and best practices to enhance understanding and proficiency in using Access for database projects.

- **Hands-On Learning Experience**: Access encourages a hands-on approach to learning database management. Students and new users can immediately apply theoretical knowledge by creating actual database applications. This practical experience is crucial for reinforcing learning and building confidence in using database technologies.

- **SQL Integration**: While Access automates many tasks, it also offers the opportunity to write and execute SQL queries directly. This feature allows learners to practice SQL in a real-world application context, bridging the gap between theoretical SQL learning and practical database management.

- **Scalability of Learning**: As learners grow more comfortable and proficient, Access grows with them. The platform supports increasingly complex database functionalities, including advanced queries, VBA programming, and integration with other software. This scalability makes Access suitable for both basic and advanced learning paths.

Benefits of Using Microsoft Access as a Learning Tool

- **Foundation for Database Concepts**: Access provides a solid foundation in database principles such as relational database design, normalization, and data integrity. Learning these concepts through Access equips students with the knowledge applicable to more complex database systems like SQL Server or Oracle.

- **Skill Development for the Workplace**: Proficiency in Access can translate directly into job skills, especially in environments where small to medium-sized database solutions are utilized. Understanding Access and its integration capabilities with the broader Microsoft Office suite can make learners more versatile and valuable in the job market.

- **Affordable Learning Platform**: For educational institutions and individuals on a budget, Access offers a cost-effective solution for database education. It requires minimal investment compared to more specialized database software, making it accessible for personal learning or for outfitting computer labs in schools.

- **Interactive and Engaging Learning**: The ability to create and manipulate databases interactively makes learning more engaging and less theoretical. Students can see the immediate impact of their actions in the database, providing instant feedback that is essential for effective learning.

Microsoft Access serves as a potent learning tool that introduces and enhances database management skills. Its combination of user-friendly interfaces, comprehensive learning resources, and practical, hands-on experience makes it an excellent entry point for individuals new to database concepts or those seeking to refine their database management abilities. Whether in academic settings or as a self-study tool, Access provides a robust platform for learning, making complex database principles more approachable and understandable.

Starting with Microsoft Access

To begin with Access, you will need to install the latest version, usually provided with Microsoft Office Professional or as a stand-alone application. Once installed, opening Access presents you with options to create a new database or open an existing one. Users can start from a blank database or choose from various templates tailored to specific tasks or industries, which can significantly speed up the development process.

Installing and Setting Up Microsoft Access:

Installing and setting up Microsoft Access is a straightforward process, crucial for beginning your journey in database management. Whether you're an individual looking to manage personal data, a student learning database fundamentals, or a business professional tasked with creating a departmental resource, the initial setup is your first step.

Step-by-Step Installation of Microsoft Access

1. **Purchasing Microsoft Access:**

   - Access can be purchased as part of the Microsoft Office Professional suite or as a standalone application. Visit the Microsoft Store or a licensed retailer to acquire your copy. Ensure your computer meets the system requirements for the version of Office or Access you are installing.

2. **Installing Access:**

   - If you have the Office 365 subscription, log in to your Microsoft account and navigate to the Office download section. If you're installing from a physical copy, insert the disk into your computer.

- Run the setup file and follow the on-screen instructions. For Office 365 users, select "Install Office" and then choose the apps you want to install, including Access.

- During installation, you might choose the installation directory if your system has specific requirements; otherwise, the default settings are suitable for most users.

3. **Launching Access for the First Time**:

- Once installed, open Microsoft Access from your Start menu or desktop shortcut. Upon first launch, you may be prompted to sign in with your Microsoft account, especially if you're using an Office 365 version.

- Access might also ask you to select a theme for your Office applications. Choose according to your preference.

Setting Up Your First Database

1. **Using a Template**:

- When you start Access, you'll be greeted with various database templates ranging from business contacts and inventory to project management. For instance, selecting the "Asset Tracking" template will create a database with pre-defined tables, forms, and reports suitable for tracking assets.

- Click on a template that suits your needs, and Access will prompt you to give a name to your database file and choose where to save it. After these selections, click "Create."

2. **Creating a Blank Database**:

- If you prefer to start from scratch, choose the "Blank database" option at the start screen.

- Enter a file name and select the location to save your database. Click "Create."

- Access will open with a blank table named "Table1" by default. You can begin defining fields immediately, such as **ID**, **FirstName**, **LastName**, etc., by typing in the "Click to Add" column header.

3. **Initial Configuration**:

    - **Table Setup**: In your blank table, set primary keys to ensure each record has a unique identifier. For example, you can right-click on the **ID** field column and select "Primary Key" to set it.

    - **Relationships**: If you plan on having multiple tables, go to the "Database Tools" tab and click on "Relationships" to define how tables connect with each other, such as linking **EmployeeID** in an Employees table to **ManagerID** in a Management table.

Installing and setting up Microsoft Access is a user-friendly process that paves the way for efficient and effective database management. Whether using a template or starting from a blank database, Access provides a robust platform for storing, managing, and analyzing data. The initial setup is crucial as it impacts how you interact with and utilize the database, setting the foundation for all your database activities. With Access installed and properly configured, you're ready to explore the powerful features it offers for personal, educational, or professional use.

Basic Concepts of Databases:

Introduction to Basic Database Concepts

Understanding the foundational elements of a database is essential for effectively using Microsoft Access. The core components—tables, queries, forms, and reports—each play a vital role in organizing, managing, and interpreting data.

Tables: The Building Blocks of a Database

- **Definition and Purpose**: Tables are the core storage units in a database, holding the actual data in rows (records) and columns (fields). Each field has a specific data type, such as text, number, date, or Boolean.

- **Example**: Consider a simple "Customers" table for a retail business. It might include fields like **CustomerID** (Primary Key), **FirstName**, **LastName**, **Email**, **Phone**, and **Address**. Each record in the "Customers" table represents one customer's information.

Queries: Accessing and Manipulating Data

- **Definition and Purpose**: Queries are tools used to retrieve and manipulate data from tables based on specific criteria. They can combine data from multiple tables, calculate new data, update records, and more.

- **Example**: If you want to find all customers from a particular city, you would use a query. For instance, a query on the "Customers" table could filter records where **City** equals "New York". This would list all customers living in New York, allowing further interaction like sending targeted promotions.

Forms: User Interfaces for Data Entry

- **Definition and Purpose**: Forms provide a user-friendly interface for entering, modifying, and viewing data from tables or queries. They help in managing data entry in a controlled manner, reducing errors and simplifying interactions with the data.

- **Example**: A "Customer Entry" form would include fields displayed on the screen where users can enter new customer data or update existing data. The form might include text boxes for first name and last name, a dropdown for selecting city, and buttons for submitting or canceling the data entry.

Reports: Organizing Data into Readable Formats

- **Definition and Purpose**: Reports are used to format, summarize, and present data in a structured way, often for printing or sharing. Reports can draw data from tables or queries and can include graphical elements like charts and tables.

- **Example**: A "Monthly Sales Report" could be created to show total sales by each product category for the past month. The report would pull data from a "Sales" table, possibly using a query that sums up sales figures, and display it in an easy-to-read format, complete with headings and perhaps a pie chart showing the sales distribution.

Putting It All Together

To illustrate how these components work together, consider a database designed for a bookstore:

1. **Tables**: You create tables to store data about **Books**, **Customers**, **Orders**, and **Employees**.

- **Books** might include fields like **ISBN**, **Title**, **Author**, and **Price**.

- **Customers** might include **CustomerID**, **Name**, and **ContactInfo**.

2. **Queries**: You set up queries to find specific information, such as "Books by Author" or "Orders Over $100".

3. **Forms**: You design a form for entering new books into the **Books** table, which includes fields for all the book's details and validation rules to ensure data accuracy.

4. **Reports**: You generate monthly sales reports from the **Orders** table to track which books are selling the best, formatted to highlight key figures and trends.

Understanding tables, queries, forms, and reports in Microsoft Access allows users to efficiently organize, manage, and use data. Each component serves a specific function, and together they form the integrated structure of a well-designed database. Whether you're managing customer information, tracking inventory, or compiling financial reports, these elements are fundamental to effective database management in Access.

Conclusion

This overview section of the book is designed to set the foundation for the subsequent detailed exploration of Microsoft Access's capabilities. By understanding what Access is and what it can do, you will be better prepared to dive deeper into its functionalities and start building your own database solutions effectively.

Chapter 2 - Understanding Database Theory

Introduction to Database Theory

Database theory provides the foundational principles for designing and managing databases effectively. It encompasses topics such as data models, relationships, integrity constraints, normalization, and transactions. These concepts are essential for creating databases that are efficient, reliable, and scalable.

Data Models

Definition and Purpose:

A data model is a conceptual representation of the data objects, the associations between different data objects, and the rules which govern data operations. It ensures that data is organized logically and consistently across systems. A data model is an abstract representation designed to structure, organize, and manage data systematically. It defines the relationships among different data elements and sets the rules and guidelines for how data can be stored, retrieved, and updated within a database system. The purpose of data models is to ensure that the database is structured in a way that supports both the efficient execution of tasks and the integrity of the data stored.

Key Aspects of Data Models in Database Theory

1. **Structural Framework**: Data models provide a framework that dictates the structure of the data. This includes the design of tables, the relationships between tables, and the constraints applied to these tables. The framework helps in visualizing complex data relationships and in maintaining data accuracy and consistency.

2. **Data Abstraction**: Data models facilitate a level of abstraction that hides the storage complexities from the database users and focuses on data usage and management. By abstracting the details of data storage, data models allow users to interact with the data through a simplified interface, enhancing usability and accessibility.

3. **Guidance on Data Interaction**: Data models dictate how data can be accessed and manipulated. They define the logical paths through which data flows within the system and the interactions between different data entities.

This guidance is crucial for ensuring that data manipulations are performed correctly and efficiently.

4. **Scalability and Flexibility**: Effective data models are scalable and flexible, allowing for the database to evolve as requirements change. A well-designed model accommodates growth in data volume and complexity without significant redesign, providing long-term stability and performance.

Examples of Data Models

*   **Relational Model**: The most widely used data model in database management, particularly in systems like Microsoft Access. It organizes data into tables (relations) that consist of rows (records) and columns (attributes). Each table represents a type of entity, and each row in the table represents an instance of that entity. Relationships between tables are established through foreign keys. This model is prized for its simplicity and robustness, making it ideal for transactional systems.

Example: In a library management system, a relational model could have tables like **Books**, **Authors**, and **Loans**. The **Books** table might include columns such as **BookID**, **Title**, and **AuthorID** where **AuthorID** links to the **Authors** table which includes **AuthorID** and **AuthorName**.

*   **Entity-Relationship Model (ER Model)**: This model focuses on the relationships between different entities in a database. It uses a graphical approach to design the database at the conceptual level, which helps in understanding data requirements and how different entities are interrelated.

Example: In an ER model for a school system, entities might include **Students**, **Teachers**, and **Classes**. Relationships could be defined as **Students** attend **Classes** taught by **Teachers**. This visual model helps in comprehensively understanding how student and teacher data interact through the classes they are associated with.

Understanding data models is fundamental to effective database design and operation. Whether one is using a relational database like Microsoft Access or any other DBMS, a solid grasp of data modeling concepts ensures that the database is capable of supporting the organization's data needs efficiently and reliably. Data models not only help in organizing data in a coherent and logical structure but also play a crucial role in maintaining data integrity, guiding database interactions, and ensuring the database's scalability and flexibility over time.

Relationships

Definition and Purpose:

Relationships between tables are crucial in a relational database. They define how tables connect and interact with each other. The three main types of relationships are one-to-one, one-to-many, and many-to-many. In the context of database theory, relationships refer to the logical connections between different entities (tables) within a database. These relationships help to structure how data in one table can be associated with data in another, reflecting how entities interact with each other in the real world. The purpose of defining relationships in a database is to maintain data integrity, enable efficient data retrieval, and ensure that the data is representative of real-world scenarios.

Key Aspects of Relationships in Database Management

1. **Maintaining Data Integrity**: Relationships enforce data integrity by ensuring that the database adheres to certain rules, such as referential integrity, which prevents orphaned records and maintains consistency across linked tables.

2. **Facilitating Data Retrieval**: By establishing clear relationships, databases can more efficiently retrieve related data across multiple tables. This is essential for performing complex queries that involve aggregating or comparing data from different sources.

3. **Reducing Data Redundancy**: Properly defined relationships help in normalizing the database, which reduces redundancy and improves storage efficiency. This not only saves space but also simplifies updates since data is not duplicated across multiple tables.

4. **Representing Real-World Relationships**: Relationships in a database model real-world interactions and dependencies between entities, providing a more intuitive and accurate structure for the data. This helps users and systems to better understand and predict data interactions.

Types of Relationships

- **One-to-One**: In a one-to-one relationship, each record in one table corresponds to one record in another table. This type of relationship is not very common but is useful when splitting a table for security reasons, storing data that is only occasionally applicable, or improving performance by segregating part of a table.

Example: In a human resources system, each employee (in an **Employees** table) might have a corresponding record in a **Salaries** table that contains sensitive salary information.

- **One-to-Many**: This is the most common type of relationship where a record in one table can relate to many records in another table. This relationship reflects most real-world scenarios where an entity can be associated with multiple instances of another entity.

Example: In a library system, one **Author** can write many **Books**. Here, the **Author** table has a one-to-many relationship with the **Books** table, where each author's unique identifier (AuthorID) is used as a foreign key in the **Books** table.

- **Many-to-Many**: A many-to-many relationship occurs when multiple records in one table relate to multiple records in another table. This type of relationship typically requires a third table, known as a junction table, which contains foreign keys that reference the primary keys in the related tables.

Example: In a school management system, a **Students** table and a **Classes** table have a many-to-many relationship, as students can enroll in multiple classes and each class can have multiple students. This relationship is managed through a **StudentClasses** junction table that contains the IDs from both the **Students** and **Classes** tables.

Understanding and correctly implementing relationships in databases are crucial for effective database design. These relationships not only enhance the functionality of the database by ensuring data integrity and reducing redundancy but also mirror the real-world interactions between entities, thereby making the database a more accurate and useful tool. In database systems like Microsoft Access, mastering relationships is key to exploiting the full potential of relational database capabilities, enabling complex, real-world data management tasks to be performed with ease and accuracy.

- **Example**:

  - **One-to-One**: Each record in one table corresponds to one record in another table. For example, **Authors** to **Biographies** where each author has one unique biography.

  - **One-to-Many**: One record in one table can be associated with multiple records in another table. For example, one **Publisher** publishes many **Books**.

- **Many-to-Many**: Records in one table can be associated with multiple records in another table and vice versa, typically managed through a junction table. For example, a **Books** table and an **Authors** table might be related through a **BooksAuthors** junction table that holds IDs from both tables.

Integrity Constraints

Definition and Purpose:

Integrity constraints ensure data accuracy and consistency. These include primary keys, foreign keys, and unique constraints. Integrity constraints are rules that are applied to database tables to ensure the accuracy and reliability of the data within the database. They are used to enforce certain conditions that data must meet to be entered into a table. The purpose of integrity constraints is to maintain the quality and integrity of the data in the database system, ensuring that it remains a true and accurate reflection of the real-world entities and relationships it is designed to model.

Key Roles of Integrity Constraints

1. **Data Accuracy**: Integrity constraints ensure that only valid data is entered into the database. This prevents errors and inconsistencies that could compromise the results of data retrieval and analysis.

2. **Consistency**: Constraints help maintain data consistency by ensuring that relationships between tables and within tables are consistently maintained. This is crucial in relational databases where related data is spread across different tables.

3. **Data Integrity**: By enforcing rules such as unique identifiers and foreign key relationships, integrity constraints ensure that the database behaves as expected, preserving the integrity of data across transactions.

4. **Prevention of Data Corruption**: Constraints prevent invalid data entry, which could lead to data corruption and faulty database operations. They serve as a first line of defense against errors in data handling by users or applications.

Types of Integrity Constraints

- **Primary Key Constraint**: Ensures that each record in a table is unique and identifiable. This is achieved by designating one or more fields in a table as the primary key, which cannot accept null values and must be unique across the table.

Example: In a **Customers** table, the **CustomerID** column might be set as the primary key to uniquely identify each customer.

- **Foreign Key Constraint**: Maintains referential integrity by ensuring that a field in one table uniquely identifies a row of another table. This constraint is crucial for maintaining accurate and consistent relationships between tables.

Example: In an **Orders** table, a **CustomerID** foreign key would reference the **CustomerID** primary key in the **Customers** table, ensuring that orders can only be placed by existing customers.

- **Unique Constraint**: Ensures that all values in a column or a set of columns are different from one another. This constraint is used when data needs to be unique but not necessarily a primary key.

Example: An **email** column in the **Customers** table may have a unique constraint to prevent two customers from having the same email address.

- **Check Constraint**: Specifies a condition that each row in the table must meet. This is used to enforce domain integrity by limiting the values that can be placed in a column.

Example: A **check** constraint on an **Age** column might specify that values must be between 0 and 120, ensuring that only valid ages are entered into the database.

- **Not Null Constraint**: Ensures that a column cannot have a null value. This is important for critical fields where data must be present for each record.

Example: In a **Employees** table, the **EmployeeName** column might be set to NOT NULL to ensure that every employee record has a name associated with it.

Integrity constraints are a fundamental aspect of database theory, essential for ensuring the correctness, consistency, and effectiveness of the data within a database. By defining and enforcing these constraints, database administrators and designers can prevent erroneous data entry and maintain a high standard of data integrity. These constraints not only facilitate reliable data management but also strengthen the database's capacity to serve its intended purposes effectively.

- **Example**: In an **Orders** table, the **OrderID** field could be set as the primary key to ensure that each order is uniquely identified. A foreign key might relate **CustomerID** in the **Orders** table to **CustomerID** in the **Customers** table, ensuring that orders are always associated with existing customers.

<u>Normalization</u>

Definition and Purpose:

Normalization is the process of organizing data in a database to reduce redundancy and improve data integrity. It involves dividing large tables into smaller, manageable ones while maintaining relationships between them. Normalization is a systematic approach used in database design to reduce redundancy and eliminate undesirable characteristics like Insertion, Update, and Deletion Anomalies in relational databases. The process involves organizing the fields and table structures of a database to minimize duplication and dependency by dividing large tables into smaller, more manageable ones, while still retaining the relationships between them. The primary purpose of normalization is to enhance a database's efficiency and maintainability, ensuring that it consumes fewer resources and provides faster responses to queries.

Key Roles of Normalization

1. **Reduce Redundancy**: Normalization minimizes or eliminates data redundancy, which is the repetition of data in the database. This reduction in redundancy helps in saving storage and makes the database more streamlined.

2. **Avoid Anomalies**: The main types of anomalies, Insertion, Update, and Deletion, are avoided through normalization. These anomalies can lead to loss of data integrity and inconsistencies within the database. Normalization ensures that each piece of data is stored only once, preventing these potential issues.

3. **Improve Data Integrity**: By establishing clear relationships and dependencies through normalization, the integrity of the database is enhanced. This approach makes the data more consistent and reliable over time and through various operations.

4. **Enhance Query Performance**: A well-normalized database can perform queries more efficiently. Smaller tables with fewer indices speed up search operations. Additionally, maintenance operations such as updates, deletions, and insertions are also more efficient in a normalized database.

5. **Facilitate Scalability**: As databases grow, a normalized structure can accommodate new data types and relationships without significant reorganization, thus supporting easier scalability.

Levels of Normalization

Normalization typically involves several stages, each called a "normal form" (NF). Most databases are normalized to the third normal form (3NF), which is considered sufficient for most applications, but higher levels of normalization, like Boyce-Codd Normal Form (BCNF), Fourth Normal Form (4NF), and Fifth Normal Form (5NF), are used to address more complex scenarios.

- **First Normal Form (1NF)**: A table is in 1NF when it contains only atomic values, meaning each field contains unique and indivisible values, and there are no repeating groups or arrays.

Example: Consider a table recording customer purchases. To comply with 1NF, separate fields for each product type purchased by a customer should be eliminated. Instead, each product type purchased should be in a separate record.

- **Second Normal Form (2NF)**: To achieve 2NF, a table must first be in 1NF, and then all non-key attributes must be fully functional and dependent on the entire primary key, not just a part of it.

Example: If a **StudentCourses** table has a composite primary key (**StudentID**, **CourseID**), then other attributes like **CourseName** and **Instructor** should depend on **CourseID** only.

- **Third Normal Form (3NF)**: A table is in 3NF if it is in 2NF and all its attributes are not only fully functionally dependent on the primary key but also independent of each other. That is, no non-key attribute should depend on another non-key attribute.

Example: A **Customers** table where **CustomerID** determines **CustomerName**, and **CustomerName** determines **CustomerCreditRating**, should be adjusted. **CustomerCreditRating** should directly depend on **CustomerID**, not indirectly through **CustomerName**.

Normalization is a critical process in database design aimed at reducing redundancy and dependency in data storage. By following the principles of normalization, database designers can create systems that are efficient, scalable, and robust, capable of supporting complex data interactions while maintaining data integrity and optimal performance.

- **Example**: Suppose a **CustomerOrders** table contains customer information along with order details. This table can be normalized into two tables: **Customers** (storing customer data) and **Orders** (storing order data). This separation reduces duplicate data entries and simplifies maintenance.

Transactions and ACID Properties

Definition and Purpose:

Transactions are a series of operations performed as a single logical unit of work, ensuring data integrity in database operations. ACID (Atomicity, Consistency, Isolation, Durability) properties guarantee that transactions are processed reliably. In database management, a transaction refers to a single unit of work that consists of one or more operations (such as updates, inserts, or deletes) which are executed as a single logical operation. The purpose of a transaction is to ensure that a database maintains consistency in the face of errors, power failures, and other mishaps. Transactions are critical for applications where accuracy and data integrity are paramount, such as in financial systems, e-commerce platforms, and any system where data must remain consistent after concurrent operations.

ACID Properties of Transactions

To ensure the reliability and integrity of transactions, database systems adhere to a set of properties known as ACID:

1. **Atomicity**: This property ensures that a transaction is treated as a single, indivisible unit, which either succeeds completely or fails completely. If any part of the transaction fails, the entire transaction is rolled back, and the database state is left unchanged.

Example: When transferring money from one bank account to another, the transaction to debit one account and credit the other must be completed in full. If either operation fails, the entire transaction must be undone to prevent an imbalance in accounts.

2. **Consistency**: Transactions must transition the database from one valid state to another valid state, maintaining all predefined rules, such as integrity constraints. No transaction should leave the database in a half-finished state.

Example: If a transaction is intended to update inventory levels, it must adjust both the quantities sold and the quantities remaining in stock to maintain consistency within inventory records.

3. **Isolation**: Changes made in a transaction should be isolated until the transaction is completed, ensuring that concurrent transactions do not affect each other. This property prevents transactions from reading or writing to the same data concurrently, which could lead to inconsistencies.

Example: If two bank customers are simultaneously updating their account balances, isolation ensures that each transaction sees a consistent view of the account balances, without interference from the other.

4. **Durability**: Once a transaction has been committed, it should remain so, even in the event of a power loss, crash, or other system failures. This property ensures that the results of the transaction are permanently recorded in the database.

Example: After a customer completes a purchase and the transaction is recorded, the sale remains on record even if the system crashes immediately afterward.

Importance of Transactions in Database Systems

Transactions play a crucial role in maintaining data integrity and consistency across database systems, especially under concurrent access scenarios. They are essential for:

- **Error Handling**: Transactions provide a mechanism for error detection and recovery. If an error occurs within a transaction, the system can revert back to the initial state before the transaction began, thus preserving the integrity of the data.

- **Synchronization**: In multi-user environments, transactions help synchronize access to database resources by controlling how data is read and modified. This prevents conflicts and ensures that all users see a consistent view of the data.

- **System Reliability**: By ensuring that changes are durable, transactions enhance the reliability of the database system. Users can trust that once a transaction is completed, the data is accurately recorded and safe, even if the system fails.

Transactions and their ACID properties are fundamental to the design and operation of reliable and robust database systems. They ensure that even in complex environments with multiple concurrent users, the database maintains integrity, consistency, and reliability. Understanding and implementing these principles is essential for any database professional, particularly when managing critical data in commercial, financial, or any high-stakes IT environment.

- **Example**: When a customer places an order, the database might need to update the **Orders** table, decrement stock in the **Inventory** table, and update the balance in the **CustomerAccounts** table. These operations should be performed as a transaction to ensure that either all updates are committed or none are, maintaining database consistency.

Introduction To Database Structures:
Overview of Database Structures

Database structures are the fundamental frameworks that define how data is stored, organized, and accessed within a database system. These structures are crucial for efficient data retrieval, data integrity, and optimal performance of database operations. Understanding database structures is essential for anyone involved in the design, implementation, and maintenance of a database.

Key Database Structures

Database structures primarily include tables, indexes, views, and schemas. Each plays a unique role in how data is managed and utilized:

1. **Tables**: The most fundamental and critical structure in a database, tables store data in rows and columns. Each table represents a specific type of entity (such as customers, orders, or products) and holds relevant data in a structured format.

Example: In a retail database, a **Products** table might include columns such as **ProductID**, **ProductName**, **Price**, and **StockLevel**. Each row in the table represents a distinct product available in the store.

2. **Indexes**: Indexes are special lookup tables that the database search engine can use to speed up data retrieval. Simply put, an index in a database

functions like an index in a book. It is particularly useful for improving the performance of query operations and is essential for large databases.

Example: An index could be created on the **ProductName** column in the **Products** table to allow quicker searches of products based on their names.

3. **Views**: A view is a virtual table based on the result-set of an SQL statement. It contains rows and columns, just like a real table. The fields in a view are fields from one or more real tables in the database. Views do not contain data themselves; they display data retrieved from other tables.

Example: A **ProductSummary** view could be created to display the product name, price, and stock level from the **Products** table but not include supplier or cost details, which might be sensitive.

4. **Schemas**: A schema is an organizational framework that defines the relationships between the different structures within the database, including tables, views, and other elements. It acts as a container that holds all the objects associated with the database.

Example: In a university database, a schema might include multiple tables like **Students**, **Courses**, **Enrollments**, and **Grades**, with views that provide summarized academic records.

Importance of Database Structures

- **Data Organization**: Properly designed database structures help in organizing data in a manner that makes it accessible and useful. Good organization supports efficient data retrieval and updates.

- **Data Integrity**: Structures like tables and schemas help enforce data integrity through constraints and rules, ensuring that the data entered into the database is accurate and consistent.

- **Performance Optimization**: Structures such as indexes optimize database performance, making it quicker to perform queries and retrieve data. This is crucial for databases with large volumes of data or high transaction rates.

- **Security and Access Control**: Views and schemas can be utilized to control access to data. Sensitive information can be hidden in views that do not expose critical data, or access can be restricted to certain schemas.

Understanding the various database structures is foundational to database management and design. Tables, indexes, views, and schemas each serve specific roles that enhance the functionality and efficiency of a database. Mastery of these structures enables database professionals to create systems that are not only robust and efficient but also scalable and secure, capable of meeting the diverse data needs of modern organizations. Whether designing a new database or managing an existing one, a clear grasp of these structures is crucial for effective database administration.

Understanding Relationships Between Data
Overview of Relationships in Databases

In database theory, understanding the relationships between different sets of data is fundamental to effective database design and operation. Relationships define how data in one table relates to data in another, reflecting the real-world interactions among entities. Properly defining and managing these relationships ensures data integrity, facilitates complex queries, and enhances data retrieval efficiency.

Types of Relationships

Relationships in a database are generally categorized into three main types: one-to-one, one-to-many, and many-to-many. Each type has specific use cases and implications for how data is organized and accessed:

1. **One-to-One Relationships**: A one-to-one relationship occurs when each record in one table corresponds to one record in another table. This type of relationship is less common but is useful when splitting data across tables for security reasons, performance improvements, or organizational clarity.

Example: In a human resources system, an **Employee** table might have a one-to-one relationship with an **EmployeeDetails** table. Each record in the **Employee** table, which stores basic information like name and employee ID, corresponds to exactly one record in the **EmployeeDetails** table, which stores sensitive data such as Social Security numbers and medical information.

Visualizing One-to-One Relationships

Diagram Setup:

- Use two tables: **Employee** and **EmployeeDetails**.

- Show that each record in the **Employee** table corresponds to exactly one record in the **EmployeeDetails** table.

- Link fields from each table with a line indicating that they reference each other uniquely.

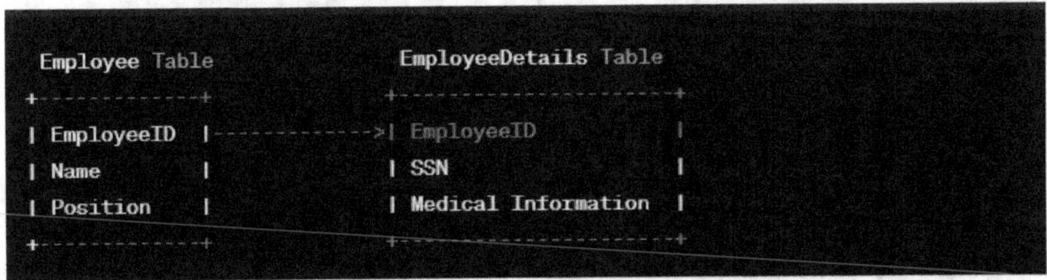

Description: Each employee ID in the **Employee** table points to a unique employee ID in the **EmployeeDetails** table, illustrating a one-to-one relationship.

2. **One-to-Many Relationships**: This is the most common relationship, where a record in one table can be associated with multiple records in another table. This relationship is used to model scenarios where one entity (represented by one record) is associated with several others.

Example: A **Customer** table and an **Orders** table exhibit a one-to-many relationship if each customer can place multiple orders. Each record in the **Customer** table can be linked to many records in the **Orders** table via a foreign key in **Orders** that points to the primary key in **Customer.**

Visualizing One-to-Many Relationships

Diagram Setup:

- Use two tables: **Customer** and **Orders**.

- Show that one record in the **Customer** table relates to multiple records in the **Orders** table.

- Use arrows to depict that multiple orders can be linked to a single customer.

Graphic:

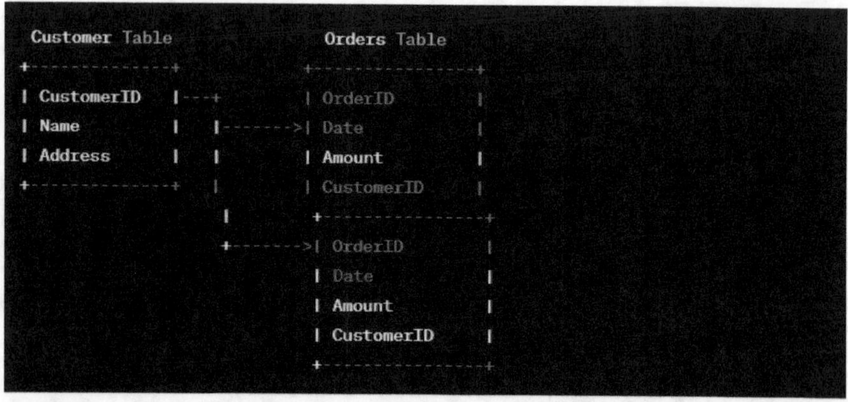

Description: The diagram shows multiple orders associated with a single customer, demonstrating a one-to-many relationship.

3. **Many-to-Many Relationships**: In a many-to-many relationship, records in one table can relate to multiple records in another table and vice versa. This type of relationship typically requires an additional table called a junction or join table, which stores the foreign keys from both related tables.

Example: A **Students** table and a **Courses** table have a many-to-many relationship because a student can enroll in multiple courses and a course can include multiple students. This relationship is managed through a **StudentCourses** join table that contains **StudentID** and **CourseID** as foreign keys.

Visualizing Many-to-Many Relationships

Diagram Setup:

*   Use three tables: **Students, Courses**, and **StudentCourses**.

*   Indicate that **Students** and **Courses** are linked through the **StudentCourses** join table.

*   Show many-to-many links between students and courses facilitated by the join table.

Graphic:

```
Students Table                  StudentCourses Table                Courses Table
+----------------+              +------------------------+          +----------------+
| StudentID      |---+          | StudentID        |---+           | CourseID       |
| Name           |   |--------> | CourseID         |   |--------->| Title          |
+----------------+   |          +------------------------+   |      +----------------+
                     +--------> | StudentID        |   |   |
                                | CourseID         |---+
                                +------------------------+
```

Description: This diagram illustrates a many-to-many relationship where students can enroll in multiple courses and courses can have multiple students, connected through the **StudentCourses** join table.

Importance of Defining Relationships

- **Data Integrity**: Relationships help maintain data integrity through the use of foreign keys that ensure only valid data is stored in the related tables. This enforcement of referential integrity prevents orphan records and inconsistent data.

- **Efficient Data Retrieval**: Properly defined relationships facilitate efficient queries that join tables based on these relationships. They enable complex SQL queries that can combine data from several tables in meaningful ways, enhancing the database's utility and performance.

- **Reduced Data Redundancy**: By defining clear relationships, the database design often naturally leads to normalization, which reduces redundancy and improves data storage efficiency.

- **Modeling Real-world Scenarios**: Accurately defining relationships in a database model ensures that the database structure mirrors the real-world interactions among data entities, making the database more intuitive and useful for users.

Understanding relationships between data is a crucial aspect of relational database management and design. Effective management of these relationships ensures robust data integrity, optimized query performance, and accurate data modeling. Whether designing a new database system or managing an existing one, database professionals must meticulously define and manage relationships to leverage the full capabilities of relational database technology, ensuring that the system is efficient, reliable, and reflective of real-world data interactions.

Principles Of Data Integrity and Normalization:
Overview

In database design, maintaining data integrity and applying normalization are crucial for ensuring reliable and efficient data management. These principles help prevent redundancy, minimize errors, and enhance the performance of database operations.

Data Integrity

Data integrity refers to the accuracy and consistency of data stored in a database. It is critical because it ensures the reliability of information throughout its lifecycle.

Key Aspects of Data Integrity

1. **Entity Integrity**: Ensures each table row has a unique identity and that the identifier (primary key) is never null.

2. **Referential Integrity**: Ensures that relationships between tables remain consistent. For example, foreign keys link only to existing primary keys or other valid foreign keys.

3. **Domain Integrity**: Ensures all entries in a given column are of the same data type or format.

4. **User-Defined Integrity**: Ensures some specific business rules are met that are not covered by other integrity types.

Example of Data Integrity

Consider a **Customer** table where **CustomerID** is the primary key. This ID must always be unique and not null to ensure each customer can be uniquely identified.

Visual Representation:

```
   Customers Table
+---------------+-------------+-------------+
| CustomerID    | FirstName   | LastName    |
+---------------+-------------+-------------+
| 001           | John        | Doe         |
| 002           | Jane        | Smith       |
+---------------+-------------+-------------+
```

Explanation: CustomerID ensures entity integrity by providing a unique identifier for each customer.

Normalization

Normalization is a process to reduce redundancy and dependency by organizing fields and table of a database. The main aim is to isolate data so that additions, deletions, and modifications of a field can be made in just one table and then propagated through the rest of the database via the defined relationships.

Levels of Normalization

Example of Normalization

Before Normalization (Not in 1NF):

```
   Orders Table
+-----------+---------------+-------------+------------+
| OrderID   | Product       | Customer    | Quantity   |
+-----------+---------------+-------------+------------+
| 1001      | Apple, Banana | John Doe    | 3, 2       |
+-----------+---------------+-------------+------------+
```

After Normalization to 1NF:

```
Orders Table
+-------------+-------------+-----------------+
| OrderID | CustomerID | Customer    |
+-------------+-------------+-----------------+
| 1001    | 001        | John Doe    |
+-------------+-------------+-----------------+


OrderDetails Table
+-------------+----------------+----------------+
| OrderID | Product    | Quantity |
+-------------+----------------+----------------+
| 1001    | Apple      | 3        |
| 1001    | Banana     | 2        |
+-------------+----------------+----------------+
```

Explanation: The original table is not in 1NF because it contains repeating groups of data. The normalized tables separate order details into a different table, where each type of product in an order is listed in its row, linked by **OrderID**.

Understanding and implementing the principles of data integrity and normalization are foundational in database management. These practices not only safeguard the data's accuracy and consistency but also optimize the database's structure for more efficient queries and maintenance. The adherence to these principles is critical for any robust database system, ensuring that it can reliably serve its intended functions.

Conclusion

Understanding and applying database theory is crucial for designing and managing effective databases. By embracing concepts such as data models, relationships, integrity constraints, normalization, and transactions, users of Microsoft Access can create well-structured, efficient, and reliable databases. These foundational principles not only enhance data handling and retrieval but also ensure the longevity and scalability of database solutions. Through practical application in Access, these theories become invaluable tools for any database administrator or developer.

Part II: Building a Database in Access

Chapter 3 - Creating and Managing Tables

Introduction to Table Management

Tables are the core components of any relational database system, including Microsoft Access. They hold all the user data entered into the database. Effective table management is crucial for ensuring data is organized logically, maintained easily, and accessed efficiently. This section explores the fundamental aspects of creating and managing tables in Microsoft Access with practical examples and visual aids.

Steps to Create and Manage Tables

1. **Designing the Table Structure**:

   - **Define Purpose**: Determine what information the table is intended to manage. Each table should hold data about one thing or concept, such as customers, orders, or products.

   - **Identify Fields**: Decide what pieces of information need to be stored in the table. Each piece of information becomes a field (column) in the table.

   - **Set Data Types**: For each field, determine the most appropriate data type (e.g., text, number, date/time).

2. **Creating a Table in Microsoft Access**:

   - **Using Design View**: This method gives you full control over the table structure. You can define the field names, data types, and other properties such as field size and default values.

   - **Using Datasheet View**: Quick and easy, suitable for when the structure is not fully planned yet. Just start typing and Access will adjust the data types automatically based on the input.

Example: Creating a **Customers** table.

   - Fields might include **CustomerID** (AutoNumber), **FirstName** (Text), **LastName** (Text), **Email** (Text), **Phone** (Text).

Graphic Example:

```
Design View of 'Customers' Table
+---------------------+-----------------+----------------+
| Field Name          | Data Type       | Description    |
+---------------------+-----------------+----------------+
| CustomerID          | AutoNumber      | Primary Key    |
| FirstName           | Text            |                |
| LastName            | Text            |                |
| Email               | Text            |                |
| Phone               | Text            |                |
+---------------------+-----------------+----------------+
```

3. **Setting Primary Keys**:

   - **Purpose**: The primary key is a unique identifier for each record in a table. It must contain unique values and cannot contain NULL values.

   - **How to Set**: In Design View, select the field or combination of fields that you want to use as the primary key, then click the 'Primary Key' button on the toolbar.

4. **Defining Relationships**:

   - **Between Tables**: Establish relationships between tables to link data logically and enforce referential integrity.

   - **Example**: Link **CustomerID** in the **Orders** table to **CustomerID** in the **Customers** table to indicate which customer placed each order.

Graphic Example:

```
Relationships Graphic
Customers Table                    Orders Table
+-------------------+              +-------------------+
| CustomerID  PK |------------| CustomerID   FK |
| FirstName      |              | OrderID      PK |
| LastName       |              | OrderDate       |
+-------------------+              +-------------------+
```

Best Practices for Managing Tables

- **Normalization**: Apply normalization rules to reduce redundancy and dependency.

- **Consistent Naming Conventions**: Use clear, descriptive names for tables and fields to make the database easier to understand and maintain.

- **Documentation**: Maintain good documentation of the table designs, especially explaining the purpose of each table and field, which is invaluable for long-term maintenance and updates.

Designing Tables and Defining Data Types
Introduction to Table Design and Data Types

In any database management system, including Microsoft Access, effective table design is crucial for ensuring data integrity, facilitating efficient data retrieval, and optimizing storage. Each table should be carefully designed to hold related data according to clear and logical patterns. This involves not only selecting appropriate data types for each field but also understanding the relationships these tables have with others.

Steps in Designing Tables and Defining Data Types

1. **Identify Entities and Relationships**:

   - **Entities**: Determine what kinds of items or objects the database needs to track. Each entity typically becomes a table.

   - **Relationships**: Understand how these entities relate to one another. This step influences how you design the tables and establish foreign keys.

   - **Example**: For a bookstore, entities might include **Books**, **Authors**, **Customers**, and **Orders**.

2. **Define Fields and Select Data Types**:

   - **Fields**: Decide what information needs to be stored for each entity. Each piece of information becomes a field.

   - **Data Types**: Choose the most appropriate data type for each field based on the kind of data it will store. This choice affects data integrity and query performance.

- **Text**: Names, descriptions, or any other alphanumeric data.

- **Number**: Quantities, prices, or anything numerical where calculations might be necessary.

- **Date/Time**: Any data point that references dates or times.

- **Boolean**: True/False values.

- **Memo**: Long text entries.

- **Others**: Currency, Hyperlink, etc.

Example: Designing a **Books** table.

- Fields might include **BookID**, **Title**, **AuthorID**, **Genre**, **Price**, **PublishDate**.

- Data Types might be **AutoNumber** for **BookID**, **Text** for **Title**, **Number** for **AuthorID** (linking to an **Authors** table), **Text** for **Genre**, **Currency** for **Price**, **Date/Time** for **PublishDate**.

Graphic Example:

```
Design View of 'Books' Table
+---------------+---------------+-------------------+
| Field Name    | Data Type     | Description       |
+---------------+---------------+-------------------+
| BookID        | AutoNumber    | Primary Key       |
| Title         | Text          | Book Title        |
| AuthorID      | Number        | FK to Authors     |
| Genre         | Text          | Book Genre        |
| Price         | Currency      | Price of Book     |
| PublishDate   | Date/Time     | Publication Date  |
+---------------+---------------+-------------------+
```

3. **Define Primary Keys:**

- **Purpose**: Ensure each record in the table can be uniquely identified.

- **Selection**: Typically, one field (or a combination of fields) is chosen as the primary key.

- **Example**: **BookID** would be a suitable primary key for the **Books** table because it uniquely identifies each book.

4. **Establishing Field Properties**:

   - **Field Size**: For text fields, define the maximum length to optimize storage.

   - **Default Values**: Set defaults where applicable to streamline data entry.

   - **Validation Rules**: Establish rules to ensure data integrity (e.g., **Price** must be greater than 0).

Best Practices for Table Design

- **Normalization**: Design tables to reduce redundancy and ensure data is logically segmented into the smallest useful parts.

- **Consistency**: Use consistent naming conventions and data types across the database to reduce confusion and errors during data entry.

- **Documentation**: Keep detailed documentation of the table design process, including descriptions of each field and the reasons for key decisions. This documentation is invaluable for maintenance and future modifications.

Designing tables and defining data types are foundational steps in setting up an effective database in Microsoft Access. By carefully planning and implementing thoughtful designs, you ensure that the database is robust, scalable, and capable of meeting both current and future needs. This systematic approach to table design not only enhances performance but also makes the database easier to manage, maintain, and expand as necessary.

Setting Primary and Foreign Keys:
Introduction to Primary and Foreign Keys

In database design, primary and foreign keys play a crucial role in establishing and enforcing relationships between tables, ensuring data integrity, and enhancing database performance. A primary key uniquely identifies each record within a table, while a foreign key links records between two tables, creating a relational structure that reflects real-world data interactions.

Setting Primary Keys

Definition: A primary key is a column or a set of columns whose values uniquely identify every row in a table. There should be no two rows in a table that share the same primary key value, and it cannot contain null values.

Example: In a **Customers** table, the **CustomerID** can serve as a primary key because it is unique to each customer.

Steps to Set a Primary Key:

1. **Choose the Column**: Identify the column that will serve as the primary key. This could be a single column like **CustomerID** or a combination of columns (composite key).

2. **Apply the Primary Key**: In Microsoft Access, you can set the primary key by selecting the column in table design view and clicking the "Primary Key" button on the toolbar.

Graphic Example:

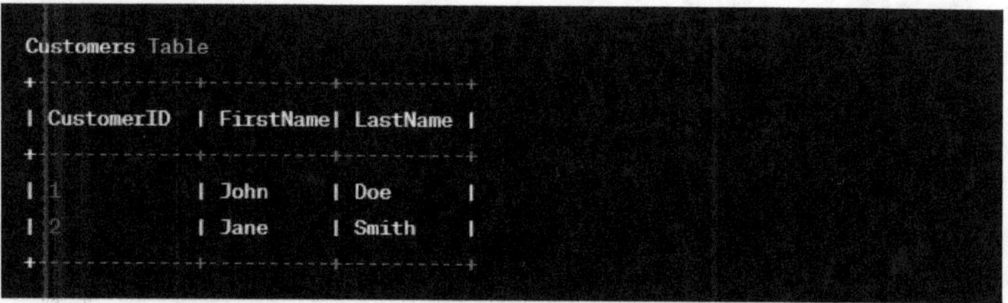

Setting Foreign Keys

Definition: A foreign key is a field (or collection of fields) in one table that uniquely identifies a row of another table or the same table. The table containing the foreign key is called the referencing table, and the table containing the candidate key is referred to as the referenced table.

Example. In an **Orders** table, the **CustomerID** can serve as a foreign key linking each order to a customer in the **Customers** table.

Steps to Set a Foreign Key:

1. **Identify the Relationships**: Determine which tables need to be connected via a foreign key.

2. **Choose the Referencing Column**: The foreign key in the referencing table (e.g., **Orders**) should match the primary key in the referenced table (e.g., **Customers**).

3. **Enforce Referential Integrity**: In Microsoft Access, you can set up foreign keys by creating relationships in the Relationships window and ensuring that referential integrity is enforced.

Graphic Example:

```
Relationships Diagram

+----------------------+        +---------------------+
| Customers            |        | Orders              |
|----------------------|        |---------------------|
| CustomerID (PK)      |------>| CustomerID (FK)     |
| FirstName            |        | OrderDate           |
| LastName             |        | Total               |
+----------------------+        +---------------------+
```

Explanation: The diagram shows a foreign key relationship where each record in the **Orders** table references a record in the **Customers** table through the **CustomerID**. This setup ensures that all orders are associated with existing customers, maintaining data integrity across tables.

Best Practices for Using Keys

- **Use AutoNumbers for Primary Keys**: In Access, using an AutoNumber data type for primary keys is a good practice as it automatically generates a unique identifier for each record.

- **Avoid Using Personal Data**: Avoid using personal data (like Social Security numbers) as primary keys for security and privacy reasons.

- **Normalize Data**: Ensure that data is normalized to reduce redundancy and improve data integrity, which often involves properly setting up primary and foreign keys.

- **Maintain Integrity**: Always enforce referential integrity to prevent orphan records and ensure consistency across your database.

Properly setting primary and foreign keys is a fundamental aspect of database design that ensures efficient and accurate data retrieval, maintains data integrity, and clearly defines the relationships between tables. By following these guidelines and examples, you can effectively manage the relational structure of your database in Microsoft Access, making it robust and reliable for handling complex data interactions.

Importing and Exporting Data:
Introduction to Data Import and Export in Microsoft Access

Efficient data management often requires the ability to import data from and export data to various formats. This capability is essential for integrating Access databases with other data sources, facilitating data backups, and sharing information with other systems or applications. Microsoft Access supports a range of formats for importing and exporting data, including Excel spreadsheets, CSV files, text files, and more.

Importing Data into Microsoft Access

Purpose: Importing data into Access is useful when you need to incorporate data from other sources into your Access database without manually entering it.

Common Formats:

- **Excel Files**: Ideal for detailed data that is already structured in columns and rows.

- **CSV Files**: Best for simpler, flat data that needs to be imported into a single table.

- **Text Files**: Useful for importing data from logs or data dumps.

Steps to Import Data:

1. **Prepare the Data Source**: Ensure the data is clean and well-structured in the source file. Columns should have headers if possible, and the data format should match the expected format in Access.

2. **Choose the Import Option**: In Access, go to the 'External Data' tab and select the appropriate import option based on the format of your data source (e.g., Excel, CSV).

3. **Follow the Import Wizard**: Access provides a step-by-step wizard for importing data. Specify the source file, and decide whether to create a new table or append the data to an existing table.

4. **Map the Fields**: If the data columns do not exactly match your Access table, the wizard allows you to map source columns to target table fields.

5. **Complete the Import**: Review any errors reported by Access during the import process and make necessary adjustments.

Example:

```
[Graphic Example: Import Wizard in Microsoft Access]
"Import Data from Excel"
+-----------------------------------+
| Step 1: Select File               |
| Step 2: Choose Sheet              |
| Step 3: Field Mapping             |
| Step 4: Finalize Import           |
+-----------------------------------+
```

Exporting Data from Microsoft Access

Purpose: Exporting data from Access allows you to share information with users who do not have Access, back up data, or use the data in other applications.

Common Formats:

- **Excel Files**: Useful for reports that might require further analysis in spreadsheet form.

- **CSV Files**: Best for creating universal file formats that can be imported into various other systems.

- **PDF Documents**: Ideal for distributing reports or data snapshots in a non-editable format.

Steps to Export Data:

1. **Select the Data to Export**: Identify the table or query results you wish to export.

2. **Choose the Export Option**: In the 'External Data' tab, select the format you want to export your data to.

3. **Configure Export Options**: Depending on the format, configure options such as file name, export location, and whether to open the file after exporting.

4. **Perform the Export**: Execute the export and check the output file to ensure the data has been correctly exported.

Example:

```
[Graphic Example: Export Options in Microsoft Access]
"Export Data to Excel"

+--------------------------------------------+
| File Name: SalesReport.xlsx      |
| Include Formatting: Yes          |
| Open File After Export: Yes      |
| Export Location: C:\Reports\     |
+--------------------------------------------+
```

Best Practices for Importing and Exporting Data

- **Data Verification**: Always verify the imported or exported data to ensure there are no discrepancies, such as missing or misaligned data.

- **Consistent Updates**: Maintain a routine for regular imports and exports, especially if the database interacts with other business systems.

- **Backup Before Major Imports/Exports**: Always create a backup of your Access database before performing large or complex data imports or exports to prevent data loss.

Mastering the processes of importing and exporting data in Microsoft Access enhances the flexibility and utility of your database. Whether integrating with other systems, sharing information, or conducting regular data updates, these functionalities are pivotal in maintaining an efficient and responsive database environment. By following the steps outlined above and adhering to best practices, you can ensure that your data remains accurate and secure across all transactions.

Conclusion

Creating and managing tables effectively is essential for building a robust database in Microsoft Access. Proper table design, including the careful selection of fields, primary keys, and relationships, lays the foundation for efficient data storage, retrieval, and integrity. By following best practices and understanding the functionalities available in Access, users can optimize their database to meet both current and future needs, ensuring scalability and reliability.

Chapter 4 - Developing Queries for Data Management

Introduction to Developing Queries

Queries are essential tools in Microsoft Access for retrieving, analyzing, updating, and manipulating data stored within database tables. They allow you to ask complex questions of your data, perform sophisticated analyses, and generate reports tailored to specific needs. Effective query design can drastically improve the functionality and efficiency of a database by enabling quick access to important information.

Types of Queries in Microsoft Access

1. **Select Queries**: The most common type of query used to retrieve data from one or more tables and display it in a specified format. These queries can be designed to filter, sort, and group data according to particular criteria.

2. **Action Queries**: These queries make changes to the data in the database and include:

   - **Update Queries**: Modify data in existing records.

   - **Delete Queries**: Remove records from tables.

   - **Append Queries**: Add new records to tables.

   - **Make-Table Queries**: Create new tables from existing data.

3. **Parameter Queries**: Allow users to provide input each time the query is run, making them dynamic and flexible.

4. **Crosstab Queries**: Summarize and display data as a cross-tabulation, showing data across rows and columns.

5. **SQL Queries**: Provide direct access to write and execute SQL statements, offering maximum flexibility and control over data manipulation.

Steps to Develop a Basic Select Query

1. **Identify the Requirement**: Determine what information you need from the database. This step defines the purpose of the query.

2. **Select Tables and Fields**: Choose which tables contain the data and which fields (columns) you want to include in your query.

3. **Specify Criteria**: Define any conditions that records must meet to be included in the query results. This could involve filtering data based on certain field values.

4. **Design the Query**:

   - Use the Query Design View in Access where you can visually select tables, drag and drop fields, and set criteria.

   - Alternatively, use the SQL View to write the SQL statement directly if you prefer or need more complex functionality.

5. **Run the Query**: Execute the query to view the results. Check the data to ensure it meets your requirements.

6. **Save and Document**: Save the query for future use and document its purpose and design for maintenance or modification later.

Example: Creating a Select Query

Scenario: You want to retrieve a list of all customers who have placed orders totaling more than $500 in the last year.

Steps:

1. **Tables Involved**: **Customers** and **Orders**.

2. **Fields to Display**: Customer name and contact details from the **Customers** table.

3. **Criteria**: Total order amount > $500; Date of order within the last year.

4. **Query Design**:

   - Link **Customers** and **Orders** tables on **CustomerID**.

   - Add fields **CustomerName**, **Contact**, **OrderAmount**, and **OrderDate**.

   - Set criteria on **OrderAmount** and **OrderDate**.

Visual Representation:

```
Query Design View
+------------------------------------------------------+
| Tables:                                              |
| Customers              Orders                        |
| +------------------+   +------------------+          |
| | CustomerID       |-->| CustomerID       |          |
| | CustomerName     |   | OrderAmount      |          |
| | Contact          |   | OrderDate        |          |
| +------------------+   +------------------+          |
|                                                      |
| Fields: CustomerName, Contact, OrderAmount           |
| Criteria: OrderAmount > 500 AND OrderDate > Date()-365 |
+------------------------------------------------------+
```

Best Practices for Query Development

- **Optimization**: Ensure queries are optimized for performance, especially those run on large datasets or complex databases.

- **Test Thoroughly**: Always test queries to verify correctness and ensure they don't produce unintended effects, particularly with action queries.

- **Security Considerations**: Be cautious with queries that modify data. Ensure they are protected against unauthorized use and consider implementing confirmation steps before data changes.

- **Documentation**: Maintain thorough documentation for all queries, including their purpose, design rationale, and any parameters they use. This is essential for maintenance and future updates.

Writing Basic to Advanced Queries:
Introduction to Query Development

Query development in Microsoft Access is a critical skill for data analysts, allowing them to extract, analyze, and manipulate data efficiently. Queries can range from simple data retrieval operations to complex data manipulations involving multiple tables and conditions. Understanding how to craft these queries from basic to advanced levels is essential for making the most of your database.

Types of Queries and Examples

1. **Basic Select Queries**: These are used to retrieve information from the database by specifying which tables to pull data from and what columns to display.

Example: A query to list all customers:

```sql
SELECT FirstName, LastName, Email
FROM Customers;
```

Visual Representation:

```
+-------------+-------------+----------------------+
| FirstName   | LastName    | Email                |
+-------------+-------------+----------------------+
| John        | Doe         | johndoe@email.com    |
| Jane        | Smith       | janesmith@email.com  |
+-------------+-------------+----------------------+
```

2. **Filtered Queries**: Add criteria to select queries to filter data based on specific conditions.

Example: A query to find customers from a specific city, e.g., "New York":

```sql
SELECT FirstName, LastName, City
FROM Customers
WHERE City = 'New York';
```

3. **Aggregate Queries**: These queries summarize data, such as counting entries, averaging numbers, or finding maximum and minimum values.

Example: A query to count the number of orders each customer has placed:

```sql
SELECT CustomerID, COUNT(OrderID) AS NumberOfOrders
FROM Orders
GROUP BY CustomerID;
```

4. **Join Queries**: Combine rows from two or more tables based on a related column between them.

Example: A query to retrieve customer names along with their orders:

```sql
SELECT Customers.FirstName, Customers.LastName, Orders.OrderDate
FROM Customers
INNER JOIN Orders ON Customers.CustomerID = Orders.CustomerID;
```

5. **Parameter Queries**: These queries prompt the user to enter a variable (parameter) each time they are run, making them flexible and interactive.

Example: A query to find orders from a specific date, where the date is provided by the user:

```sql
SELECT OrderID, OrderDate
FROM Orders
WHERE OrderDate = [Enter the order date];
```

6. **Action Queries**: Modify data in the database. These include Update, Delete, and Append queries.

Example of an Update Query: Increasing the price of all products by 10%:

```sql
UPDATE Products
SET Price = Price * 1.10;
```

Best Practices in Query Development

- **Clarity and Simplicity**: Keep queries as simple and clear as possible. Complex queries can be broken down into subqueries if they become too convoluted.

- **Use Comments**: When writing SQL directly, use comments to explain parts of the query, especially in more complex queries.

- **Optimization**: Consider the performance implications of your queries. Use indexes effectively, and be mindful of the cost of joins and subqueries.

- **Testing and Validation**: Test queries thoroughly to ensure they return expected results and do not negatively impact database performance.

Visual Tools and SQL View in Access

- **Query Design Tool**: Microsoft Access provides a Query Design tool that allows users to visually create queries. It's particularly useful for joins, where dragging and dropping fields can create links between tables.

- **SQL View**: For more control or complex queries, switch to SQL View in Access and write or paste your SQL code directly.

Developing queries from basic to advanced is a foundational skill for leveraging the full potential of Microsoft Access. By understanding different types of queries and applying best practices in their creation, users can efficiently manage and analyze their data, unlocking deeper insights and supporting effective data-driven decision-making.

Using SQL Within Access:
Introduction to SQL in Microsoft Access

SQL (Structured Query Language) is the standard language for managing and manipulating databases. Microsoft Access supports SQL, allowing users to directly write and execute queries, beyond the graphical query design tools. Using SQL in Access can enhance your ability to perform complex data operations, giving you more flexibility and control over your database management tasks.

Basics of Using SQL in Access

SQL in Access allows you to:

- Directly query data tables.

- Create, modify, and delete tables.

- Define relationships.

- Perform complex filtering and calculations.

Writing Basic SQL Queries in Access

1. **Select Query**: Retrieving data from one or more tables.

```sql
SELECT FirstName, LastName, Email
FROM Customers
WHERE City = 'New York';
```

This SQL command selects the first name, last name, and email from the **Customers** table where the city is New York.

2. **Insert Query**: Adding new records to a table.

```
INSERT INTO Customers (FirstName, LastName, City, Email)
VALUES ('Alice', 'Johnson', 'Los Angeles', 'alice.johnson@example.com');
```

This command adds a new record to the **Customers** table.

3. **Update Query**: Modifying existing records.

```
UPDATE Customers
SET Email = 'new.email@example.com'
WHERE CustomerID = 1;
```

This updates the email address for the customer with **CustomerID** of 1.

4. **Delete Query**: Removing records from a table.

```
DELETE FROM Customers
WHERE CustomerID = 1;
```

This command deletes the record from **Customers** where **CustomerID** is 1.

Visual Representation

Example of SQL Query Editor in Access:

Figure: The SQL view in Microsoft Access where users can directly type and execute SQL queries.

(Note: This is a hypothetical representation as images can't be displayed directly in this text-only format.)

Using SQL to Perform Advanced Operations

1. **Join Operations**: Combining rows from two or more tables based on a related column.

```sql
SELECT Customers.FirstName, Customers.LastName, Orders.OrderDate
FROM Customers
INNER JOIN Orders ON Customers.CustomerID = Orders.CustomerID;
```

This SQL statement retrieves customer names along with their order dates by joining the **Customers** and **Orders** tables on the **CustomerID**.

2. **Aggregate Functions**: Using functions like **SUM**, **AVG**, **MIN**, **MAX**, and **COUNT** to perform calculations on a set of values.

```sql
SELECT AVG(Price) AS AveragePrice
FROM Products;
```

This calculates the average price of all products in the **Products** table.

3. **Group By and Having Clauses**: Grouping records and filtering them based on a condition after aggregation.

```sql
SELECT CustomerID, COUNT(OrderID) AS NumberOfOrders
FROM Orders
GROUP BY CustomerID
HAVING COUNT(OrderID) > 5;
```

This SQL query groups orders by customer and filters to show only those customers who have more than five orders.

Best Practices When Using SQL in Access

- **Consistent Formatting**: Write SQL with a consistent style, such as capitalizing SQL keywords and ensuring proper indentation, to enhance readability.

- **Comment Your SQL**: Include comments in your SQL scripts to explain the purpose of complex queries or unusual decisions in your code.

- **Test Queries**: Always test your SQL queries on a subset of data or in a test environment to ensure they perform as expected without affecting live data.

Using SQL within Access offers a powerful way to handle complex data operations that go beyond the capabilities of the built-in query design tools. It provides precision control over data manipulation and retrieval, making it an essential skill for advanced database users. By understanding and applying SQL effectively within Access, you can optimize your database management and unlock more advanced functionalities for data analysis and reporting.

Creating Calculated Fields and Aggregate Data: Introduction to Calculated Fields and Aggregate Data

In database management, particularly within Microsoft Access, calculated fields and aggregation are powerful tools for data analysis. Calculated fields allow you to create new data from existing data through mathematical, string, or logical operations directly within your queries. Aggregate data functions summarize or analyze groups of data, such as counting, averaging, or finding minimum and maximum values. These tools enhance the capability to derive meaningful insights directly from your database without manual data manipulation.

Creating Calculated Fields in Access

Calculated fields use expressions to transform data within a query. They can combine data from different fields, incorporate functions, and reference constants or other calculations.

Example 1: Combining First and Last Names

```
SELECT FirstName & " " & LastName AS FullName
FROM Customers;
```

This query concatenates the first and last names of customers with a space between, creating a new field called **FullName**.

Example 2: Calculating Total Price

```
SELECT Quantity, Price, (Quantity * Price) AS TotalPrice
FROM OrderDetails;
```

This calculates the total price for each order detail by multiplying the quantity of items by their price, resulting in a new field **TotalPrice**.

Using Aggregate Functions in Queries

Aggregate functions perform a calculation on a set of values and return a single value. They are used with the **GROUP BY** clause to group rows that have the same values in specified columns into summary rows.

Common Aggregate Functions:

- **SUM()**: Calculates the total sum of a numeric column.

- **AVG()**: Calculates the average value.

- **COUNT()**: Counts the number of rows.

- **MIN()** and **MAX()**: Get the minimum and maximum value.

Example: Summarizing Order Data

```
SELECT CustomerID, SUM(TotalPrice) AS TotalSpent
FROM Orders
GROUP BY CustomerID;
```

This query sums the **TotalPrice** of orders for each customer, providing a quick insight into total spending per customer.

Visual Representation

Diagram of a Query with Calculated Fields and Aggregate Functions:

```
[Query Design Grid]
+-------------------------------------------------------+
|                                                       |
| Field        | Table      | Sort | Show | Criteria |
+-------------------------------------------------------+
|                                                       |
| CustomerID | Orders       |      | Yes |          |
| TotalPrice | Orders       |      | No  |          |
| SUM(TotalPrice) AS TotalSpent |   | Yes |       |
+-------------------------------------------------------+
```

(Note: Visual representations like this are hypothetical and illustrative.)

Best Practices for Using Calculated Fields and Aggregations

1. **Efficiency**: Although powerful, calculated fields and aggregations can slow down queries, especially on large datasets. It's important to use them judiciously.

2. **Accuracy**: Ensure that your expressions and aggregate functions are correctly specified to avoid errors in your calculations.

3. **Testing**: Always test your queries to verify that calculated and aggregated data is correct and meaningful.

4. **Documentation**: Maintain clear documentation of the logic behind each calculated field and aggregation to aid in future maintenance and understanding.

Calculated fields and aggregate functions are indispensable tools in database query design, particularly within Access. They provide enhanced flexibility in data analysis, allowing for sophisticated manipulation and summarization of data directly within your database queries. With careful use, these tools can significantly enhance your ability to analyze and interpret data efficiently and accurately, leading to better-informed business decisions.

Conclusion

Developing effective queries in Microsoft Access is crucial for managing and analyzing data efficiently. By understanding the different types of queries and following structured steps for query development, you can harness the full power of Access to retrieve meaningful insights from your data and perform essential data operations. Whether for simple data retrieval or complex data manipulations, queries are indispensable tools in the arsenal of any database manager.

Chapter 5 - Designing Forms for Data Entry

Introduction to Form Design in Microsoft Access

Forms in Microsoft Access serve as the primary interface for users to interact with data. Well-designed forms improve data entry accuracy, efficiency, and user satisfaction. They allow users to input, modify, and view data in a structured and intuitive way, directly linked to the underlying database tables.

Key Principles of Form Design

User-Friendly Layout:

Ensure the form layout is logical and user-friendly. Group related fields, use clear labels, and maintain consistent formatting to guide users through data entry tasks smoothly.

Introduction to User-Friendly Layout

Creating a user-friendly layout for data entry forms in Microsoft Access or any database system is crucial for enhancing user experience and efficiency. A well-designed form layout not only facilitates smoother data entry but also reduces errors, improves data quality, and increases user satisfaction. It involves thoughtful organization, clear labeling, and intuitive navigation elements that align with the natural workflow of the users.

Principles of User-Friendly Form Layout

1. **Logical Grouping of Fields**:

- **Purpose**: Group related data fields together in clearly defined sections or tabs. This helps users quickly understand where to enter data and reduces the cognitive load by categorizing information logically.

- **Implementation**: Use frame controls to visually separate different sections, such as personal information, contact details, and payment information on a customer form.

2. **Consistent and Clear Labeling**:

- **Purpose**: Ensure that every data entry field is accompanied by a concise and clear label. This helps users understand what information is required without guessing or assumptions.

- **Implementation**: Place labels close to the corresponding fields to prevent eye movement from straying too far, which can cause confusion and errors.

3. **Alignment and Grid Structure**:

- **Purpose**: Align fields to create a clean, organized appearance that is easy to navigate. Proper alignment reduces the effort required to process the form visually and helps users enter data more quickly.

- **Implementation**: Align labels consistently, either to the left of the fields or right-aligned and close to the input area, depending on the form design. Use a grid layout to arrange fields and labels in a structured manner.

4. **Minimize Clutter**:

- **Purpose**: Reduce unnecessary elements on the form to focus the user's attention on important actions. A cluttered form can be overwhelming and lead to mistakes or overlooked fields.

- **Implementation**: Only display fields that are necessary for the specific task of the form. Consider using collapsible sections or multi-step forms if large amounts of data are necessary.

5. **Responsive Design**:

- **Purpose**: Ensure that the form is usable on different devices, including desktops, tablets, and smartphones. A responsive design adapts to the screen size and orientation, providing a consistent experience across devices.

- **Implementation**: Test form layouts on multiple devices to ensure controls are accessible and visible without excessive scrolling or resizing.

6. **Aesthetic and Visual Comfort**:

- **Purpose**: Enhance the visual appeal of the form, which can improve user engagement and reduce fatigue during data entry tasks.

- **Implementation**: Use subtle color schemes that are easy on the eyes, sufficient white space to avoid feeling cramped, and fonts that are easy to read.

Example: Customer Registration Form Layout

Here's a conceptual layout for a customer registration form designed with user-friendly principles:

Visual Representation:

```
+-----------------------------------------------+
| Customer Registration                         |
+-----------------------------------------------+
| Personal Information                          |
| [First Name     ] [Last Name        ]         |
| [Date of Birth ]                              |
+-----------------------------------------------+
| Contact Details                               |
| [Email           ]                            |
| [Phone Number   ]                             |
+-----------------------------------------------+
| Address                                       |
| [Street          ] [City          ]          |
| [State           ] [Postal Code   ]           |
+-----------------------------------------------+
| [  Submit  ] [  Cancel  ]                     |
+-----------------------------------------------+
```

A user-friendly layout is foundational for designing effective forms for data entry. By adhering to principles of logical grouping, consistent labeling, alignment, and minimal clutter, forms can be made intuitive and efficient. Such well-designed forms not only streamline the data entry process but also enhance overall user satisfaction and data accuracy.

Data Entry Efficiency:

Design forms to minimize the time and effort required for data entry. This can include default values, drop-down lists, and checkboxes for quick selections.

Introduction to Data Entry Efficiency

Efficient data entry is a critical aspect of form design in database applications like Microsoft Access. The goal is to minimize the time and effort required to input data accurately, thereby enhancing productivity and reducing the possibility of errors. This involves optimizing the form's layout and functionality to streamline the interaction between the user and the form.

Principles for Enhancing Data Entry Efficiency

1. **Minimize Data Entry:**

- **Purpose**: Reduce the amount of typing and interaction required to enter data.

- **Implementation**: Where possible, use pre-populated fields, default values, and dropdown lists that allow users to select options rather than typing. For example, use a dropdown for states in an address form or set the current date as a default value in a date field.

2. **Use of AutoComplete**:

- **Purpose**: Assist users in filling out forms by predicting the information they might enter based on initial characters.

- **Implementation**: Implement AutoComplete on fields such as city names, product codes, or other common entries to speed up the form-filling process and reduce typographical errors.

3. **Tab Order and Logical Flow**:

- **Purpose**: Ensure the tab order follows the natural flow of data entry, typically from left to right and top to bottom.

- **Implementation**: Set the tab stops in a logical sequence that matches the intended flow of data entry to prevent users from having to manually click each field or use inconsistent navigation, which can slow down the data entry process.

4. **Input Masks and Data Formatting**:

- **Purpose**: Guide users on how data should be entered and ensure consistency.

- **Implementation**: Use input masks in fields where data needs to be entered in a specific format, such as phone numbers, social security numbers, or dates. This not only helps in maintaining data consistency but also reduces the likelihood of errors.

5. **Real-time Data Validation**:

- **Purpose**: Provide immediate feedback on the correctness of the data entered.

- **Implementation**: Validate data as it is entered. For example, verify that email addresses contain an "@" sign and a period, or ensure that numeric fields do not contain letters. Highlight errors in real-time and provide clear instructions on how to correct them.

6. **Keyboard Shortcuts and Accessibility**:

- **Purpose**: Allow power users and those with disabilities to navigate and use forms more efficiently.

- **Implementation**: Implement keyboard shortcuts for common actions, such as submitting the form (**Ctrl+Enter**) or moving to the next section (**Ctrl+Right Arrow**). Ensure accessibility features are supported, like screen reader compatibility and high-contrast modes.

Example: Implementing Efficiency in a Customer Order Form

Here's how efficiency principles could be applied in a customer order form:

Layout and Functionality:

- **Customer ID Field**: AutoComplete based on initial customer name input, fetching relevant customer data to auto-populate other fields like address and phone number.

- **Product Selection**: Dropdown list populated with product names or codes. Selecting a product auto-fills its price and available stock.

- **Quantity Field**: Numeric stepper control allowing users to click up or down to adjust the quantity.

- **Order Date**: Defaulted to today's date, editable via a date picker.

- **Submit Button**: Positioned prominently at the bottom and accessible via the **Alt+S** keyboard shortcut.

Efficient form design is essential for ensuring quick and accurate data entry. By carefully considering each aspect of the form's interaction with the user—from the placement and choice of controls to the logical flow and accessibility—designers can create forms that not only meet the functional requirements but also enhance user satisfaction and operational productivity. These principles, when effectively implemented, make data entry tasks less cumbersome and more error-free.

<u>Validation and Error Handling</u>:

Implement data validation rules to prevent errors during data entry. Provide clear error messages to help users correct data entry mistakes effectively.

Introduction to Validation and Error Handling

Validation and error handling are critical components of form design in database management systems like Microsoft Access. Effective validation ensures that data entered into the system adheres to specified formats and rules, preventing corrupt or inaccurate data from being stored. Error handling complements validation by informing users of mistakes in a way that enables them to correct those errors effectively and efficiently.

Principles of Validation and Error Handling

1. **Field-Level Validation:**

- **Purpose**: Ensure that data entered in each field meets specific criteria before it is accepted. This can include checks for data type, format, and logical consistency.

- **Implementation**: Utilize built-in validation features in form controls to specify criteria—such as text length, numerical ranges, or format patterns (e.g., date formats, telephone numbers). For example, setting a field in a customer form to reject anything other than numerical input for an age field.

2. **Form-Level Validation:**

- **Purpose**: Confirm that the data across different fields within a form collectively satisfies broader validation rules before the form is submitted.

- **Implementation**: Use form submission triggers (like a save or submit button) to initiate validation scripts that check various fields for logical consistency. For instance, ensuring that end dates are not earlier than start dates in a booking form.

3. **Real-Time Feedback:**

- **Purpose**: Provide immediate, context-sensitive feedback as soon as a user makes an error. This helps correct mistakes at the moment they occur.

- **Implementation**: Implement event handlers that react to user actions, such as leaving a field (**On Exit** event) or changing a field's content (**On Change** event). For example, validating an email address for the correct format as soon as the user moves to the next field.

4. **Error Messaging**:

- **Purpose**: Clearly communicate the nature of the error to the user in a friendly and constructive manner.

- **Implementation**: Use clear, concise, and non-technical language in error messages. Indicate both the error and the expected action to correct it. For instance, instead of saying "Invalid entry," use "Please enter a valid email address, such as user@example.com."

5. **Visual Cues for Errors**:

- **Purpose**: Visually highlight fields that contain errors to guide users directly to the problem area.

- **Implementation**: Change the border color of erroneous fields to a bright color like red, or add an error icon next to the field. Optionally, tooltips can appear when the user hovers over the error icon, providing additional guidance.

6. **Preventative Measures**:

- **Purpose**: Reduce the chance of errors by guiding user inputs from the outset.

- **Implementation**: Incorporate dropdown menus, checkboxes, and radio buttons to limit user choices to valid options, reducing the chance for error. For example, using a dropdown menu for state selection ensures that users can only choose from a list of valid states.

Example: Implementing Effective Error Handling in a Registration Form

Scenario: A user is filling out a registration form but forgets to fill out a mandatory email address field and enters an invalid date format for their birthdate.

Visual Representation:

```
+------------------------------------------------+
| Registration Form                              |
+------------------------------------------------+
| Name: [John Doe                  ]             |
| Email: [                      ] *Required      |
| Birthdate: [dd-mm-yyyy] *Invalid date format   |
| [Submit]                                       |
+------------------------------------------------+
```

Error Handling:

- **Email Field**: If left blank, the field border turns red, and a message appears below: "Please enter your email address."

- **Birthdate Field**: If the date format is incorrect, the field border turns red, and a message appears below: "Please enter your birthdate in the format dd-mm-yyyy."

Proper validation and error handling are vital for maintaining the integrity of data entered through forms. By implementing these principles effectively, you can ensure that data collected is accurate, errors are minimized, and users are provided with a clear, guided experience that facilitates correct data entry. This not only enhances user satisfaction but also reduces the workload involved in data cleanup and correction down the line.

Navigation and Usability:

Include navigation buttons, such as 'Next', 'Previous', 'Submit', and 'Cancel', to facilitate easy movement around the form and between records. Tooltips and status information can enhance user interaction by providing additional context or help.

Introduction to Navigation and Usability in Form Design

In the context of form design, particularly within database applications like Microsoft Access, navigation and usability are crucial for ensuring that users can interact with the form efficiently and intuitively. Good navigation helps users move between different parts of a form or between different forms without confusion or unnecessary delays. Usability focuses on making the form easy to use and understand, minimizing user errors and enhancing user satisfaction.

Principles of Navigation and Usability

1. **Clear Navigation Controls**:

- **Purpose**: Provide users with clear pathways to move through form fields and actions effortlessly.

- **Implementation**: Include buttons for common actions such as 'Submit', 'Cancel', 'Next', 'Previous', and 'Close'. Position these buttons in consistent locations across forms, typically at the bottom or top-right corner of the form.

2. **Logical Flow**:

- **Purpose**: Arrange fields in a logical sequence that follows the natural data entry or review process.

- **Implementation**: Organize fields in the order they are typically filled out or processed. For instance, personal information should come before payment details on a registration form.

3. **Progress Indicators**:

- **Purpose**: Inform users of their progress when filling out multi-page or complex forms.

- **Implementation**: Use progress bars or step indicators on forms that span multiple pages or sections to show users how much they have completed and how much remains.

4. **Minimize Page Transitions**:

- **Purpose**: Reduce the need for navigating between different pages to complete related data entry tasks.

- **Implementation**: Where possible, use expandable sections, tabs, or modal dialogs to keep the user on the same page while entering or editing related information, reducing the load time and the risk of losing data between transitions.

5. **Consistent Layout and Design**:

- **Purpose**: Ensure that the form's layout and design remain consistent across different forms within the application to reduce learning time and confusion.

- **Implementation**: Use a standard template for all forms including the same color scheme, font style, and control layout. This consistency helps users become familiar with the application's interface more quickly.

6. **Accessibility**:

- **Purpose**: Ensure that forms are accessible to users of all abilities, including those with disabilities.

- **Implementation**: Design forms that are compatible with screen readers, provide keyboard navigation, and use high contrast colors. Labels should be associated with form controls for better screen reader support.

7. **Responsive Design**:

- **Purpose**: Ensure forms are usable on various devices, including desktops, tablets, and smartphones.

- **Implementation**: Design forms so that they adjust gracefully to different screen sizes and orientations. Use responsive design techniques to ensure that controls are easy to interact with on any device.

Example: User Registration Form Usability Features

Visual Representation:

```
+--------------------------------------------------+
| Registration Form                                |
| [Progress: Step 2 of 4]                          |
+--------------------------------------------------+
| Name: [John Doe                    ]             |
| Email: [john.doe@example.com     ]               |
| [Next Page] [Previous Page] [Cancel Registration] |
+--------------------------------------------------+
```

Explanation:

- **Progress Indicator**: Shows the current step in a multi-step registration process.

- **Navigation Buttons**: Located at the bottom for easy access, allowing users to move forward, go back, or cancel the registration.

- **Field Order**: Arranged logically from personal to more specific information.

Effective navigation and usability in form design are essential for creating user-friendly database applications. By implementing these principles, designers can ensure that users can complete forms quickly and with fewer errors, leading to a more efficient data entry process and a better overall user experience. These practices not only aid in the accuracy of the data collected but also enhance the satisfaction of the users interacting with the application.

Steps to Designing Effective Forms:

<u>Define the Purpose</u>:

Clearly define what the form is meant to achieve. Is it for creating new records, editing existing ones, or perhaps a combination of both?

Introduction to Defining the Purpose of a Form

At the core of effective form design is a clear understanding of the form's purpose. Defining the purpose is the first and most critical step in the design process as it directly influences all subsequent design decisions, from the selection of fields to the layout and interactions the form will support. This foundational step ensures that the form not only meets the functional requirements but also aligns with the broader goals of the database system or business process.

Importance of Defining the Purpose

1. **Clarity in Functionality**: Understanding the purpose allows designers to determine exactly what the form needs to do, which can range from collecting specific information, facilitating data updates, processing transactions, or serving as a navigation hub within the application.

2. **Targeted Design**: By clearly defining the purpose, designers can tailor the form's structure and interface to the intended users, making it intuitive and efficient for those who will use it most frequently.

3. **Efficiency in Development**: A well-defined purpose helps streamline the development process by focusing efforts on necessary features and avoiding the inclusion of irrelevant functionalities that can clutter the form and complicate maintenance.

4. **Enhanced User Experience**: Forms designed with a clear purpose in mind are more likely to provide a satisfying user experience because they meet the users' needs without extraneous complications or distractions.

Steps to Define the Purpose of a Form

1. **Identify User Needs**: Start by understanding who will use the form and what they need to achieve with it. This involves discussions with stakeholders, user surveys, or analyzing the tasks that the form is intended to support.

2. **Define the Data Requirements**: Determine what data needs to be collected or displayed through the form. This includes identifying which fields are necessary for input, which are for display only, and the sources of this data, such as which tables in the database will interact with the form.

3. **Determine Form Actions**: Decide on the actions that users need to perform using the form, such as creating new records, editing existing ones, deleting data, or simply viewing data. This will help in defining the controls and functionalities that need to be included in the form.

4. **Consider Integration Needs**: Understand how the form fits into the larger workflow or system. Does it need to interact with other forms or systems? Does it trigger other processes like sending emails or updating other databases?

5. **Set Success Criteria**: Establish what makes the form successful. This could be based on efficiency metrics (e.g., reducing data entry time, minimizing errors), user satisfaction scores, or other performance indicators.

Example: Customer Feedback Form

Purpose: Collect valuable customer feedback for service improvement.

- **User Needs**: Easy way for customers to submit feedback after receiving a service.

- **Data Requirements**: Collect customer name, service date, feedback type (e.g., complaint, suggestion, compliment), and detailed description.

- **Form Actions**: Allow users to submit their feedback, which triggers a confirmation email to the customer and an alert to the service manager.

- **Integration Needs**: The form should integrate with the customer relationship management (CRM) system to pull in customer details automatically if the customer is logged in.

- **Success Criteria**: High completion rates, positive user feedback on the form's ease of use, and actionable insights gained from the feedback provided.

Defining the purpose of a form is a critical step in form design that ensures the end product is effective, efficient, and user-friendly. This process helps in aligning the form's functionality with the user's needs and the organization's objectives, thereby enhancing the overall data management strategy and user satisfaction.

Select Fields and Controls:

Decide which fields are necessary for the form and choose appropriate controls for each field based on the type of data (e.g., text boxes for free text, combo boxes for selections).

1. **Layout and Grouping**:

- **Grid Layout**: Align fields in a grid layout to ensure the form is tidy and organized.

- **Grouping**: Group related fields into sections or tabs to make the form easier to understand and use.

2. **Implement Validation**:

- **Field-Level Validation**: Use field properties to enforce rules like required fields, data types (number, text, date), and range limits.

- **Form-Level Validation**: Write event-driven VBA code to perform more complex validations when users submit the form.

3. **Test and Iterate**: Test the form with end-users to gather feedback on its functionality and usability. Refine the design based on this feedback to enhance user experience and data integrity.

Example: Customer Entry Form

Layout Example:

```
+-----------------------------------------------------+
| Customer Entry Form                                 |
+-----------------------------------------------------+
| [Name      ] [John Doe              ]               |
| [Address   ] [123 Apple Street      ]               |
| [City      ] [New York              ] [State] [NY]  |
| [Email     ] [john.doe@example.com  ]               |
|                                                     |
| [          Save          ] [      Cancel          ] |
+-----------------------------------------------------+
```

Functionality:

- **Name, Address, Email**: Text boxes for user input.

- **City**: A combo box populated with city names for user selection.

- **State**: A drop-down list with state abbreviations.

Best Practices for Form Design in Access

- **Keep It Simple**: Avoid clutter by only including necessary elements. A clean interface helps users focus on the task at hand.

- **Consistency**: Use consistent element sizing, spacing, and fonts. Consistent interfaces are easier for users to understand and use effectively.

- **Feedback**: Provide immediate feedback for actions (e.g., saving data), so users know the status of their inputs.

- **Accessibility**: Design forms to be accessible to users with disabilities, considering color contrasts and keyboard navigability.

Building Forms and Form Controls:
Introduction to Form Construction

In database management systems like Microsoft Access, building effective forms is crucial for facilitating user interaction and ensuring efficient data management. Forms act as the interface through which users view, enter, and modify data stored in the database. Well-designed forms use a variety of form controls tailored to the specific needs of data entry, thereby enhancing user experience and promoting accurate data collection.

Key Components of Form Building

1. **Layout Design**:

    - **Purpose**: To provide a clear, logical, and aesthetically pleasing structure for users to interact with.

    - **Implementation**: Arrange form controls in a grid layout, group related fields, and use whitespace effectively to prevent clutter. Ensure the form is responsive to different device screens if accessed via web or mobile.

2. **Selection of Form Controls**:

    - **Purpose**: To offer appropriate tools for data entry and modification that match the type of data being collected.

    - **Implementation**: Choose from a variety of controls such as text boxes, combo boxes, check boxes, radio buttons, date pickers, and command buttons, depending on the nature of data. For example, use combo boxes for fields with a predefined set of options and checkboxes for binary choices.

3. **Data Binding**:

    - **Purpose**: To connect form controls directly to data sources, allowing for real-time updates and data integrity.

    - **Implementation**: Bind controls to specific fields in a database table or query. For instance, bind a text box to a "Customer Name" field in a "Customers" database table to display and update real-time data.

4. **Validation Rules**:

    - **Purpose**: To ensure data entered into the form meets certain criteria before being submitted to the database.

    - **Implementation**: Implement validation directly in form controls or through event-driven scripts. For example, validate email formats in a text box using a simple script to check for the presence of an "@" symbol and a period.

5. **Navigation Controls**:

   - **Purpose**: To facilitate easy movement within the form and between other forms or reports.

   - **Implementation**: Include buttons for navigating to the next record, previous record, first record, last record, submitting data, and cancelling changes. Add shortcuts and tooltips to enhance usability.

Step-by-Step Process to Build a Form

1. **Plan the Form**:

   - Outline the purpose of the form and the type of data it will handle. Sketch a draft layout on paper or use a wireframing tool to visualize the placement of form controls.

2. **Create the Form in Access**:

   - Use the Form Wizard for a guided setup or start with a blank form for more custom designs.

   - Drag tables or queries onto the form where data sources are automatically linked.

3. **Arrange and Configure Controls**:

   - Place controls according to the planned layout. Adjust properties like size, font, and colors for better readability and consistency.

   - Bind each control to the corresponding field in the data source.

4. **Implement Validation and Error Handling**:

   - Set up input masks for data formatting, validation rules for data integrity, and error handling routines to guide users for correction.

5. **Test and Refine**:

   - Conduct user testing to gather feedback on the form's functionality and usability.

   - Make necessary adjustments based on user input to enhance performance and ease of use.

Example: Customer Contact Form

Visual Example:

```
[Customer Contact Form]

+-------------------------------------------------+
| Name: [John Doe              ]                  |
| Email: [john.doe@example.com]                   |
| Contact No: [123-456-7890   ]                   |
| [ ] Subscribe to newsletter                     |
|                                                 |
| [Submit]                       [Cancel]         |
+-------------------------------------------------+
```

Description:

- **Text Boxes** for name, email, and contact number.

- **Checkbox** for optional newsletter subscription.

- **Command Buttons** for submitting or cancelling the form.

Building forms in Microsoft Access involves more than just placing controls on a layout. It requires thoughtful design, strategic control selection, and rigorous testing to ensure that the forms not only look good but also function effectively, facilitating smooth and efficient data entry and management. By adhering to best practices in form design and leveraging Access's robust form-building tools, developers can create powerful user interfaces that enhance the overall database application.

Enhancing Form Functionality With VBA:
Introduction to Using VBA in Form Design

Visual Basic for Applications (VBA) is a powerful scripting language provided by Microsoft Access to enhance and automate functionality within forms. VBA can be used to customize forms beyond the capabilities offered through standard form properties and events, allowing for more dynamic interactions and tailored user experiences.

Importance of VBA in Form Functionality

1. **Customization**: VBA enables deep customization of form behavior, allowing developers to specify how forms react to specific user inputs, system events, and external data changes.

2. **Automation**: It automates repetitive tasks and complex sequences of actions that would otherwise require manual intervention, thus increasing efficiency and reducing errors.

3. **Integration**: VBA facilitates interaction between the form and other parts of the Access application, other Microsoft Office applications, and even external systems, making it versatile for integration needs.

4. **Conditional Logic**: Implement complex conditional logic that adjusts the user interface and flow based on user input, data values, or external conditions.

Enhancing Form Functionality with VBA

1. **Dynamic Field Validation:**

   - **Purpose**: To validate data entries dynamically and provide immediate feedback.

   - **Example**: Automatically verify the correctness of an email address format as soon as the user exits the email text box.

```
Private Sub txtEmail_LostFocus()

  If Not txtEmail.Text Like "*@*.*" Then

    MsgBox "Please enter a valid email address.", vbExclamation, "Invalid Email"

    txtEmail.SetFocus

  End If

End Sub
```

2. **Conditional Visibility and Accessibility:**

   - **Purpose**: Adjust the visibility or accessibility of form controls based on specific criteria.

- **Example**: Enable a submit button only after all mandatory fields are filled.

Private Sub Form_Current()

cmdSubmit.Enabled = (Not IsNull(txtName) And Not IsNull(txtEmail))

End Sub

3. **Automating Data Entry**:

- **Purpose**: Automate data entries based on predefined rules or external data.

- **Example**: Automatically fill in the city and state fields when a user enters a ZIP code.

Private Sub txtZIP_AfterUpdate()

Dim rs As Recordset

Set rs = CurrentDb.OpenRecordset("SELECT City, State FROM ZipCodes WHERE ZIP = '" & txtZIP.Text & "'")

If Not rs.EOF Then

txtCity.Value = rs!City

txtState.Value = rs!State

End If

rs.Close

Set rs = Nothing

End Sub

4. **Event-Driven Actions**:

- **Purpose**: Trigger actions like emails, calculations, or updates based on user actions within the form.

- **Example**: Send a confirmation email when a user submits a form.

Private Sub cmdSubmit_Click()

If MsgBox("Are you sure you want to submit?", vbYesNo) = vbYes Then

Call SendEmail(txtEmail.Text, "Thank you for your submission", "Here are the details you submitted...")

MsgBox "Submission successful and email sent.", vbInformation

End If

End Sub

Visual Representation of Enhanced Form

Diagram: A flowchart showing the logic implemented via VBA:

```
+---------------------+      +---------------------+      +---------------------+
| Enter Email         | ---> | Validate Format     | ---> | On Error: Show Msg  |
+---------------------+      +---------------------+      +---------------------+
          | Valid Email                 |
          V                             V
+---------------------+      +---------------------+
| Enter ZIP Code      | ---> | Auto-fill City,     |
+---------------------+      | State based on ZIP|
                             +---------------------+
```

Utilizing VBA in Microsoft Access forms significantly enhances their functionality, allowing for a customized, dynamic, and user-friendly experience. By automating tasks, validating user input in real-time, and implementing sophisticated business logic directly within forms, developers can create efficient and powerful applications that go beyond simple data entry tasks. This capability enables Access forms to handle complex scenarios, making them invaluable tools in any data-driven environment.

Form Validation Techniques:
Introduction to Form Validation

Form validation is a critical aspect of form design in database applications like Microsoft Access. It ensures that the data entered by users meets predefined criteria before it's submitted or saved to the database. Effective validation not only prevents errors but also enhances data integrity and user experience by preventing incorrect data from being stored.

Types of Validation Techniques

1. **Client-side Validation**:

- **Purpose**: Validates data on the user's computer as soon as an entry is made or before the form is submitted.

- **Implementation**: Typically involves checking the validity of field values using condition checks and providing immediate feedback.

2. **Server-side Validation**:

- **Purpose**: Checks the data on the server after it has been submitted, ensuring it adheres to business rules and security measures not enforced on the client side.

- **Implementation**: This involves re-validating data on the backend before committing it to the database.

3. **Field-Level Validation**:

- **Purpose**: Ensures that each individual field contains data formatted correctly and according to requirements.

- **Implementation**: Can include checking if the field is not empty, verifying the format (e.g., email or phone number), or ensuring the data does not exceed specified limits.

4. **Form-Level Validation**:

- **Purpose**: Checks the validity of data across multiple fields to ensure overall form accuracy and coherence.

- **Implementation**: Involves conditions that compare data between fields, such as ensuring a start date is earlier than an end date.

Examples of Form Validation Techniques

1. **Using Input Masks**:

- **Purpose**: Enforces specific formatting for field entries.

- **Example**: An input mask in an "Phone Number" field ensures entries are in the format (XXX) XXX-XXXX.

- **Code Sample** (Microsoft Access):

Set the Input Mask property in the field properties to "(000) 000-0000;0;_"

2. **Built-in Data Validation Rules**:

*   **Purpose**: Provides a way to enforce rules directly within table design or form controls.

*   **Example**: Setting a validation rule in a "Date of Birth" field to ensure the date is reasonable (e.g., not in the future).

*   **Code Sample** (Microsoft Access):

Validation Rule: <=Date() AND >Date()-365*150

Validation Text: "Enter a valid date of birth."

Event-Driven Validation with VBA:

*   **Purpose**: Offers complex and custom validation logic that can be triggered by form events.

*   **Example**: Ensuring that a user confirms their email address correctly before submitting.

*   **VBA Example**:

```vba
Private Sub txtEmail_Exit(Cancel As Integer)
  If txtEmail.Value <> txtConfirmEmail.Value Then
    MsgBox "Email addresses do not match. Please re-enter."
    txtConfirmEmail.SetFocus
    Cancel = True
  End If
End Sub
```

Visual Representation of Form Validation

Diagram Example:

```
+---------------------------------------------------------------+
|                    Registration Form                          |
+---------------------------------------------------------------+
| [Name          ]                                              |
| [Email         ] <Validating: Must contain '@' and '.'>       |
| [Confirm Email] <Validating: Must match Email>                |
| [Date of Birth] <Validating: Must be a past date>             |
| [Submit] <Enabled only if all fields are valid>               |
+---------------------------------------------------------------+
```

Form validation is an indispensable part of designing effective data entry forms in Microsoft Access. By incorporating various validation techniques, developers can ensure that data captured through forms is accurate and compliant with specified requirements. This proactive approach to data quality reduces the need for error handling after data submission, streamlining data processing, and improving overall system reliability and user satisfaction.

Conclusion

Effective form design in Microsoft Access is crucial for ensuring efficient and accurate data entry. By focusing on user-friendly layouts, efficient data handling, and robust validation, forms can greatly enhance the usability and functionality of a database application. Regularly revisiting and revising form designs based on user feedback and changing needs is essential for maintaining an effective data entry environment.

Chapter 6 - Crafting Reports for Analysis

In database management systems like Microsoft Access, reports are vital tools used to compile and present data in a structured, readable format. Crafting effective reports allows organizations to analyze data, support decision-making processes, and communicate information clearly to stakeholders. A well-designed report transforms raw data into actionable insights through careful layout, calculated fields, and visualization elements.

Key Components of Effective Report Design

1. **Data Selection and Organization**:

- **Purpose**: Ensure that the report provides all necessary information in an organized manner to answer specific business questions or track performance metrics.

- **Implementation**: Include relevant data fields, use grouping and sorting to organize data logically, and ensure data is filtered appropriately to focus on key areas of interest.

2. **Layout and Aesthetics**:

- **Purpose**: Enhance the readability and appeal of the report.

- **Implementation**: Use headers and footers for consistency, employ charts or graphs for visual data representation, and adhere to a clean layout with appropriate use of whitespace and fonts.

3. **Interactivity**:

- **Purpose**: Allow users to interact with the report dynamically, exploring different facets of the data as needed.

- **Implementation**: Implement features like drill-downs, parameter queries for dynamic filtering, and interactive sorting.

4. **Accuracy and Timeliness**:

- **Purpose**: Ensure that reports reflect the most current and accurate data available, maintaining credibility and relevance.

- **Implementation**: Automate data updates where possible and provide clear timestamps to indicate when data was last refreshed.

Steps to Crafting an Analytical Report in Microsoft Access

1. **Define the Report's Objective**:

- Determine what questions the report needs to answer and identify the target audience. For instance, a sales report might aim to show monthly sales trends and identify top-performing products.

2. **Select and Query Data**:

- Use queries to gather and prepare data for the report. This might involve aggregating sales data by month and product category or filtering data to exclude irrelevant entries.

3. **Design the Report Layout**:

- Start with a template or a blank report. Arrange data elements and controls like text boxes, labels, and data fields on the report canvas. Prioritize the most important data (like key metrics or trends) and place it prominently.

4. **Incorporate Visual Elements**:

- Add charts, graphs, and images to visually summarize data and highlight key points. For example, use a bar chart to show comparative sales figures across different regions.

5. **Test and Refine**:

- Preview the report to check for data accuracy and visual alignment. Adjust the design based on feedback from potential users to ensure the report meets its intended purpose effectively.

6. **Deploy and Schedule Updates**:

- Once the report is finalized, make it available to end-users, either through direct access in Access or via scheduled email distributions. Set up periodic updates to the report data to maintain its relevance.

Example: Monthly Sales Report

Visual Example:

```
+-----------------------------------------------------------+
|                   Monthly Sales Report                    |
+-----------------------------------------------------------+
| Sales Trends (Jan - Dec)          | Top 5 Products        |
| [Bar Chart]                       | [Pie Chart]           |
+-----------------------------------------------------------+
| Detailed Sales Data                                       |
| Product | Jan | Feb | Mar | ... | Dec | Total | % of Total |
+-----------------------------------------------------------+
| Prod A  | $20K| $25K| $30K| ... | $45K| $350K | 15%       |
| Prod B  | $15K| $20K| $25K| ... | $40K| $300K | 12%       |
+-----------------------------------------------------------+
|                     [Print] [Export]                      |
+-----------------------------------------------------------+
```

Description:

- **Sales Trends**: A bar chart displays monthly sales trends over the year, providing a quick visual analysis of sales performance.

- **Top 5 Products**: A pie chart shows the revenue contribution of the top 5 products, highlighting the most successful products.

- **Detailed Sales Data**: A table lists sales by product per month with totals and percentage contributions, offering a detailed breakdown for deeper analysis.

Designing Readable Reports:

Readable reports are essential in data analysis as they directly influence the ability of stakeholders to understand and act upon the information presented. The design of a report in database systems like Microsoft Access involves not just the presentation of data, but also ensuring that the data is accessible, clear, and effectively communicated. This process is critical in turning raw data into actionable insights.

Principles of Designing Readable Reports

1. **Clear Hierarchy and Structure:**

- **Purpose**: Facilitate easy navigation through the report by establishing a visual hierarchy and logical structure.

- **Implementation**: Use headings and subheadings to denote different sections clearly. Employ consistent formatting styles (e.g., bold for headings, italics for subheadings) to guide the reader's eye through the report.

2. **Consistent Layout**:

- **Purpose**: Enhance the readability by maintaining a consistent layout throughout the report.

- **Implementation**: Align text and data consistently across pages. Use grid systems to layout elements neatly. Ensure that margins, font sizes, and spacing are uniform.

3. **Legible Typography**:

- **Purpose**: Ensure that the text is easy to read and understand.

- **Implementation**: Choose fonts that are easy to read (e.g., Arial, Calibri, Times New Roman) and appropriate for the medium (print or screen). Use font sizes that are large enough to be read comfortably. Reserve decorative fonts for titles or headings only.

4. **Effective Use of Color**:

- **Purpose**: Utilize colors to draw attention, indicate status, or differentiate data without overwhelming the user.

- **Implementation**: Use a color palette that provides good contrast and is accessible to those with color vision deficiencies. Use color sparingly to highlight key data points or sections.

5. **Data Visualization**:

- **Purpose**: Help the reader to quickly comprehend complex data and identify patterns.

- **Implementation**: Incorporate charts, graphs, and tables where appropriate. Choose the type of visualization based on what best represents the data (e.g., bar charts for comparisons, line graphs for trends).

6. **Interactive Elements** (if applicable):

- **Purpose**: Enhance user engagement and provide a dynamic way to explore data.

- **Implementation**: Include interactive elements such as drill-downs, tooltips, or hyperlinks that allow users to explore layers of data or access related information seamlessly.

Example: Sales Performance Report

Visual Description of a Well-Designed Sales Report:

- **Title**: Bold and centered at the top of the first page.

- **Headers**: Distinct style, perhaps shaded with a light color for easy identification.

- **Text**: Consistent font type and size across the report, with larger fonts for headings.

- **Colors**: Use a subtle color scheme with blue for text headers, gray for grid lines, and a soft color background for charts.

- **Charts**: A pie chart illustrating product category sales mix; a line graph showing monthly trends.

- **Tables**: Clearly delineated rows and columns with alternate row coloring for ease of reading.

```
+-----------------------------------------------------------------+
|                    Sales Performance Report                     |
|                       Fiscal Year 2023                          |
+-----------------------------------------------------------------+
| Sales Trends by Month                                           |
| [Line Graph: Jan-Dec]                                           |
+-----------------------------------------------------------------+
| Sales Breakdown by Product Category                             |
| [Pie Chart: Category A, B, C, D]                                |
+-----------------------------------------------------------------+
| Detailed Sales Data                                             |
| +-------------+---------+---------+---------+-----------+ |
| | Product     | Jan '23 | Feb '23 | Mar '23 | ...       | |
| +-------------+---------+---------+---------+-----------+ |
| | Product A   | $5,000  | $7,000  | $6,500  | ...       | |
| | Product B   | $3,000  | $4,000  | $2,500  | ...       | |
| +-------------+---------+---------+---------+-----------+ |
+-----------------------------------------------------------------+
| Notes:                                                          |
| * All figures are in USD.                                       |
| * For detailed product-wise data, refer to Appendix A.          |
+-----------------------------------------------------------------+
```

Designing readable reports is a crucial skill in data management that enhances the utility and effectiveness of the data presented. By adhering to principles of good design, such as clarity, consistency, and effective use of visual aids, you can ensure that your reports are not only informative but also engaging and easy to understand. This approach not only facilitates better decision-making but also significantly enhances user interaction with the data.

Data Grouping and Summarization:

In the context of report crafting, particularly within database applications like Microsoft Access, data grouping and summarization are crucial techniques for presenting complex information in an organized and digestible manner. These techniques allow users to see patterns, compare grouped data, and make informed decisions quickly. Effective use of grouping and summarization transforms extensive data sets into clear insights through structured presentation and calculated summaries.

Key Techniques for Effective Data Grouping and Summarization

1. **Grouping Data**:

- **Purpose**: Organize data into categories that make the data easier to understand and analyze.

- **Implementation**: Data can be grouped by specific attributes, such as date, category, department, or any other relevant criterion. In Microsoft Access, grouping is typically done through query design, where data is sorted and grouped under a specific field.

2. **Summarization**:

- **Purpose**: Reduce detailed data into essential summaries using various aggregation functions.

- **Implementation**: Common summarization functions include counting the number of items in a group, calculating totals, or computing averages, minimums, and maximums. This is often achieved in Access using SQL aggregation functions like **SUM()**, **AVG()**, **COUNT()**, **MIN()**, and **MAX()** within grouped queries.

Steps to Implement Grouping and Summarization in Reports

1. **Identify Grouping and Summarization Needs**:

- Determine what information stakeholders need to see and how best to categorize that information. For example, a sales report might be grouped by region and summarized by total sales and average transaction value.

2. **Design the Query**:

- Create queries in Access that pull and group the necessary data. Use SQL **GROUP BY** clauses to organize data and **SUM()**, **AVG()**, or other functions to provide summarized data.

3. **Create the Report**:

- Use the grouped and summarized query as the source for the report. In Access, when designing the report, set grouping and sorting rules to define how data is displayed.

4. **Format the Report for Clarity**:

- Clearly label each group and ensure that summarization points are prominently displayed. Use formatting options like bold text, different font sizes, or color highlights to distinguish summary data from detailed data.

Example: Monthly Sales Report by Region

Scenario: You need to create a report in Microsoft Access that shows total sales and average sale value by region for each month.

Query Design:

```
SELECT Region, Month, SUM(Sales) AS TotalSales, AVG(Sales) AS AverageSale

FROM SalesData

GROUP BY Region, Month

ORDER BY Month, Region;
```

Report Layout:

- **Header**: Report title, date range of the data.

- **Body**: Data grouped first by month, then by region. Each region shows total sales and average sale.

- **Footer**: Overall totals and averages for the report period.

Visual Example:

```
+---------------------------------------------+
|              Monthly Sales Report           |
|              January - June                 |
+---------------------------------------------+
| January                                     |
|   Northeast                                 |
|     Total Sales: $120,000                   |
|     Average Sale: $1,200                    |
|   Midwest                                   |
|     Total Sales: $90,000                    |
|     Average Sale: $1,000                    |
+---------------------------------------------+
| February                                    |
|   Northeast                                 |
|     Total Sales: $150,000                   |
|     Average Sale: $1,250                    |
|   Midwest                                   |
|     Total Sales: $95,000                    |
|     Average Sale: $950                      |
+---------------------------------------------+
| Totals                                      |
|   Total Sales: $455,000                     |
|   Overall Average Sale: $1,125              |
+---------------------------------------------+
```

Data grouping and summarization are powerful techniques in report crafting that enhance the comprehensibility and usefulness of reports. By effectively organizing and summarizing data, reports can highlight key information and trends that support strategic business decisions. Implementing these techniques in Microsoft Access involves careful query design and thoughtful report layout planning, ensuring that the final product is both informative and easy to navigate.

Incorporating Charts and Graphics:

Incorporating charts and graphics into reports is an effective way to visually represent data, making complex information easier to understand and more engaging for the audience. In database management systems like Microsoft Access, the integration of visual elements such as charts, graphs, and other illustrative graphics can transform textual data into visual stories, enhancing the report's ability to communicate insights clearly and effectively.

Benefits of Using Charts and Graphics

<u>Enhanced Comprehension</u>:

In the realm of data analysis and report crafting, the use of charts and graphics plays a pivotal role in enhancing comprehension. Visual representations of data help to distill complex information into accessible and immediately understandable formats, facilitating quicker and more intuitive analysis. This capability is crucial in supporting stakeholders to grasp detailed datasets and insights effortlessly.

Why Visuals Enhance Comprehension

1. **Simplification of Complex Data**:

- **Explanation**: Charts and graphics transform large quantities of data and complex relationships into simpler, more digestible visual formats. This allows users to recognize patterns, trends, and outliers more quickly than they could through tables of raw data.

- **Example**: A line graph showing sales trends over several years immediately highlights growth patterns, seasonal variations, and any anomalies, far more quickly than a table could convey.

2. **Immediate Data Interpretation**:

- **Explanation**: Visual tools enable the instant interpretation of data contexts and magnitudes, which text or tables alone may fail to communicate effectively.

- **Example**: A bar chart comparing the performance of different departments within an organization allows managers to instantly see which are under- or over-performing, without needing to delve into specific numbers.

3. **Facilitates Better Memory Retention**:

- **Explanation**: Visuals are more memorable than text-based data. People tend to recall information that they have seen depicted graphically much more easily than data they have read in text form.

- **Example**: An infographic summarizing customer satisfaction ratings and key feedback points is more likely to be remembered than a similar summary presented in a text-based report.

4. **Supports Pattern Recognition**:

- **Explanation**: Charts and graphs excel at revealing patterns in data, whether they are trends over time, correlations between variables, or distributions.

- **Example**: A scatter plot might be used to illustrate the relationship between advertising spend and sales revenue, clearly showing how changes in one variable relate to changes in the other.

Implementing Effective Visuals for Enhanced Comprehension

1. **Choose the Right Type of Chart**:

- Depending on what you need to communicate, select a chart that best fits the data. Use pie charts for proportions, line graphs for trends, bar charts for comparisons, and scatter plots for relationships.

2. **Keep it Simple**:

- Avoid cluttering visuals with too much information. Focus on key data points, and use labels and legends only where necessary to make the graph understandable.

3. **Use Color Effectively**:

- Utilize color to highlight important data points or to distinguish between different data sets within a chart. However, ensure that the color contrasts used are accessible to all users, including those with color vision deficiencies.

4. **Incorporate Data Labels and Tooltips**:

- When hovering over or clicking on a specific part of a chart, tooltips can provide additional information or precise data values. Data labels can offer immediate clarity and should be used judiciously to enhance readability without overcrowding the visual.

Visual Example: Sales Volume Over Five Years

Line Graph Description:

```
+------------------------------------------------+
|              Sales Volume Over Five Years      |
|    (X-axis: Years, Y-axis: Sales in $)         |
|                                                |
| 120K ------------------------------------o     |
| 100K --------------------------------o---/     |
|  80K ----------------------------o----/        |
|  60K ----------------------o-----/             |
|  40K ----------o----/                          |
|  20K --o-----/                                 |
|  0K -/                                         |
| 2016  2017  2018  2019  2020                   |
+------------------------------------------------+
```

Explanation:

This line graph depicts a clear upward trend in sales volume from 2016 to 2020, allowing viewers to quickly grasp the growth trajectory without needing to process individual data points from a table.

The strategic use of charts and graphics significantly enhances the comprehension of complex data in reports. By transforming numerical data into visual formats, stakeholders can quickly understand, retain, and act upon the insights derived from data analysis, making visualizations an indispensable tool in any data-driven decision-making process.

Increased Engagement:

In data analysis and reporting, engaging the audience is crucial to ensure the information presented is not only understood but also retains the attention of viewers long enough to make an impact. Incorporating charts and graphics into reports significantly enhances engagement by making the data more visually appealing and easier to digest. This visual approach can transform a standard report into a compelling data narrative that captures and maintains audience interest.

Why Visuals Increase Engagement

1. **Visual Appeal**:

- **Explanation**: Humans are naturally drawn to visual content. Well-designed charts and graphics can make reports more visually attractive, encouraging users to explore the data further.

- **Example**: A colorful pie chart showing market share distribution among competitors can immediately draw attention compared to a table listing the same data.

2. **Simplifies Complex Information**:

- **Explanation**: Graphics can simplify complex information, making it more accessible and less intimidating for users who may not be experts in data analysis.

- **Example**: A complex correlation between demographic factors and product preferences can be easily represented through a heat map, simplifying the understanding of dense statistical data.

3. **Storytelling**:

- **Explanation**: Visuals can tell a story with data, guiding the viewer through a logical narrative that explains trends, correlations, or patterns in a way that words alone cannot.

- **Example**: A series of line graphs depicting the growth of a company's revenue over several years, accompanied by bar charts of market conditions, can narrate the story of the company's success and the market dynamics influencing that growth.

4. **Interactive Elements**:

- **Explanation**: Interactive charts and graphics invite users to engage with the data by exploring different views, drilling down into specifics, or even modifying the data scope.

- **Example**: An interactive dashboard that allows users to select different time ranges or product categories to see how sales figures change accordingly.

Implementing Engaging Visuals in Reports

1. **Use Diverse Visualization Types**:

- To cater to different data types and insights, utilize a mix of visualization tools like bar charts, scatter plots, timelines, and area charts to maintain viewer interest and cater to different analytical needs.

2. **Incorporate Motion or Animation**:

- Where possible, use subtle animations when transitioning between states in interactive reports or dashboards to draw attention and provide a dynamic viewing experience.

3. **Optimize for Clarity and Aesthetics**:

- Ensure that visuals are not only informative but also aesthetically pleasing. Pay attention to color schemes, font choices, and layout designs that enhance the overall visual impact without sacrificing clarity.

4. **Design for Interactivity**:

- Develop interactive elements in online or digital reports where users can hover, click, or scroll to discover additional data layers. This functionality increases engagement by making the user an active participant in data exploration.

Example: Annual Sales Performance Dashboard

Visual Example:

```
+------------------------------------------------------+
|                 Annual Sales Dashboard               |
|                                                      |
| [Revenue Growth] [Line Chart: 2016-2021]             |
|   - Highlight key growth periods with animation      |
|                                                      |
| [Market Share]  [Pie Chart: 2021]                    |
|   - Interactive: Hover to see % of each segment      |
|                                                      |
| [Sales by Region] [Heat Map]                         |
|   - Interactive: Click on region for more detail     |
|                                                      |
| [User Engagement]                                    |
| [Scatter Plot: Usage vs. Satisfaction]               |
|   - Dynamic elements adjust as data filters change   |
+------------------------------------------------------+
```

Charts and graphics significantly enhance the engagement level of reports by providing visually appealing and interactive ways to explore data. This increased engagement not only makes the data more accessible but also encourages a deeper understanding and retention of the information presented, ultimately supporting better-informed decisions based on the analysis. By carefully designing and implementing thoughtful visuals, data analysts can transform standard reports into engaging, insightful tools for data storytelling.

<u>Effective Comparison</u>:

Effective comparison is a critical aspect of data analysis that allows stakeholders to evaluate differences, trends, and performance metrics across various dimensions. Charts and graphics significantly enhance the ability to perform these comparisons by visually distinguishing data in an intuitive and immediate way. This visual approach can simplify the understanding of complex data sets, making comparisons not only faster but also clearer and more impactful.

Why Visuals are Crucial for Effective Comparisons

1. **Immediate Visual Distinctions**:

- **Explanation**: Visual elements like colors, shapes, and sizes can be used to quickly highlight differences between data sets.

- **Example**: A clustered bar chart displaying sales performance across multiple regions can use different colors for each region, allowing viewers to instantly see which regions are performing better or worse.

2. **Simplification of Complex Data**:

- **Explanation**: Graphics can condense complex data into simple visual forms, making it easier to compare large amounts of data at once.

- **Example**: A stacked line graph could show the evolution of market shares of different companies over time, making it easy to compare growth trajectories and market dynamics.

3. **Enhanced Pattern Recognition**:

- **Explanation**: Charts organize data in patterns that the human eye is adept at recognizing. This organization helps in identifying trends, outliers, and anomalies more efficiently.

- **Example**: A scatter plot illustrating the relationship between advertising spend and sales revenue across different media channels helps identify which channels yield the highest ROI.

4. **Scalability of Data Presentation**:

- **Explanation**: Graphics can effectively represent varying scales of data, from very small to very large, without losing readability.

- **Example**: Logarithmic scales in line charts can help compare growth rates of companies starting from different foundational revenues.

Implementing Visuals for Effective Comparisons

1. **Choose the Right Type of Chart**:

- Different types of data and comparisons might require different types of charts. Use bar charts for direct comparisons of quantities, line charts for trends over time, pie charts for proportions, and scatter plots for correlational data.

2. **Use Consistent and Distinguishing Features**:

- Employ consistent visual features (like color schemes, symbols, or line styles) across similar data types to aid in recognition and comparison. Distinctive features should be used to highlight key differences or important data points.

3. **Highlight Key Comparisons**:

- Use graphical tools like trend lines, reference lines, or differing opacity to draw attention to important comparisons or significant findings within the data.

4. **Interactive and Dynamic Visuals**:

- Enhance static charts with interactive elements such as tooltips, clickable legends that toggle data sets on and off, or sliders that adjust the range of displayed data. This allows users to make custom comparisons based on their specific interests or needs.

Example: Comparative Revenue Analysis by Product

Visual Description:

```
+-------------------------------------------------+
|                Revenue by Product               |
|                                                 |
| [2019]           [2020]           [2021]        |
| [Bar Chart]      [Bar Chart]      [Bar Chart]   |
|                                                 |
| - Each bar represents a product                 |
| - Different colors for each year highlight trends |
| - Hover to see exact revenue figures            |
+-------------------------------------------------+
```

Explanation:

Three bar charts are placed side by side, each representing a different year. Each chart includes the same set of products, allowing for direct year-over-year revenue comparisons. Color coding by year across all charts helps to track the performance of each product over time.

Using charts and graphics for effective comparison in data reports offers a robust method for presenting data that enhances understanding, accelerates decision-making, and reveals deeper insights into patterns and trends. By carefully designing visuals that highlight key data differences and relationships, analysts can provide stakeholders with powerful tools to interpret complex information with clarity and precision.

Types of Charts and Graphics for Reports

1. **Bar Charts:**

- **Use Case**: Ideal for comparing quantities across different categories.

- **Example**: Comparing monthly sales across different regions.

2. **Line Graphs:**

- **Use Case**: Best for illustrating trends over time.

- **Example**: Showing sales growth from month to month within a year.

3. **Pie Charts:**

- **Use Case**: Useful for showing proportions and percentages that make up a whole.

- **Example**: Displaying the market share of different product categories.

4. **Scatter Plots**:

- **Use Case**: Effective for identifying relationships and distributions between two variables.

- **Example**: Analyzing the correlation between advertising spend and sales volume.

5. **Infographics**:

- **Use Case**: Combining data visualization with text to explain complex information succinctly.

- **Example**: Summarizing customer demographics alongside purchasing trends.

Steps to Incorporate Charts and Graphics in Microsoft Access Reports

1. **Data Preparation**:

- Ensure that data is clean and well-organized. Aggregate or summarize data as necessary to support the chosen visual representations.

2. **Selecting Appropriate Charts**:

- Choose a chart type that best represents the data and supports the report's objectives. Consider the message that the chart needs to convey and select accordingly.

3. **Creating Charts in Access**:

- Use the Chart Wizard in Microsoft Access to insert charts:

- Choose the chart type and specify the data source.

- Configure the axes and data fields. For example, set the x-axis as time (months) and the y-axis as sales figures.

- Customize the chart's appearance with titles, legends, and colors.

4. **Integrating Charts into Reports**:

- Place charts strategically within the report to support the textual content.

- Ensure that each graphic has a clear title and labels for easy understanding.

5. **Testing and Refinement**:

- Preview the report to assess the clarity and impact of the charts and graphics.

- Adjust layouts and settings as needed to improve visibility and effectiveness.

Visual Example of a Report with Charts

```
+-------------------------------------------------+
|               Annual Sales Report               |
+-------------------------------------------------+
| Sales Growth by Month                           |
| [Line Graph: Jan - Dec]                         |
+-------------------------------------------------+
| Sales Distribution by Product Category          |
| [Pie Chart: Category A, B, C, D]                |
+-------------------------------------------------+
| Comparative Regional Sales                      |
| [Bar Chart: Northeast, Midwest, South, West]|
+-------------------------------------------------+
| Detailed Sales Data Table                       |
| +-------+-------+-------+-------+                |
| | Jan   | Feb   | Mar   | Apr   | ...           |
| +-------+-------+-------+-------+                |
| | $20K  | $25K  | $30K  | $35K  | ...           |
| +-------+-------+-------+-------+                |
+-------------------------------------------------+
```

Charts and graphics are essential components of modern reports, enhancing both the aesthetic appeal and the communicative power of the data presented. In Microsoft Access, the integration of these visual tools into reports not only helps in portraying data in a more accessible manner but also supports a deeper and more immediate understanding of the underlying trends and messages. Properly implemented, these visual elements can significantly elevate the effectiveness of business reports.

Conclusion

Crafting reports in Microsoft Access is an essential skill for transforming data into insightful, actionable, and visually appealing formats. Effective reports are meticulously designed to meet specific analytical needs, ensuring that stakeholders can make informed decisions based on reliable and timely data. By following structured steps in report design and leveraging Access's powerful reporting tools, users can significantly enhance the value of their data.

Part III: Advanced Access Features

Chapter 7 - Automation and Macros

Automation in database management systems, particularly through the use of macros, simplifies repetitive tasks, enhances consistency, and improves the efficiency of database operations. Macros are sequences of actions or commands that can be initiated by a single command or trigger. They are extensively used in systems like Microsoft Access to automate processes such as data entry, report generation, and routine data maintenance.

Benefits of Using Macros for Automation

Increased Efficiency:

In the realm of database management, especially in systems like Microsoft Access, macros play a crucial role in enhancing operational efficiency. Macros automate repetitive tasks that would otherwise require manual intervention, thus speeding up processes and reducing the workload for users. This automation is particularly beneficial in large databases or applications where consistency and speed are essential.

Understanding the Efficiency Gains from Macros

1. **Time Savings:**

- **Explanation**: Macros execute a series of commands automatically and much faster than manual processing. This speed is critical in environments where time-sensitive data updates are necessary, such as in inventory control or order processing systems.

- **Example**: A macro that automatically updates inventory levels and reorders stocks when quantities fall below a predetermined threshold can save substantial time compared to performing these tasks manually.

2. **Reduced User Interaction:**

- **Explanation**: By minimizing the steps users must take to complete a task, macros reduce the risk of errors and the physical effort involved in data entry and processing.

- **Example**: A macro could be set to run data validation checks across multiple fields upon form submission, ensuring all data meets business rules without requiring manual checks by the user.

3. **Streamlining Complex Processes**:

- **Explanation**: Macros can handle complex sequences of tasks that would be cumbersome and error-prone if performed manually. This capability is particularly valuable in data-intensive tasks such as monthly reporting or batch data processing.

- **Example**: A macro in Microsoft Access that extracts data from various tables, performs calculations, and generates a consolidated monthly sales report, all with a single trigger.

Steps to Implement Macros for Increased Efficiency

1. **Identify Repetitive Tasks**:

- Analyze daily operations to identify actions that are performed frequently and are candidates for automation.

- Focus on tasks that involve multiple steps, require data from various sources, or involve complex logic.

2. **Design the Macro**:

- Map out the sequence of actions that the macro must perform.

- Use tools like Microsoft Access Macro Builder to assemble these actions into a macro. Ensure that the macro handles exceptions or errors to avoid disruptions in automated processes.

3. **Deploy and Monitor**:

- Implement the macro in a live environment.

- Monitor its performance to ensure it operates as intended and refines the actions or logic as necessary to optimize efficiency.

Example: Auto-generating Email Reminders

Scenario: A database system that tracks project deadlines and automatically sends email reminders to team members a week before each deadline.

Macro Setup:

- **Trigger**: Set to check project deadlines daily.

- **Action Sequence**:

1. Query the database for projects whose deadlines are one week away.

2. Generate email reminders listing pending tasks.

3. Send emails to the respective project managers and team members.

- **Outcome**: Ensures timely reminders without requiring manual tracking, significantly reducing the administrative burden and enhancing project management efficiency.

Visual Diagram: Macro Workflow

```
+-------------------------------------+
|      Daily Deadline Check Macro     |
|-------------------------------------|
| [Start]                             |
|    ↓                                |
| [Query Projects]                    |
|    "Find projects with deadlines    |
|    within the next 7 days"          |
|    ↓                                |
| [Generate Emails]                   |
|    "Compose reminder emails"        |
|    ↓                                |
| [Send Emails]                       |
|    "Distribute reminders to         |
|    project teams"                   |
|    ↓                                |
| [End]                               |
+-------------------------------------+
```

Macros significantly increase the efficiency of database operations by automating repetitive and time-consuming tasks. This automation not only saves time but also reduces the likelihood of errors and frees up resources for other critical activities. By leveraging the power of macros, organizations can ensure their database systems are not only more efficient but also more effective in supporting business operations.

Error Reduction:

In data-intensive environments, human error can lead to inconsistencies, data integrity issues, and inefficiencies. Automating tasks with macros in database systems like Microsoft Access significantly reduces these risks. Macros ensure that operations are carried out in a uniform manner, minimizing the likelihood of errors typically associated with manual data entry and processing.

Why Macros Minimize Errors

1. **Consistent Execution**:

- **Explanation**: Macros perform tasks in exactly the same way every time they are run, eliminating the variations that can occur with manual processes.

- **Example**: A macro that automatically updates customer records ensures that all entries are processed under the same criteria, reducing the chance of data being incorrectly updated or omitted.

2. **Automated Validation Checks**:

- **Explanation**: Macros can include validation rules that check data for errors before it is entered into the database, ensuring compliance with data standards.

- **Example**: A macro that verifies data formats and mandatory fields before submitting a form can prevent incorrect data from being saved.

3. **Scheduled Operations**:

- **Explanation**: Macros can be scheduled to run at specific times, ensuring that routine database maintenance tasks such as backups, data cleanups, and updates are performed regularly without human intervention.

- **Example**: A nightly macro that cleans up temporary data and backs up the database ensures that these critical tasks are not overlooked.

Implementing Macros for Error Reduction

1. **Identify Error-Prone Processes**:

- Review processes that frequently result in errors. Common areas include data entry, data transfer between systems, and complex calculations.

- Prioritize automation in these areas to maximize impact on error reduction.

2. **Design and Develop Macros:**

- Develop macros using Microsoft Access's Macro Builder or VBA programming, incorporating error handling routines to manage exceptions gracefully.

- Include validation logic within macros to check data for accuracy and completeness before processing.

3. **Test and Refine:**

- Thoroughly test macros in a controlled environment to ensure they perform as expected.

- Monitor the macros post-deployment to refine their operations based on real-world feedback and error logs.

Example: Automating Invoice Processing

Scenario: Automating the invoice entry process in a financial system to reduce manual entry errors.

Macro Setup:

- **Trigger**: Activation upon form submission in the invoice entry form.

- **Action Sequence:**

1. Validate invoice details against purchase orders to ensure matching data.

2. Calculate totals and apply discounts automatically.

3. Check for duplicate entries before saving to the database.

- **Outcome**: Reduces errors in financial reporting and improves the reliability of financial data.

Visual Diagram: Invoice Processing Macro

```
+----------------------------------------------------+
|           Invoice Entry Automation Macro           |
|----------------------------------------------------|
| [Start]                                            |
|    ↓                                               |
| [Validate Invoice Against PO]                      |
|    ↓                                               |
| [Calculate Totals and Discounts]                   |
|    ↓                                               |
| [Check for Duplicates]                             |
|    ↓                                               |
| [Save to Database]                                 |
|    ↓                                               |
| [End]                                              |
+----------------------------------------------------+
```

Description:

This diagram outlines the automated steps involved in processing an invoice, ensuring that each step is validated and errors are minimized before data is committed to the database.

Utilizing macros for automation not only streamlines operations but also significantly reduces the potential for human error in database management systems. By ensuring consistent execution, validating data automatically, and scheduling routine tasks, macros enhance the accuracy and reliability of data across systems. This proactive approach to error reduction is essential for maintaining high data quality and operational efficiency in any organization.

<u>Improved Workflow:</u>

Macros are a powerful tool in database management systems for enhancing workflow efficiency and effectiveness. By automating routine and complex tasks, macros streamline operations, reduce the need for manual intervention, and ensure that processes are carried out consistently and correctly. This not only accelerates the pace of work but also improves the overall reliability of the business processes.

Benefits of Macros for Workflow Improvement

1. **Streamlined Processes:**

- **Explanation**: Macros automate sequences of tasks that typically require multiple steps, reducing the process to a single action or event.

- **Example**: A macro in Microsoft Access can automate the process of importing data, processing it according to business rules, and then exporting it to a report format, all triggered by a single user action or scheduled event.

2. **Consistency in Task Execution**:

- **Explanation**: Every time a macro runs, it performs tasks in exactly the same way, ensuring that all data is processed consistently without variations that might occur with different human operators.

- **Example**: A macro used for monthly financial closings ensures that all entries are accounted for and that calculations are performed uniformly, minimizing discrepancies.

3. **Error Handling and Reduction**:

- **Explanation**: Macros can include sophisticated error-checking and handling mechanisms that detect, log, and even correct errors as they occur.

- **Example**: A data validation macro can check entries for errors, alert users to discrepancies, and prevent the saving of incorrect data.

4. **Integration of Multiple Systems**:

- **Explanation**: Macros can serve as a bridge to connect disparate systems within an organization, facilitating smooth data flow between them.

- **Example**: A macro might extract customer data from a CRM system, process it in Access for analysis, and then push needed updates to an inventory management system.

Steps to Implement Macros for Improved Workflow

1. **Identify Bottlenecks and Repetitive Tasks**:

- Analyze current workflows to identify areas where tasks are repetitive, prone to error, or where bottlenecks frequently occur.

- Prioritize these areas for automation.

2. **Design the Macro**:

- Map out the workflow that the macro will automate. Define each step of the process, the data inputs and outputs, and any decision points or conditions that affect how the macro should function.

- Develop the macro using Microsoft Access's Macro Builder or Visual Basic for Applications (VBA), depending on the complexity of the tasks involved.

3. **Test and Deploy the Macro**:

- Rigorously test the macro in a controlled environment to ensure it functions correctly and handles errors appropriately.

- Deploy the macro in a live environment, monitor its performance, and make adjustments as necessary.

Example: Order Processing System Automation

Scenario: Automating the order entry, processing, and invoicing system in a sales department to reduce manual entry and speed up order fulfillment.

Macro Design:

- **Trigger**: Activation when a new order is entered into the system.

- **Action Sequence**:

1. Validate product availability from inventory.

2. Calculate total order cost, including applicable discounts and taxes.

3. Generate an invoice and email it to the customer.

4. Update inventory levels.

- **Outcome**: Reduces order processing time from several hours to minutes, increases accuracy, and enhances customer satisfaction.

Visual Workflow Diagram: Order Processing Automation

```
+- - - - - - - - - - - - - - - - - - - - - - - - - - - - - - - - +
|                    Order Processing Macro                      |
|- - - - - - - - - - - - - - - - - - - - - - - - - - - - - - - - |
| [New Order Entered]                                            |
|     ↓                                                          |
| [Check Inventory]                                              |
|     ↓                                                          |
| [Calculate Costs and Discounts]                                |
|     ↓                                                          |
| [Generate and Send Invoice]                                    |
|     ↓                                                          |
| [Update Inventory]                                             |
|     ↓                                                          |
| [End]                                                          |
+- - - - - - - - - - - - - - - - - - - - - - - - - - - - - - - - +
```

Description:

This diagram illustrates the automated steps involved in processing an order, showing how multiple tasks are consolidated into a streamlined workflow through macro automation.

Using macros to automate workflows in Microsoft Access and other database management systems significantly enhances operational efficiency, consistency, and reliability. By reducing the need for manual interventions and ensuring that processes are executed consistently, macros help organizations to optimize their workflows, thereby saving time, reducing errors, and improving overall productivity.

Types of Macros in Microsoft Access

1. **Data Macros**: Similar to triggers in other database systems, data macros perform actions automatically in response to table events like adding, updating, or deleting records.

2. **User Interface (UI) Macros**: These are used to automate tasks related to the user interface, such as opening forms, generating reports, or customizing navigation within an application.

Examples of Commonly Used Macros

1. **Autoexec Macro**:

- **Purpose**: Automatically perform specific actions when a database is opened.

- **Example**: A macro that opens a specific form, checks for updates, or performs a security check when the database starts.

2. **Form Automation Macro**:

- **Purpose**: Control form behaviors like opening other forms, querying data, or updating fields based on user interactions.

- **Example**: A macro attached to a button on a form that submits data, then opens another form based on the entered information.

3. **Report Generation Macro**:

- **Purpose**: Automate the process of generating and formatting reports at scheduled times or in response to user actions.

- **Example**: A macro that runs a sales report at the end of each day, formats it, and then emails it to specified users.

Implementing a Simple Macro in Microsoft Access

Scenario: You want to create a macro that automatically sends a thank you email to a customer after a new order is placed.

Steps:

1. **Open the Macro Builder**: Navigate to the 'Create' tab in Access and click on 'Macro'. This opens the Macro Builder tool.

2. **Choose the Action**: Select the 'SendEmail' action from the list of available actions.

3. **Configure the Action**:

- **To**: Add a field that dynamically inserts the customer's email address.

- **Subject**: "Thank you for your order!"

- **Message**: Construct a generic thank you message, or personalize it using data from the order.

4. **Trigger the Macro**: Attach this macro to the 'After Insert' event on the Orders table, ensuring it executes each time a new order is recorded.

Visual Example: Macro in Action

```
+------------------------------------------------------+
| [Database: Customer Orders]                          |
|                                                      |
| [Table: Orders]                                      |
|  - [New Record Entered]                              |
|      -> Trigger: After Insert                         |
|      -> Action: SendEmail                             |
|          To: [CustomerEmail]                         |
|          Subject: "Thank you for your order!"        |
|          Message: "We appreciate your business..."   |
+------------------------------------------------------+
```

Automating Repetitive Tasks with Macros:

In database management systems like Microsoft Access, automating repetitive tasks with macros can significantly enhance efficiency and accuracy. Macros are powerful tools that execute a series of commands automatically to perform operations that would otherwise be manual and time-consuming. This automation is crucial for tasks that are mundane, error-prone, or too complex to perform manually on a consistent basis.

Benefits of Automating Repetitive Tasks

1. **Time Savings**:

-   Automating repetitive tasks frees up valuable time for users to focus on more strategic activities that require human intervention and decision-making.

2. **Increased Accuracy**:

-   Macros execute the same steps in the same order every time, dramatically reducing the likelihood of errors associated with manual processes.

3. **Consistency**:

-   Automation ensures that tasks are performed consistently, regardless of who is using the system or other external factors, leading to reliable and predictable outcomes.

Common Repetitive Tasks Suitable for Automation

1. **Data Entry**:

- **Task**: Entering customer information into a database.

- **Automation**: A macro that pulls data from input forms and populates database tables, ensuring all data fields are filled correctly.

2. **Report Generation**:

- **Task**: Generating daily sales reports.

- **Automation**: A macro scheduled to run at the end of each day, compiling sales data into a report format and distributing it via email to relevant stakeholders.

3. **Data Backup**:

- **Task**: Backing up database files.

- **Automation**: A macro that runs nightly to copy database files to a secure location, ensuring data integrity and availability.

Steps to Automate Repetitive Tasks with Macros

1. **Identify Repetitive Processes**:

- Analyze daily operations to pinpoint tasks that are performed frequently and consume substantial time or are prone to human error.

2. **Design the Macro**:

- Use Microsoft Access Macro Builder or VBA (Visual Basic for Applications) to create a macro that encapsulates the necessary commands and logic.

- Include error handling within the macro to manage exceptions and ensure the macro can handle unexpected situations gracefully.

3. **Implement and Test the Macro**:

- Integrate the macro into the daily workflow.

- Test the macro extensively to ensure it functions as intended under various scenarios.

- Gather feedback from users and refine the macro based on real-world usage.

4. **Deploy and Monitor**:

- Roll out the macro for regular use.

- Monitor its performance and impact on workflow efficiency.

- Make adjustments as necessary to optimize its functionality.

Example: Automating Customer Onboarding Emails

Scenario: Automating the process of sending welcome emails to new customers upon their registration.

Macro Design:

- **Trigger**: Activation when a new customer record is added to the database.

- **Action Sequence**:

1. Check the completion of the customer profile.

2. Retrieve the customer's email address from the database.

3. Generate a personalized welcome email.

4. Send the email using predefined email templates.

- **Outcome**: Ensures every new customer receives a timely welcome email, enhancing customer engagement and satisfaction.

Visual Diagram: Email Automation Process

```
+-------------------------------------------------+
|           Email Automation Workflow             |
|-------------------------------------------------|
| [New Customer Added]                            |
|     ↓                                           |
| [Verify Profile Completion]                     |
|     ↓                                           |
| [Retrieve Email Address]                        |
|     ↓                                           |
| [Generate Personalized Email]                   |
|     ↓                                           |
| [Send Email]                                    |
|     ↓                                           |
| [Log Activity]                                  |
|     ↓                                           |
| [End]                                           |
+-------------------------------------------------+
```

Description:

This flowchart illustrates the automated steps involved in sending a welcome email to new customers, showing how a macro can streamline a key communication process.

Automating repetitive tasks with macros in database systems is an effective way to enhance operational efficiency, improve data accuracy, and ensure consistency in processes. By leveraging macros, organizations can reduce the burden of mundane tasks, allowing staff to concentrate on more critical aspects of their work, thus optimizing overall productivity and performance.

Connecting Forms and Reports to Macros:

In database management systems like Microsoft Access, connecting forms and reports to macros significantly enhances the functionality and user experience. This integration allows automated actions based on user inputs or report triggers, streamlining processes, and ensuring data consistency and accuracy throughout the application.

Benefits of Connecting Macros to Forms and Reports

1.   **Automated Data Processing:**

- Macros can automatically process data entered in forms, reducing manual effort and improving efficiency.

2. **Dynamic Report Generation**:

- Connecting reports to macros can facilitate dynamic generation of reports based on current data and specific user criteria, ensuring reports are always up-to-date and relevant.

3. **Enhanced User Interactivity**:

- Macros can respond to user actions in forms, such as button clicks or field changes, enhancing interactivity and responsiveness of the database application.

Common Use Cases for Macros in Forms and Reports

1. **Form Submission Actions**:

- **Task**: Processing data when a form is submitted.

- **Automation**: A macro that validates form data, updates records in the database, and then triggers a confirmation message or updates related content.

2. **Conditional Report Actions**:

- **Task**: Generating reports based on specific conditions or user inputs.

- **Automation**: A macro that runs when a user specifies certain parameters (e.g., date range, department) and generates a tailored report reflecting those parameters.

Steps to Connect Macros to Forms and Reports

1. **Identify Interaction Points**:

- Determine where users interact with forms or where reports need to respond dynamically to data or input conditions.

2. **Design the Macro**:

- Using Microsoft Access's Macro Builder, design macros that perform necessary actions based on the identified interaction points.

3. **Link Macros to Forms/Reports**:

- Connect the macros to specific events in forms (e.g., **On Click, After Update**) or report triggers (e.g., **On Open, On Close**).

4. **Test and Refine**:

- Rigorously test the integrated system to ensure that the macros execute correctly and enhance the form or report functionality as intended.

Example: Automated Email Notification on Form Submission

Scenario: Sending an automated email notification when a user submits a project completion form.

Macro Design:

- **Trigger**: Form submission (**On Click** event of the Submit button).

- **Actions**:

1. Validate the data entered in the form.

2. Update the project status in the database.

3. Send an email to the project manager notifying them of the completion.

- **Tools**: Microsoft Access Macro Builder for setting up the macro, linked to VBA scripts for handling the email sending functionality.

Visual Diagram: Email Notification Macro Process

```
+------------------------------------------------------+
|        Project Completion Notification Flow          |
|------------------------------------------------------|
| [Form Submission]                                    |
|    ↓                                                 |
| [Validate Data]                                      |
|    ↓                                                 |
| [Update Project Status]                              |
|    ↓                                                 |
| [Generate Email]                                     |
|    ↓                                                 |
| [Send Email to Project Manager]                      |
|    ↓                                                 |
| [Confirmation Message to User]                       |
|    ↓                                                 |
| [End]                                                |
+------------------------------------------------------+
```

Description:

This flowchart illustrates the sequence of actions triggered by the submission of a project completion form. It shows how macros facilitate the automated processing of form data and communication of completion to relevant stakeholders.

Connecting forms and reports to macros in Microsoft Access or similar database systems provides a powerful way to automate and enhance data handling processes. By automating repetitive tasks and responding dynamically to user inputs, macros increase the efficiency, accuracy, and responsiveness of database applications. This integration not only saves time but also improves the overall user experience, making database interactions more intuitive and effective.

Error Handling in Macros:

Error handling is a crucial component of designing robust macros in database management systems like Microsoft Access. It involves anticipating, detecting, and responding to errors or exceptions that may occur during the execution of a macro. Proper error handling ensures that your application behaves predictably under all circumstances, preventing data corruption, system crashes, and enhancing user experience by providing informative feedback.

Importance of Error Handling

1. **Prevents Data Loss**:

*   Well-implemented error handling can prevent actions that might lead to data loss or corruption, especially in complex data manipulation tasks.

2. **Enhances Reliability**:

*   Macros that can gracefully handle errors are more reliable and less likely to cause unexpected crashes or undesirable outcomes.

3. **Improves User Confidence**:

*   By managing errors effectively and informing users about issues, macros enhance the perceived stability and reliability of your database application.

Strategies for Error Handling in Macros

1. **Try-Catch Blocks**:

- **Explanation**: This method involves wrapping potentially error-prone code in a "try" block. If an error occurs, control is passed to the "catch" block where the error is handled.

- **Example**: In VBA (used within Access macros), this can be implemented using **On Error GoTo** handlers that redirect to error-handling routines.

2. **Validation Before Execution**:

- **Explanation**: Performing checks before executing actions can prevent many common errors.

- **Example**: Before performing a division operation, validate that the denominator is not zero to avoid a divide-by-zero error.

3. **Logging Errors**:

- **Explanation**: Keeping a record of when and where errors occur can help in troubleshooting and improving the macro.

- **Example**: Write error details to a log file or database table whenever an error is caught.

Implementing Error Handling in Microsoft Access Macros

1. **Identify Common Errors**:

    - Review the macro's operations to identify potential points of failure such as data type mismatches, database lookup failures, or arithmetic errors.

2. **Use Built-in Error Handling Options**:

    - Utilize Access's built-in error handling features in the Macro Builder by selecting actions and specifying conditions that check for specific errors.

3. **Custom Error Handling with VBA**:

    - For more complex macros, use VBA to write detailed error-handling code. Use **On Error GoTo** to divert execution to a label that handles the error.

Example: Error Handling in a Data Import Macro

Scenario: A macro in Access is designed to import data from an external file into a database table.

Macro Design with Error Handling:

- **Step 1**: Open the external file.

    - **Error Check**: Confirm the file exists before attempting to open it.

- **Step 2**: Read data and insert into the database.

    - **Error Check**: Validate data formats and handle any type conversion errors.

- **Step 3**: Close the file.

    - **Error Check**: Ensure the file is not already closed.

VBA Example:

```
On Error GoTo ErrorHandler

' Step 1: Attempt to open the file

Open "C:\Data\importfile.txt" For Input As #1

' Step 2: Process file data

While Not EOF(1)

    Line Input #1, LineData

    ' Insert data into table

    DoCmd.RunSQL "INSERT INTO DataTable (DataField) VALUES ('" &
LineData & "')"

Wend

ExitHere:

    ' Step 3: Close file

    Close #1

    Exit Sub

ErrorHandler:
```

MsgBox "An error occurred: " & Err.Description

Resume ExitHere

Visual Diagram: Error Handling Process

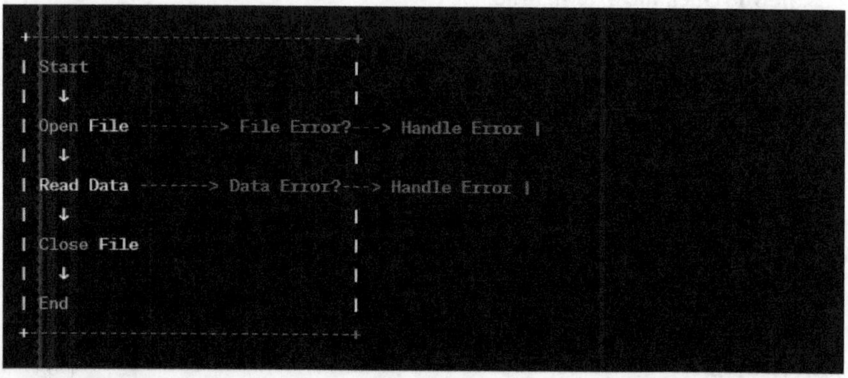

```
+----------------------------------+
| Start                            |
|   ↓                              |
| Open File --------> File Error?---> Handle Error |
|   ↓                              |
| Read Data -------> Data Error?---> Handle Error |
|   ↓                              |
| Close File                       |
|   ↓                              |
| End                              |
+----------------------------------+
```

Effective error handling in macros is vital for maintaining the integrity and reliability of database applications. By anticipating potential errors and implementing strategies to deal with them, developers can create more robust macros that safeguard against data loss and provide a better user experience. This practice not only enhances the functionality of the application but also contributes to its overall stability and trustworthiness.

Conclusion

Automation and macros are essential tools in database management systems that not only enhance operational efficiency but also ensure data integrity and streamline user interactions. By effectively using macros, organizations can automate mundane tasks, reduce the likelihood of human error, and provide more reliable and responsive services to their users.

Chapter 8 - Using VBA for Enhanced Functionality

Visual Basic for Applications (VBA) is a powerful programming language integrated into Microsoft Office applications, including Access. It allows developers to go beyond default database management features and create custom functions, automate tasks, and enhance user interfaces. VBA is essential for developing complex functionalities that are not possible through standard Access tools alone.

Benefits of Using VBA:

<u>**Customization**</u>:

Visual Basic for Applications (VBA) is a powerful scripting language that provides extensive customization capabilities in Microsoft Access and other Office applications. Through VBA, developers can tailor applications to fit specific business needs, creating custom functionalities that go beyond the out-of-the-box features. This customization enhances user interaction, data handling, and overall application efficiency.

Advantages of VBA Customization

1. **Tailored User Experiences**:

- **Explanation**: Customize user interfaces and workflows to meet the unique requirements of different user groups within an organization.

- **Example**: Designing custom forms that dynamically adjust their content and available options based on user role or input, providing a more relevant and streamlined user experience.

2. **Advanced Data Manipulation**:

- **Explanation**: Execute complex data calculations and transformations that are not possible with standard Access queries and expressions.

- **Example**: Automatically calculating weighted averages or financial forecasts based on variable user-defined parameters.

3. **Conditional Logic Implementation**:

- **Explanation**: Embed sophisticated decision-making processes directly into database operations.

- **Example**: Developing VBA scripts that trigger specific actions like notifications or updates when data meets certain conditions.

4. **Integration of External Data**:

- **Explanation**: Seamlessly integrate and manipulate data from other sources and systems, enhancing the capabilities of your Access database.

- **Example**: Importing and automatically processing CSV files from an external system into an Access database, with error handling to manage discrepancies.

Implementing VBA for Customization

1. **Identifying Customization Needs**:

- Work with end-users and stakeholders to identify areas where customization could improve efficiency, accuracy, or user satisfaction.

- Prioritize customizations that have a direct impact on productivity or critical business processes.

2. **Developing Custom Solutions**:

- Utilize the VBA editor in Access to write and debug custom scripts.

- Create modular, reusable VBA procedures that can be applied across multiple forms or reports to maintain consistency and reduce redundancy.

3. **User Interface Customization**:

- Design dynamic forms and reports using VBA to show or hide elements based on user actions or data conditions.

- Customize navigation within applications to guide users through complex tasks or workflows.

4. **Testing and Deployment**:

- Thoroughly test custom functionalities in a development environment to ensure they work correctly and handle exceptions gracefully.

- Deploy updates in stages to minimize disruption and gather feedback to refine functionalities further.

Example: Custom Sales Dashboard

Scenario: Developing a custom sales dashboard that aggregates sales data from multiple sources, provides interactive charts, and displays real-time performance metrics.

VBA Implementation:

- **Data Aggregation**: Use VBA to query, aggregate, and present sales data from various databases and external APIs.

- **Interactive Charts**: Create interactive VBA-driven charts that users can customize and explore, such as drilling down to see sales by region or product.

- **Performance Metrics**: Calculate key performance indicators (KPIs) in real-time using VBA, displaying them on the dashboard for quick executive review.

Visual Diagram: Custom Sales Dashboard Process

```
+------------------------------------------------------------+
|                  Custom Sales Dashboard                    |
|------------------------------------------------------------|
| [Fetch Data] ---> [Process Data] ---> [Display Data] |
|             ↓             ↓             ↓                  |
|           [Calculate KPIs] [Generate Charts]               |
|             ↓             ↓                                |
|           [Interactive Elements] [Real-Time Updates]|
+------------------------------------------------------------+
```

Description:

This flowchart illustrates how VBA scripts interact within a custom sales dashboard, showing data flow from collection and processing to display, including dynamic elements and real-time updates facilitated by VBA.

Customization with VBA allows developers to create highly specialized and efficient applications tailored to specific organizational needs. By leveraging VBA's powerful scripting capabilities, businesses can enhance their database applications in Microsoft Access with advanced functionalities that improve decision-making, automate complex processes, and provide superior user experiences.

Automation:

Automation through Visual Basic for Applications (VBA) offers transformative capabilities within Microsoft Access and other Office platforms. VBA enables the automation of repetitive tasks, complex data handling processes, and interactive report generation, reducing manual efforts and enhancing efficiency and accuracy.

Advantages of VBA Automation

1. **Efficiency and Time Savings**:

- **Explanation**: Automating repetitive tasks and complex procedures saves significant time and effort, allowing users to focus on higher-value activities.

- **Example**: Automatically importing data from external sources and processing it according to predefined rules without manual intervention.

2. **Consistency and Accuracy**:

- **Explanation**: Automation ensures tasks are performed consistently and without human error, enhancing the reliability of data operations.

- **Example**: Regularly scheduled data backups and integrity checks that run without requiring manual execution.

3. **Enhanced Data Processing**:

- **Explanation**: Complex data calculations and transformations can be automated to occur instantly and accurately, facilitating more sophisticated data analysis.

- **Example**: Periodic financial reconciliations that require aggregating data from various accounts and applying complex financial rules.

4. **Streamlined Workflows**:

- **Explanation**: VBA can automate the flow of tasks between different stages of a process, ensuring smooth transitions and adherence to business logic.

- **Example**: An automated workflow in a CRM system that moves customer inquiries from initial contact to assignment to the relevant salesperson based on specific customer data criteria.

Implementing VBA for Automation

1. **Identify Automation Opportunities**:

- Review processes to identify repetitive tasks or areas where human error frequently occurs, prioritizing these for automation.

2. **Design and Develop VBA Scripts**:

- Use the VBA editor to write scripts tailored to specific automation tasks. Incorporate error handling to manage potential issues gracefully.

3. **Integrate with Database Activities**:

- Connect VBA scripts directly with Access database activities such as querying, report generation, and record updates.

4. **Test and Refine**:

- Thoroughly test all automated processes in a controlled environment to ensure they function as expected. Monitor the scripts regularly and make adjustments based on feedback or changing business needs.

Example: Automated Monthly Sales Reporting

Scenario: Developing an automated system in Microsoft Access to generate and distribute monthly sales reports.

VBA Implementation:

- **Data Gathering**: Automatically compile sales data from various internal databases at the end of each month.

- **Report Generation**: Use VBA to format this data into a comprehensive report, adding analytical insights such as sales trends and performance metrics.

- **Distribution**: Email the report to stakeholders and save a copy in a designated network folder, all managed by VBA.

Visual Diagram: Monthly Sales Report Automation

```
+-------------------------------------------------------+
|       Monthly Sales Report Automation Flow            |
|-------------------------------------------------------|
| [Compile Data] ---> [Generate Report]                 |
|        ↓                      ↓                        |
| [Analyze Trends] ---> [Format Report]                 |
|        ↓                      ↓                        |
| [Distribute Report]                                   |
|        ↓                                               |
| [Log Completion & Errors]                             |
|        ↓                                               |
| [End]                                                 |
+-------------------------------------------------------+
```

Description:

This diagram outlines the automated monthly sales reporting process, highlighting the sequence of actions from data compilation to distribution and logging, all facilitated by VBA.

Automation with VBA not only enhances the functionality and efficiency of Microsoft Access applications but also introduces a high level of precision and reliability to database management tasks. By leveraging VBA to automate complex and repetitive tasks, businesses can achieve significant improvements in productivity, data accuracy, and operational efficiency.

Integration:

Integration through Visual Basic for Applications (VBA) significantly expands the capabilities of Microsoft Access and other Office applications, enabling them to communicate with various external systems and services. This facilitates seamless data exchanges and functional cooperation between different software environments, enhancing the utility and efficiency of business processes.

Advantages of VBA Integration

1. **Seamless Data Exchange:**

- **Explanation**: VBA allows for the automated transfer of data between Access and other systems, such as Excel, Outlook, SQL Server, and even web services.

- **Example**: Automatically importing or exporting data between Access and Excel to utilize Excel's advanced analytical and visualization tools.

2. **Consolidated Workflows**:

- **Explanation**: Integration capabilities enable unified workflows that cross software boundaries, simplifying user interactions and reducing the need for manual data handling.

- **Example**: Updating a database record in Access can trigger an email via Outlook or a calendar event, ensuring all relevant systems are synchronized.

3. **Enhanced Functionality**:

- **Explanation**: Access can leverage the specialized functionalities of other applications, enhancing its own capabilities without requiring complex, standalone development.

- **Example**: Using SQL Server for handling larger, more complex datasets, while employing Access for user interface and simpler data manipulations.

4. **Real-Time Updates**:

- **Explanation**: With VBA, Access can interact with live data feeds or connected devices, allowing for real-time data updates and monitoring.

- **Example**: Connecting to IoT devices in a manufacturing process to track production metrics directly within an Access database.

Implementing VBA for Integration

1. **Identify Integration Needs**:

- Determine which systems and processes would benefit from integration. Consider the data flow, required interactions, and the potential for automation.

2. **Develop VBA Scripts for Integration**:

- Use the VBA editor to write custom scripts that handle data transfer, synchronization, or any specific interaction between Access and other applications or services.

3. **Use API Calls**:

- For integrating with web-based services or external databases, make HTTP requests or use web service APIs within VBA scripts to fetch or send data.

4. **Test and Monitor**:

- Rigorously test the integration functionality to ensure stability and accuracy. Monitor the integration for any potential issues and make adjustments as needed.

Example: Automated Report Distribution System

Scenario: Developing an automated system in Microsoft Access that generates reports and distributes them via email through Outlook, based on data stored both in Access and external SQL databases.

VBA Implementation:

- **Data Compilation**: Aggregate data from Access and SQL Server into a comprehensive dataset suitable for reporting.

- **Report Generation**: Utilize VBA to dynamically create reports within Access based on the latest data.

- **Email Distribution**: Automatically email the generated reports to a list of predefined recipients using Outlook.

Visual Diagram: Report Distribution Automation

```
+----------------------------------------------------+
|         Report Distribution Automation Flow        |
|----------------------------------------------------|
| [Aggregate Data from SQL & Access]                 |
|        ↓                                           |
| [Generate Report in Access]                        |
|        ↓                                           |
| [Distribute via Outlook Email]                     |
|        ↓                                           |
| [Log Activity & Errors]                            |
|        ↓                                           |
| [End]                                              |
+----------------------------------------------------+
```

Description:

This flowchart illustrates the process of aggregating data, generating reports, and distributing them via email, showcasing how VBA facilitates integration across different platforms and applications.

Integration via VBA enhances the functionality of Microsoft Access by enabling it to interact with a variety of external systems and services. This capability not only extends the use cases for Access databases but also ensures that data and workflows can be seamlessly managed across different platforms, increasing efficiency and reducing the potential for errors.

User Interface Enhancement:

Improve user interfaces with dynamic elements and user-driven interactions to create a more engaging user experience.

Examples of Enhanced Functionality Using VBA

1. **Dynamic Forms**:

- **Purpose**: Customize forms based on user inputs or other runtime conditions.

- **Example**: Create a form that adjusts its layout and available options based on the user's role or choices. For instance, a form for entering order details might show different fields to a salesperson compared to a manager.

2. **Automated Reports**:

- **Purpose**: Automate the generation and distribution of reports.

- **Example**: Use VBA to automatically generate a monthly sales report and email it to specified recipients at scheduled times.

3. **Data Validation and Processing**:

- **Purpose**: Enforce complex data validation rules or perform sophisticated data processing that is not supported by default Access functionalities.

- **Example**: Implement a VBA script that checks for duplicate entries before allowing a new customer record to be saved, ensuring data integrity.

4. **Custom Workflow Implementations**:

- **Purpose**: Create workflows that require conditional logic and sequential task execution based on business rules.

- **Example**: Develop a multi-step approval process for expense claims where each step involves different stakeholders and is triggered based on the amount or type of expense.

Implementing VBA in Access

1. **Access VBA Editor**:

- Open the VBA editor by pressing **ALT + F11** in Access. This is where you can write and edit VBA code.

2. **Writing VBA Code**:

- Use the VBA editor to write functions and subroutines. For example, to handle form events or automate data processing.

Example Code for sending an email:

```vba
Sub SendReportByEmail()

    Dim objOutlook As Object

    Set objOutlook = CreateObject("Outlook.Application")

    Dim objEmail As Object

    Set objEmail = objOutlook.CreateItem(0)

    With objEmail

        .To = "email@example.com"

        .Subject = "Monthly Sales Report"

        .Body = "Attached is the monthly sales report."

        .Attachments.Add "C:\Reports\MonthlySales.pdf"

        .Send

    End With

    Set objEmail = Nothing
```

Set objOutlook = Nothing

End Sub

3. **Testing and Debugging**:

- Use the VBA editor's debugging tools to step through code, watch variable values, and handle errors. Testing is crucial to ensure that the VBA scripts perform as expected without causing disruptions.

Visual Diagram: VBA Process Flow

```
+-------------------------------------------------+
| Start                                           |
|    ↓                                            |
| User submits form                               |
|    ↓                                            |
| VBA checks for duplicates                       |
|    ↓                                            |
| Data valid? ----> Yes ----> Save record         |
|              |                                  |
|             No ----> Show error message         |
|    ↓                                            |
| End                                             |
+-------------------------------------------------+
```

Introduction to VBA in Access:

Visual Basic for Applications (VBA) is an event-driven programming language provided by Microsoft as a tool to enhance productivity in its Office suite, including Access. VBA in Access allows users to write scripts that can automate repetitive tasks, integrate with other Office applications, and customize forms, reports, and user interactions. This powerful tool transforms Access from a mere data-handling application into a dynamic and customizable data management system.

Key Features of VBA in Microsoft Access

1. **Automation**:

- Automate repetitive tasks such as data entry, updates, and report generation, reducing manual errors and saving time.

2. **Custom User Interfaces**:

- Create tailored forms and controls that adapt to user inputs or specific business logic.

3. **Complex Data Handling**:

- Perform sophisticated data analysis and manipulation that goes beyond the capabilities of standard SQL queries.

4. **Integration**:

- Seamlessly interact with other applications in the Microsoft Office suite (like Excel and Outlook) or even external databases and APIs.

5. **Event-Driven Programming**:

- React to specific events within the database, such as button clicks, form submissions, or changes in data.

Examples of VBA Applications in Access

1. **Dynamic Forms**:

- **Example**: A VBA script automatically populates dropdown menus in a form based on another field's selection. This dynamic interaction enhances the user experience by simplifying how data is entered and ensuring data consistency.

2. **Automated Reporting**:

- **Example**: A monthly sales report is automatically generated and emailed to executives. VBA scripts gather data, format it into a report, and use Outlook to distribute this report based on a scheduled task within Access.

3. **Data Validation**:

- **Example**: Before saving data entered into a form, VBA scripts check the validity of the data against predefined rules, prompting the user with custom error messages if the data entered is incorrect.

Step-by-Step Guide to Getting Started with VBA in Access

1. **Access the VBA Editor**:

- Open Microsoft Access and press **ALT + F11** to open the VBA editor, where you can write, edit, and manage VBA code.

2. **Explore the Object Browser**:

- Use the Object Browser in the VBA editor to explore available classes, methods, and properties that you can use to interact with Access objects.

3. **Create Modules and Procedures**:

- Start by creating modules which are containers for your VBA procedures. Procedures can be either subroutines (which perform actions) or functions (which return values).

4. **Write Your First Script**:

- Write a simple script to automate a task, such as a subroutine that exports data to Excel.

5. **Attach Scripts to Events**:

- Link your VBA scripts to events in forms, such as **OnClick** events for buttons or **AfterUpdate** events for fields.

Visual Example: Automating Data Export to Excel

Flowchart of a VBA Script:

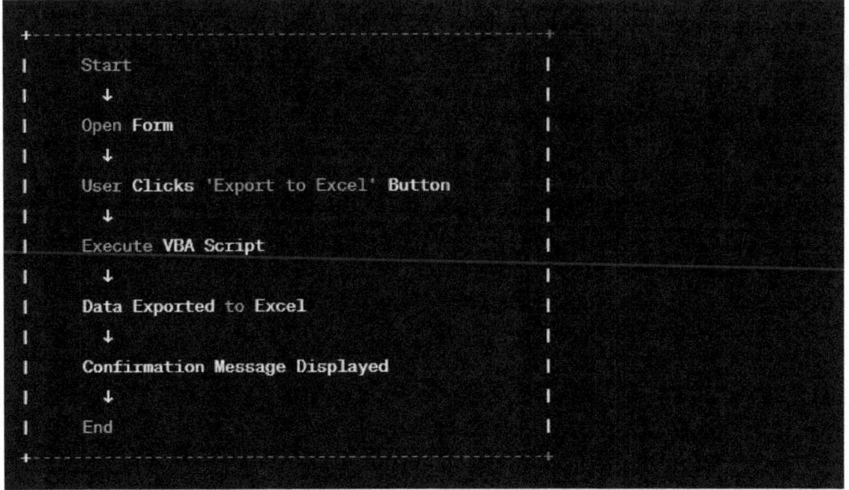

Description:

This flowchart represents the process of exporting data to Excel using a VBA script in Access, triggered by a user action. The script handles the data extraction and export, providing feedback to the user upon completion.

VBA in Microsoft Access is a powerful tool that extends the functionality of database applications, enabling automation, customization, and integration. By understanding and utilizing VBA, users can significantly enhance the efficiency and effectiveness of their database solutions, tailor their applications to specific needs, and create a more dynamic user experience.

Writing Custom Functions and Procedures:

Visual Basic for Applications (VBA) allows for the creation of custom functions and procedures within Microsoft Access, providing tailored solutions to specific business or data management needs. Functions and procedures are blocks of VBA code designed to perform specific tasks; functions return values, while procedures carry out actions. By writing custom functions and procedures, users can extend the capabilities of Access applications, automate complex tasks, and integrate more sophisticated data processing features.

Benefits of Custom Functions and Procedures

1. **Reusability**:

- Create reusable code blocks that can be applied across multiple parts of an application, enhancing consistency and reducing redundancy.

2. **Modularity**:

- Divide complex processes into manageable, discrete components, simplifying debugging, maintenance, and updates.

3. **Efficiency**:

- Improve performance by optimizing specific operations and automating repetitive tasks, saving time and reducing errors.

Types of Custom VBA Code

1. **Functions**:

- Return a value and can be used in expressions, queries, and calculations within Access.

- Example: A custom function to calculate tax based on variable regional tax rates.

2. **Sub Procedures**:

- Perform actions but do not return a value.

- Example: A procedure to automatically update customer records based on transaction data.

Writing Custom Functions and Procedures

1. **Identifying Needs**:

- Determine which tasks require customization or automation. This might include complex calculations, data validation, or specific user interactions.

2. **Opening VBA Editor**:

- Press **ALT + F11** in Access to open the VBA editor where you can write and manage your VBA code.

3. **Creating a Module**:

- In the VBA editor, insert a new module where your functions and procedures will reside.

4. **Writing the Code**:

- Use the VBA programming language to script your custom functions and procedures.

Example: Custom Function to Calculate Discounted Prices

Function Code:

```
Function CalculateDiscount(Price As Double, DiscountRate As Double) As Double

    CalculateDiscount = Price - (Price * DiscountRate / 100)

End Function
```

This function calculates a discounted price given an original price and a discount rate.

Procedure to Update Prices:

```vba
Sub UpdateDiscountedPrices()

    Dim rs As Recordset

    Set rs = CurrentDb.OpenRecordset("SELECT ProductID, Price FROM Products")


    Do While Not rs.EOF

        rs.Edit

        rs!DiscountedPrice = CalculateDiscount(rs!Price, 10)  'Assuming a 10% discount rate

        rs.Update

        rs.MoveNext

    Loop


    rs.Close

    Set rs = Nothing

    MsgBox "Prices updated successfully!"

End Sub
```

This procedure iterates through a recordset of products, applies the **CalculateDiscount** function to update prices, and provides user feedback when complete.

Visual Diagram: Discount Calculation Process

```
+----------------------------------------+
|   Start                                |
|      ↓                                 |
|   Open Products Recordset              |
|      ↓                                 |
|   Loop Through Each Product            |
|      ↓                                 |
|   Calculate New Price                  |
|      ↓                                 |
|   Update Record with New Price         |
|      ↓                                 |
|   Move to Next Record                  |
|      ↓                                 |
|   Close Recordset & Confirm            |
|      ↓                                 |
|   End                                  |
+----------------------------------------+
```

Custom functions and procedures in VBA provide a powerful way to enhance the functionality of Microsoft Access databases. By leveraging these tools, developers can create applications that are more efficient, reliable, and tailored to specific requirements. Whether automating routine tasks, performing complex calculations, or facilitating user interactions, VBA enables significant improvements in database application capabilities.

Interacting With Other Applications Via VBA:

VBA (Visual Basic for Applications) extends beyond the confines of a single application, enabling seamless interaction with other programs within the Microsoft Office suite and beyond. This capability allows Microsoft Access databases to leverage the features of other applications like Excel, Outlook, and Word, facilitating comprehensive workflows that harness the strengths of multiple tools.

Benefits of VBA Inter-application Communication

1. **Enhanced Productivity**: Automate tasks across applications, reducing manual data transfer and manipulation, thus saving time and minimizing errors.

2. **Data Consolidation**: Gather and synthesize information from various sources, providing a unified view of data spread across different platforms.

3. **Extended Functionality**: Utilize the specialized functionalities of other applications that are not natively available in Access.

Common Use Cases for Inter-application Communication

1. **Data Export/Import**: Transfer data between Access and Excel for advanced analysis and visualization.

2. **Automated Emailing**: Use Outlook to send emails from Access, automating communication based on database triggers.

3. **Document Generation**: Create Word documents from Access data for reports, letters, and other documentation needs.

Implementing VBA for Inter-application Communication

1. **Identify Requirements**:

- Determine the data flow and interaction required between applications. Pinpoint which tasks need automation and the data dependencies involved.

2. **Setup References**:

- In the VBA editor, set up references to other applications' object libraries (e.g., Microsoft Excel Object Library) to gain access to their functionalities.

3. **Develop VBA Scripts**:

- Write VBA scripts in Access that utilize the objects and methods of other applications to perform tasks.

4. **Error Handling**:

- Implement comprehensive error handling to manage issues that may arise during inter-application interactions.

Example: Exporting Data to Excel and Sending Email via Outlook

Scenario: Automatically exporting a sales report from Access to Excel and emailing it to a distribution list using Outlook.

VBA Implementation:

1. **Export to Excel**:

```
Sub ExportDataToExcel()
```

```vba
Dim rs As Recordset

Set rs = CurrentDb.OpenRecordset("SELECT * FROM SalesReport")


Dim xlApp As Object

Set xlApp = CreateObject("Excel.Application")

xlApp.Visible = True


Dim xlBook As Object

Set xlBook = xlApp.Workbooks.Add

Dim xlSheet As Object

Set xlSheet = xlBook.Sheets(1)


Dim col As Integer

For col = 0 To rs.Fields.Count - 1

    xlSheet.Cells(1, col + 1).Value = rs.Fields(col).Name

Next col


Dim row As Integer

row = 2

Do While Not rs.EOF

    For col = 0 To rs.Fields.Count - 1

        xlSheet.Cells(row, col + 1).Value = rs.Fields(col).Value

    Next col

    row = row + 1

    rs.MoveNext
```

```
    Loop

    rs.Close

    xlBook.SaveAs "C:\Reports\SalesReport.xlsx"

    xlApp.Quit

End Sub
```

2.   **Send Email via Outlook**:

```
Sub SendEmailWithAttachment()

    Dim olApp As Object

    Set olApp = CreateObject("Outlook.Application")


    Dim olMail As Object

    Set olMail = olApp.CreateItem(0)

    With olMail

      .To = "sales@company.com"

      .CC = "managers@company.com"

      .Subject = "Monthly Sales Report"

      .Body = "Please find attached the latest sales report."

      .Attachments.Add "C:\Reports\SalesReport.xlsx"

      .Send

    End With

    Set olMail = Nothing

    Set olApp = Nothing

End Sub
```

Visual Diagram: Workflow Between Access, Excel, and Outlook

```
+-------------------------------------------+
| Access Database                           |
|   ↓                                       |
| Export Data to Excel  -------------------->|
|   ↓                                       |
| Generate Report in Excel                  |
|   ↓                                       |
| Save Excel File                           |
|   ↓                                       |
| Create Email in Outlook  ---------------->|
|   ↓                                       |
| Attach Excel Report                       |
|   ↓                                       |
| Send Email                                |
|   ↓                                       |
| End                                       |
+-------------------------------------------+
```

Interacting with other applications via VBA enhances the functionality of Microsoft Access by allowing it to operate within a broader ecosystem of tools. This interaction not only facilitates sophisticated workflows but also enables more comprehensive data management practices, such as advanced data analysis, automated communications, and dynamic report generation. Through careful implementation of VBA scripts, businesses can leverage the full potential of their software investments, achieving higher efficiency and effectiveness in their operations.

Conclusion

VBA provides a versatile and powerful toolset for enhancing the functionality of database applications in Microsoft Access. By leveraging VBA, developers can introduce a level of customization and automation that significantly improves efficiency, data integrity, and user experience. Whether it's through sophisticated data handling, dynamic user interface elements, or seamless integration with other applications, VBA can transform the capabilities of standard Access databases into highly functional, tailored information systems.

Chapter 9 - Security Features in Access

Microsoft Access provides several security features designed to protect data and ensure that only authorized users can access information. These features range from simple password protections to more complex encryption methods and user-level security controls.

Key Security Features in Access

1. **Database Passwords**:

- **Purpose**: Prevent unauthorized access to an Access database file by requiring a password to open it.

- **Example**: Setting a database password through the 'Set Database Password' option under the 'File' menu in Access.

2. **Encryption**:

- **Purpose**: Protect data integrity and privacy by encrypting the contents of an Access database.

- **Example**: Using the 'Encrypt with Password' feature, Access encrypts the database file, making it unreadable without the correct password.

3. **User-Level Security** (for Access versions prior to 2007):

- **Purpose**: Control access to various parts of the database based on user roles, limiting what different users can view and modify.

- **Example**: Setting up a multi-user environment where different users have distinct permissions based on their job requirements.

4. **Access Workgroup Security**:

- **Purpose**: Manage user accounts, groups, and permissions within a shared database environment.

- **Example**: Creating groups for different departments (e.g., Sales, HR) and assigning specific data access permissions to each group.

5. **VBA Code Signing**:

- **Purpose**: Ensure the integrity and origin of VBA code by signing it with a digital certificate.

- **Example**: Developers can sign their VBA projects with a digital certificate so users know the code has not been altered and is from a trusted source.

Implementing Security Features in Microsoft Access

1. **Setting a Database Password**:

- Navigate to the 'File' menu, choose 'Info', then 'Encrypt with Password'. Enter and confirm your password.

2. **Encrypting a Database**:

- Under the same 'Info' tab, use the 'Encrypt with Password' feature. This adds a layer of security by encrypting the data stored in the database file.

3. **Using User-Level Security** (for legacy Access databases):

- Access the security settings through the 'Tools' menu in older versions of Access. Set up user and group IDs, then define their permissions throughout the database.

4. **Applying Workgroup Security**:

- For databases that require detailed access control, configure a workgroup file (system.mdw) where you can define user roles and associate them with specific permissions.

5. **Signing VBA Projects**:

- In the VBA editor, go to 'Tools' > 'Digital Signature' and choose a digital certificate to sign your VBA projects.

Example: Setting Up a Secure Multi-User Environment

Scenario: An organization needs to configure its Access database for use by multiple departments with varying levels of access.

Steps:

1. **Create User Accounts and Groups**: Define groups for each department and create user accounts assigning them to the appropriate groups.

2. **Set Permissions**: Assign permissions to each group, limiting access to specific tables, queries, forms, and reports as necessary.

3. **Implement Passwords and Encryption**: Secure the database file with a password and encrypt it to protect sensitive data.

Visual Diagram: Security Setup Workflow

```
+------------------------------------------------+
| Start                                          |
|    ↓                                           |
| Create Groups (HR, Sales, Admin)               |
|    ↓                                           |
| Create User Accounts                           |
|    ↓                                           |
| Assign Users to Groups                         |
|    ↓                                           |
| Define Permissions for Each Group              |
|    ↓                                           |
| Implement Database Password & Encryption       |
|    ↓                                           |
| Test Security Settings                         |
|    ↓                                           |
| Deployment                                     |
|    ↓                                           |
| End                                            |
+------------------------------------------------+
```

Setting User Permissions:

User permissions in Microsoft Access are crucial for controlling access to data based on user roles and responsibilities. This feature helps in maintaining data confidentiality and integrity by ensuring that users can only access and manipulate data necessary for their tasks. Setting user permissions involves defining what specific users or groups can view, modify, delete, or enter data within the database.

Importance of User Permissions

<u>**Data Protection:**</u>

In Microsoft Access, setting user permissions is a critical security measure for protecting sensitive data within a database. Properly configured permissions ensure that data is accessible only to authorized users, thus preventing unauthorized access, data breaches, and potential misuse of information. This level of control is essential not only for maintaining the integrity and confidentiality of data but also for complying with data protection regulations such as GDPR or HIPAA.

The Role of User Permissions in Data Protection

1. **Controlled Access:**

- **Explanation**: Permissions limit who can view, edit, delete, or add data within the database. This selective access helps in protecting personal and sensitive information from being exposed to unauthorized personnel.

- **Example**: A healthcare database may restrict access to patient records to only those medical professionals who are directly involved in the patient's care.

2. **Prevention of Data Leaks:**

- **Explanation**: By restricting user capabilities, the risk of accidental or intentional data leaks can be significantly reduced.

- **Example**: A financial institution could configure its Access database to ensure that lower-level staff cannot access or export detailed financial reports.

3. **Auditing and Compliance:**

- **Explanation**: Permissions help in maintaining detailed logs of who accessed the database and what changes were made, which is crucial for auditing and regulatory compliance.

- **Example**: Access logs that record data queries and modifications can be used to demonstrate compliance with data protection laws during audits.

4. **Minimizing Data Manipulation Errors:**

- **Explanation**: Restricting the ability to modify data to authorized personnel reduces the likelihood of errors that can occur when data is improperly handled or altered.

- **Example**: In a manufacturing database, only designated engineers may have the permission to alter the design specifications of products to prevent unintended modifications.

Implementing User Permissions for Data Protection in Access

1. **Assessment of Data Sensitivity**:

- Identify and classify data based on its sensitivity and the potential impact of its exposure or misuse.

2. **Role-Based Access Control (RBAC)**:

- Design user roles based on job functions and assign permissions that correspond to the needs and responsibilities of each role.

3. **Permissions Setup**:

- Utilize Access's built-in security features to set up and manage permissions. For databases that require finer-grained control, consider using additional network or application-layer security solutions.

4. **Regular Reviews**:

- Periodically review user permissions to ensure they still align with current roles and responsibilities, especially after organizational changes.

Visual Example: Role-Based Permissions Flowchart

```
+- - - - - - - - - - - - - - - - - - - - - - - - - - - - - - -+
|               Role-Based Permissions Setup            |
|- - - - - - - - - - - - - - - - - - - - - - - - - - - - - - -|
| [Identify Sensitive Data]                             |
|      ↓                                                |
| [Define User Roles]                                   |
|      ↓                                                |
| [Assign Permissions]                                  |
|      ↓                                                |
| [Implement & Monitor Access]                          |
|      ↓                                                |
| [Regular Audits and Updates]                          |
+- - - - - - - - - - - - - - - - - - - - - - - - - - - - - - -+
```

Description:

This flowchart outlines the process of setting up role-based permissions in an Access database, emphasizing the structured approach to protecting sensitive data.

User permissions are a cornerstone of data protection strategies within Microsoft Access databases. By effectively managing access rights, organizations can safeguard sensitive information against unauthorized access and potential data breaches, thereby enhancing data security and ensuring compliance with relevant legal and regulatory requirements. Proper implementation and ongoing management of user permissions are essential for maintaining the integrity and security of database systems.

Operational Integrity:

Operational integrity in database management involves ensuring that all transactions and data manipulations are performed correctly, consistently, and securely. In Microsoft Access, setting user permissions plays a pivotal role in maintaining this integrity by regulating who can perform certain actions within the database. Properly configured permissions help prevent unauthorized actions that could disrupt business operations or compromise data accuracy.

Key Aspects of User Permissions in Maintaining Operational Integrity

1. **Ensuring Accurate Data Transactions**:

- **Explanation**: By controlling who can add, delete, or modify data, user permissions ensure that only qualified personnel make database changes, thus maintaining data accuracy and integrity.

- **Example**: Only allowing financial officers to update payment entries in a financial database ensures that transactions are handled by those with the appropriate expertise.

2. **Preventing Unauthorized Changes**:

- **Explanation**: Permissions restrict the ability of users to make unauthorized changes to the database structure or critical data, which could otherwise lead to data loss or system failures.

- **Example**: Restricting the ability to alter table designs or delete records to database administrators prevents accidental or malicious modifications.

3. **Supporting Segregation of Duties**:

- **Explanation**: Implementing user permissions supports the segregation of duties, a key control in many compliance frameworks that reduces the risk of fraud and error.

- **Example**: In a payroll system, one user may be permitted to register employee hours, while another is responsible for processing payments, ensuring no single user has control over the entire process.

4. **Facilitating Audit Trails**:

- **Explanation**: With proper permissions, it's easier to track who did what in the database, supporting effective audit trails that can identify and rectify issues quickly.

- **Example**: Logging actions based on user permissions allows auditors to trace specific changes back to individual users, simplifying accountability and issue resolution.

Implementing User Permissions for Operational Integrity in Access

1. **Role Identification and Definition**:

- Assess business functions and define roles that match job responsibilities, ensuring that users have access only to the data and functions necessary for their roles.

2. **Setup and Configuration**:

- Use Access's security features to assign detailed permissions based on the defined roles. This might involve configuring table-level permissions and access rights to forms and reports.

3. **Continuous Monitoring and Review**:

- Regularly review and update permissions to adapt to changes in roles or business processes. This helps in maintaining the relevance and effectiveness of the permissions setup.

4. **Enforcement of Best Practices**:

- Enforce best practices such as least privilege and periodic access reviews to minimize risks associated with excessive or outdated permissions.

Example: Managing Sales Data Integrity

Scenario: A sales database where sales representatives enter daily sales data, managers approve entries, and only database administrators can modify the structure of the database.

Steps:

1. **Sales Representatives**: Granted permissions to add new sales records but cannot delete or alter existing records once submitted.

2. **Managers**: Have the authority to review, approve, or reject sales entries. They can also generate and access various sales reports.

3. **Database Administrators**: Responsible for structural changes and overall maintenance of the database. They have no roles in the daily sales entries or approvals to maintain segregation of duties.

Visual Diagram: Permissions Structure for Sales Database

```
+---------------------------------------------------------------+
|                   Sales Database Permissions                  |
|---------------------------------------------------------------|
| [Sales Representatives]                                       |
|   ↓ (Add Records)                                            |
|                                                               |
| [Managers]                                                   |
|   ↓ (Review, Approve, Access Reports)                        |
|                                                               |
| [Database Administrators]                                    |
|   ↓ (Modify Structure, Maintain Database)                    |
+---------------------------------------------------------------+
```

Description:

This diagram illustrates the distribution of permissions among different roles in a sales database, highlighting how user permissions are aligned with operational responsibilities to maintain data integrity and prevent unauthorized activities.

User permissions in Microsoft Access are fundamental to ensuring operational integrity by controlling access to data and database functions. Properly managed permissions safeguard against unauthorized data manipulation, support compliance and auditing processes, and help maintain the accuracy and reliability of business operations. By carefully defining and enforcing these permissions, organizations can protect their operational processes and enhance overall system security.

<u>Compliance</u>:

In many industries, regulatory compliance dictates how data should be handled, stored, and accessed. Microsoft Access databases that contain sensitive or regulated information must implement strict controls to comply with legal and industry standards such as GDPR, HIPAA, or Sarbanes-Oxley. User permissions in Access are crucial for ensuring that these standards are met, providing a framework to control and monitor access to sensitive data systematically.

Benefits of User Permissions in Ensuring Compliance

1. **Data Access Control**:

- **Explanation**: User permissions restrict access to sensitive data based on the principle of least privilege, ensuring that individuals can only access information necessary for their job functions.

- **Example**: In a healthcare database, permissions ensure that only healthcare providers can access patient records, while administrative staff can only access non-sensitive patient information like appointment schedules.

2. **Audit Trails**:

- **Explanation**: Permissions help in maintaining detailed logs of who accessed or modified data, crucial for audits and compliance checks.

- **Example**: Access logs that track user activities and data changes can be used to demonstrate compliance with data protection regulations during audits.

3. **Prevention of Unauthorized Data Disclosure**:

- **Explanation**: By carefully managing who can view, edit, or delete data, organizations can prevent unauthorized disclosure and manipulation of sensitive information.

- **Example**: Financial databases can be configured so that only authorized personnel can view or process transactions, protecting against internal and external threats.

4. **Segregation of Duties**:

- **Explanation**: User permissions facilitate the segregation of duties, a compliance requirement in many regulatory frameworks, which reduces the risk of fraud and error.

- **Example**: In an accounting system, one user's role might be to initiate transactions, another to approve them, and a third to reconcile them, with each role having distinct permissions.

Implementing User Permissions for Compliance in Access

1. **Identify Compliance Requirements**:

- Understand the specific compliance requirements related to data privacy and security for your industry and region. Determine what data is covered and the relevant controls needed.

2. **Design a Permissions Matrix**:

- Create a detailed matrix that maps user roles to permissible actions within the database. This matrix should reflect compliance requirements concerning data access and manipulation.

3. **Configure User Permissions**:

- Use Access's security features to implement the permissions as defined in the matrix. Ensure that all data access points are covered, including tables, queries, forms, and reports.

4. **Regular Audits and Updates**:

- Conduct regular audits of user activities and permission settings to ensure ongoing compliance. Update permissions as necessary to reflect changes in regulations, business operations, or roles.

5. **Educate Users and Enforce Policies**:

- Provide training for users on compliance policies and the importance of following prescribed protocols. Enforce these policies strictly to maintain the integrity of the data management system.

Example: Ensuring HIPAA Compliance in a Patient Data System

Scenario: A medical facility uses an Access database to manage patient information and needs to comply with HIPAA regulations, which require strict controls on patient data access and confidentiality.

Steps:

1. **Define User Roles**: Identify different user roles such as doctors, nurses, administrative staff, and IT personnel.

2. **Permissions Setup**: Configure user permissions so that:

- Doctors and nurses can access full medical records.

- Administrative staff can access only demographic and appointment data.

- IT staff have permissions for system maintenance but no access to medical or personal information.

3. **Audit Configurations**: Implement logging to track access and changes to sensitive data by all users.

Visual Diagram: User Permissions for HIPAA Compliance

```
+-------------------------------------------------------------------+
|            HIPAA Compliance: User Permissions                     |
|-------------------------------------------------------------------|
| [Doctors]                                                         |
|   ↓ (Full Access to Medical Records)                              |
|                                                                   |
| [Nurses]                                                          |
|   ↓ (Access to Medical Records, No Financial Data)                |
|                                                                   |
| [Administrative Staff]                                            |
|   ↓ (Access to Demographic and Appointment Data Only)             |
|                                                                   |
| [IT Personnel]                                                    |
|   ↓ (System Maintenance, No Access to Patient Data)               |
+-------------------------------------------------------------------+
```

Description:

This diagram illustrates the segregation of duties and tailored access permissions designed to comply with HIPAA regulations within a healthcare database managed in Microsoft Access.

Setting user permissions in Microsoft Access is a fundamental security practice that not only protects sensitive information but also ensures that organizations meet regulatory compliance requirements. By carefully managing access to data according to user roles, businesses can safeguard against unauthorized data breaches, maintain operational integrity, and fulfill audit requirements, thus upholding the standards set forth by compliance regulations.

Setting Up User Permissions in Microsoft Access

User permissions in Microsoft Access are set through a combination of Access security features and, in more complex cases, through network permissions if the database is shared over a network.

1. **Define User Roles**:

- Determine the various roles required within your organization (e.g., Administrator, Data Entry, Viewer) and the permissions each role should have.

2. **Create User Accounts and Groups**:

- In versions of Access that support user-level security (typically versions prior to 2007), create user accounts and organize them into groups that reflect their roles.

3. **Assign Permissions**:

- Set permissions on tables, queries, forms, reports, and macros. Permissions can include Read, Write, Update, Delete, and Execute.

4. **Use Access Security Wizard** (for older versions):

- Use the User-Level Security Wizard to help set up security settings, including user groups and permissions.

5. **Implement Network Security** (for shared databases):

- For databases shared over a network, configure network security settings to control who can access the database file on the server.

Example: Implementing User Permissions for a Sales Database

Scenario: A company uses an Access database to manage sales data and wants to set permissions to ensure sales representatives can only modify data relevant to their sales while managers can view all entries and generate reports.

Steps:

1. **Create Groups**:

- **Sales Reps**: Can update their sales records.

- **Managers**: Can view all records, generate reports, and make changes to all data.

2. **Set Table Permissions**:

- Sales Reps are given 'Update' permissions on records they own and 'Read' permissions on other data.

- Managers receive 'Read', 'Write', 'Update', and 'Delete' permissions on all sales data.

3. **Form and Report Permissions**:

- Sales Reps can access forms to enter their sales but cannot access financial summary reports.

- Managers have access to all forms and reports, including detailed financial analytics.

Visual Diagram: User Permissions Workflow

```
+-------------------------------------------------------+
| User Permissions Setup in Sales Database              |
|-------------------------------------------------------|
| [Define Roles]                                        |
|     ↓                                                 |
| [Create Groups in Access]                             |
|     ↓                                                 |
| [Assign Table Permissions]                            |
|     ↓                                                 |
| [Configure Form & Report Access]                      |
|     ↓                                                 |
| [Apply & Test Permissions]                            |
|     ↓                                                 |
| [Monitor & Adjust as Needed]                          |
+-------------------------------------------------------+
```

Description:

This flowchart describes the sequential steps involved in setting up user permissions within a sales database, highlighting the role-specific access control for different user groups.

Setting user permissions in Microsoft Access is a fundamental aspect of database security management. Proper implementation ensures that sensitive data is adequately protected and that users have the appropriate level of access for their roles. While more recent versions of Access do not include the same level of built-in user-level security features as earlier versions, similar outcomes can be achieved through careful planning of database design, use of Access features like encryption and password protection, and network security measures.

Protecting Data with Encryption:

Encryption is a critical security feature in Microsoft Access that enhances data protection by encoding database contents to prevent unauthorized access. This security measure is essential for safeguarding sensitive information from being read or altered by individuals without the proper decryption key or password.

Importance of Encryption in Access

Confidentiality:

Encryption in Microsoft Access is a critical security measure designed to ensure the confidentiality of data stored within databases. By transforming readable data into an encoded format that can only be accessed with a specific key or password, encryption helps protect sensitive information from unauthorized access, ensuring that only authorized users can view or manipulate it.

The Role of Encryption in Ensuring Data Confidentiality

1. **Protection Against Unauthorized Access**:

- **Explanation**: Encryption acts as a barrier against unauthorized users who attempt to access sensitive data within an Access database. Without the correct decryption key or password, the encrypted data remains unreadable and secure.

- **Example**: Encrypting client financial records in a consultancy firm's database ensures that even if the database file is stolen or mistakenly shared, the information remains secure and inaccessible to unauthorized parties.

2. **Data Security in Shared Environments**:

- **Explanation**: In environments where database files are stored on shared network drives or cloud storage, encryption protects data as it travels across the network and when it is stored on shared systems.

- **Example**: An HR database containing personal employee details, when encrypted, ensures that sensitive information is protected against potential snooping by other network users or IT personnel not authorized to view this data.

3. **Compliance with Privacy Regulations**:

- **Explanation**: Many industries are governed by regulations that require the protection of personal and sensitive data. Encryption helps organizations comply with these regulations by ensuring data confidentiality.

- **Example**: Healthcare providers use encryption in Access databases to secure patient medical records, complying with HIPAA regulations that mandate the protection of patient health information.

Implementing Encryption for Confidentiality in Access

1. **Setting Up Database Encryption**:

- Use the built-in encryption tool in Microsoft Access by selecting **File** > **Info** > **Encrypt with Password**. Enter a strong, secure password to encrypt the database file.

2. **Managing Encryption Keys**:

- Safely manage and store encryption keys or passwords. Only distribute keys to authorized users through secure channels to maintain the confidentiality of the encryption.

3. **Regular Security Audits**:

- Conduct periodic security audits to ensure that the encryption measures in place effectively protect data and comply with applicable regulations.

4. **Training and Policy Development**:

- Train users on the importance of encryption and secure data handling practices. Develop clear policies regarding who can access encryption keys and under what circumstances.

Example: Encryption in a Legal Firm's Database

Scenario: A legal firm stores sensitive case files and client information in an Access database. To maintain client confidentiality, the firm decides to implement encryption.

Steps to Encrypt:

1. **Back Up the Database**: Ensure there is a backup before applying encryption in case of any issues.

2. **Enable Encryption**: Follow the steps to apply a strong password for the database encryption.

3. **Verify Security**: Test the encryption by attempting to access the database file from unauthorized accounts to ensure the data is unreadable.

Visual Diagram: Implementing Encryption for Confidentiality

```
+-----------------------------------------------------+
|                                                     |
|          Implementing Encryption in Access          |
|                                                     |
|-----------------------------------------------------|
| [Backup Database]                                   |
|     ↓                                               |
| [Enable Encryption via Access Settings]             |
|     ↓                                               |
| [Set Strong Password]                               |
|     ↓                                               |
| [Encrypt Database]                                  |
|     ↓                                               |
| [Verify Encryption & Test Access Controls]          |
|     ↓                                               |
| [Distribute Keys to Authorized Personnel]           |
|     ↓                                               |
| [Ongoing Monitoring & Audits]                       |
+-----------------------------------------------------+
```

Description:

This flowchart illustrates the process of encrypting a database in Microsoft Access to maintain confidentiality. It highlights critical steps from backup to verification and ongoing management to ensure effective protection.

Encryption is essential for maintaining the confidentiality of data within Microsoft Access databases. By implementing strong encryption measures, organizations can protect sensitive information from unauthorized access, ensure compliance with regulatory requirements, and maintain the trust of clients and stakeholders. Effective management of encryption keys and regular audits are crucial to sustaining these security measures over time.

Data Integrity:

In Microsoft Access, encryption does more than just protect data from unauthorized access—it also plays a critical role in maintaining data integrity. Encryption ensures that data remains unchanged and undamaged during storage and transmission, guarding against tampering and corruption. This safeguard is essential for maintaining the accuracy and reliability of the information within the database.

The Role of Encryption in Ensuring Data Integrity

1. **Guarding Against Tampering**:

- **Explanation**: Encryption helps prevent unauthorized users from altering data. Even if they gain access to the database, the encrypted data cannot be modified without the appropriate decryption key.

- **Example**: In a financial database, encryption prevents tampering with transaction records, ensuring that financial audits reflect true transactions.

2. **Protection During Transmission**:

- **Explanation**: When data is transmitted over networks, encryption ensures it arrives at its destination without being altered or intercepted.

- **Example**: When an Access database is backed up to a cloud storage service, encryption protects the data from being intercepted or altered during transfer.

3. **Error Detection**:

- **Explanation**: Many encryption algorithms include integrity checks that help detect if data has been altered or corrupted, either intentionally or due to transmission errors.

- **Example**: AES encryption, commonly used in Access, includes mechanisms to verify data integrity when decrypted, ensuring the data has not been corrupted.

4. **Compliance with Regulatory Standards**:

- **Explanation**: Several industries are governed by regulations that require not only data privacy but also strict data integrity. Encryption helps meet these regulatory requirements.

- **Example**: Organizations dealing with personal health information must comply with HIPAA, which mandates safeguards for the integrity of electronic health records.

Implementing Encryption for Data Integrity in Access

1. **Choose Strong Encryption**:

- Use robust encryption standards such as AES (Advanced Encryption Standard) to ensure that both the confidentiality and integrity of data are maintained.

2. **Apply Encryption at Rest and In Transit**:

- Encrypt data both at rest (when data is stored) and in transit (when data is being transmitted) to protect data integrity at all stages.

3. **Manage Encryption Keys Securely**:

- Securely manage encryption keys, ensuring that they are only accessible to authorized users and are stored separately from encrypted data to prevent unauthorized decryption.

4. **Regularly Update and Patch Systems**:

- Keep your database and its environment updated with the latest security patches to protect against vulnerabilities that could compromise data integrity.

Example: Secure Client Information Database

Scenario: A law firm uses an Access database to store sensitive client information and case details. To ensure the integrity of this data, the firm implements encryption both for data stored on their servers and data transmitted to remote users.

Steps to Implement Encryption:

1. **Enable Database Encryption**: Encrypt the Access database using built-in tools with a strong password.

2. **Encrypt Data Connections**: Use VPNs or other secure protocols when transmitting data between the law firm's server and remote users to ensure the data remains intact and private.

3. **Regular Audits and Integrity Checks**: Conduct regular audits and use tools to verify the integrity of the encrypted data, ensuring it has not been altered or corrupted.

Visual Diagram: Data Integrity Protection Process

```
+----------------------------------------------------+
|        Protecting Data Integrity with Encryption   |
|----------------------------------------------------|
| [Encrypt Database at Rest]                         |
|      ↓                                             |
| [Secure Data Transmissions]                        |
|      ↓                                             |
| [Monitor and Audit Data Integrity]                 |
|      ↓                                             |
| [Manage Encryption Keys Securely]                  |
|      ↓                                             |
| [Regular System Updates and Patches]               |
+----------------------------------------------------+
```

Description:

This diagram outlines the process for maintaining data integrity in an Access database through encryption. It highlights essential steps like encrypting data at rest and in transit, along with ongoing monitoring and management practices.

Encryption is a fundamental aspect of ensuring data integrity in Microsoft Access databases. By protecting data from unauthorized alterations and detecting potential corruption, encryption not only secures data but also maintains its accuracy and reliability. Implementing strong encryption practices is essential for any organization that values the integrity of its data and seeks to comply with industry standards and regulations.

<u>Regulatory Compliance</u>:

In many sectors, regulatory frameworks dictate stringent data security practices, including mandatory encryption of sensitive or personal data. Microsoft Access, when used to store such data, must employ encryption to ensure compliance with these regulations. This not only protects data from unauthorized access but also helps organizations avoid legal penalties and maintain trust with stakeholders.

The Role of Encryption in Meeting Compliance Requirements

1. **Adherence to Data Protection Laws**:

- **Explanation**: Laws such as the General Data Protection Regulation (GDPR) in the EU, the Health Insurance Portability and Accountability Act (HIPAA) in the US, and others require that personal and sensitive data be encrypted both at rest and in transit.

- **Example**: A healthcare provider using Access to store patient records must encrypt these databases to comply with HIPAA's requirements for protecting patient health information.

2. **Preventing Data Breaches**:

- **Explanation**: Encryption reduces the risk and potential impact of data breaches, a key concern of regulatory bodies. In the event of a breach, encrypted data remains secure, mitigating the consequences.

- **Example**: If an educational institution's student database (managed in Access) is accessed illegally, encryption ensures that student records are unreadable and protected from misuse.

3. **Ensuring Data Privacy**:

- **Explanation**: Encryption is crucial for maintaining the privacy of data as mandated by privacy laws, ensuring that only authorized individuals can access and interpret the data.

- **Example**: Financial institutions using Access for client data management must encrypt this data to ensure client financial details remain confidential, as required by regulations like the Sarbanes-Oxley Act (SOX).

4. **Building Trust with Users**:

- **Explanation**: Compliance with data protection laws through encryption not only avoids penalties but also builds trust with clients and partners by demonstrating a commitment to data security.

- **Example**: A legal firm storing sensitive case information in Access can reinforce client trust by employing encryption, aligning with best practices and legal requirements.

Implementing Encryption for Compliance in Access

1. **Assessment of Data Sensitivity**:

- Evaluate the types of data stored in Access databases to determine what information requires encryption based on regulatory guidelines.

2. **Enable Built-in Encryption**:

- Utilize Microsoft Access's built-in encryption tools to secure databases, typically under File > Info > Encrypt with Password.

3. **Third-Party Encryption Solutions**:

- Consider additional third-party encryption tools for enhanced security, especially for databases containing highly sensitive or regulated data.

4. **Regular Compliance Audits**:

- Conduct periodic audits to ensure encryption practices align with evolving regulations and to address any new compliance requirements.

5. **Training and Policy Development**:

- Train employees on the importance of encryption and establish clear policies regarding data handling and security to support compliance efforts.

Example: Encrypting a Database for GDPR Compliance

Scenario: An international marketing firm uses an Access database to store customer data, including EU citizens' information, necessitating compliance with GDPR.

Steps to Implement Encryption:

1. **Identify Sensitive Data**: Determine which customer data elements fall under GDPR protection.

2. **Implement Encryption**: Use Access to encrypt the database, ensuring that all data pertaining to EU citizens is secure.

3. **Document Compliance Measures**: Maintain documentation of encryption practices and compliance measures as proof of GDPR adherence.

Visual Diagram: Compliance Through Encryption

```
+------------------------------------------------------+
|        Implementing Encryption for Compliance        |
|------------------------------------------------------|
| [Identify Regulatory Requirements]                   |
|      ↓                                                |
| [Assess Data Sensitivity]                            |
|      ↓                                                |
| [Enable Encryption in Access]                        |
|      ↓                                                |
| [Implement Third-Party Encryption (if needed)]       |
|      ↓                                                |
| [Conduct Regular Compliance Audits]                  |
|      ↓                                                |
| [Train Staff & Develop Security Policies]            |
+------------------------------------------------------+
```

Description:

This flowchart outlines the steps for implementing and managing encryption in Microsoft Access to meet regulatory compliance requirements, highlighting the comprehensive approach from assessment to training.

Encryption plays a pivotal role in ensuring regulatory compliance for organizations using Microsoft Access to store sensitive or personal data. By implementing and managing appropriate encryption measures, organizations can protect themselves from data breaches, meet legal obligations, and maintain trust with their customers and partners.

Implementing Encryption in Microsoft Access

1. **Database Encryption**:

- Microsoft Access provides a straightforward option to encrypt and password-protect a database file via its interface. This process encrypts the entire database file, making the data unreadable without the correct password.

2. **Encryption via VBA**:

- For more advanced scenarios, VBA can be used to implement custom encryption on specific data fields before they are stored in the database, providing an additional layer of security.

3. **Back-end Database Encryption**:

- For split databases, where the back-end contains the data, it is crucial to secure the back-end file using encryption, ensuring that data stored on shared network locations is protected.

Step-by-Step Guide to Enabling Encryption in Access

1. **Open the Database**:

- Start by opening the database file that you want to encrypt in Microsoft Access.

2. **Enable Encryption**:

- Go to 'File' > 'Info' > 'Encrypt with Password'. Enter a strong password when prompted. Microsoft Access will encrypt the database using the AES encryption algorithm, providing robust protection.

3. **Secure Backup**:

- Before applying encryption, ensure you have a secure backup of the database. Encryption can complicate recovery processes if the password is lost.

4. **Distribute Credentials**:

- Safely distribute the encryption password to authorized users. Consider using a secure password manager or other secure methods for sharing credentials.

Example: Encrypting a Customer Data Database

Scenario: An Access database stores sensitive customer information that includes names, addresses, and payment details. To comply with privacy regulations and protect customer data, the database needs to be encrypted.

Steps to Encrypt:

1. **Backup the Database**: Create a full backup of the database to ensure data is not lost in case of issues during the encryption process.

2. **Apply Encryption**: Follow the steps mentioned above to enable encryption through the Access interface.

3. **Verify Access**: Ensure that once encrypted, the database is accessible only by entering the correct password, confirming the encryption is active and functioning.

Visual Diagram: Encryption Process in Access

```
+-------------------------------------------------+
|                                                 |
|        Database Encryption Workflow             |
|                                                 |
|-------------------------------------------------|
| [Backup Database]                               |
|      ↓                                          |
| [Open Database in Access]                       |
|      ↓                                          |
| [Enable Encryption]                             |
|      ↓                                          |
| [Enter and Confirm Password]                    |
|      ↓                                          |
| [Database Encrypted Successfully]               |
|      ↓                                          |
| [Test Encrypted Database Access]                |
|      ↓                                          |
| [Distribute Password Securely]                  |
+-------------------------------------------------+
```

Description:

This flowchart outlines the necessary steps to encrypt a database in Microsoft Access, highlighting the importance of backing up data and securing the encryption password.

Encrypting data in Microsoft Access is a vital security practice that protects sensitive information from unauthorized access and ensures compliance with data protection regulations. By implementing encryption, businesses can significantly enhance the security posture of their Access databases, safeguarding critical data against potential threats.

Database Security Best Practices:
Implementing robust security practices is crucial for safeguarding data within Microsoft Access databases. These practices help mitigate risks such as unauthorized data access, data corruption, and loss, ensuring that sensitive information remains protected. By adhering to a set of best practices, organizations can enhance the security of their databases effectively.

Core Database Security Best Practices

1. **Regular Updates and Patch Management**:

- **Explanation**: Keeping Microsoft Access and its environment updated ensures that any security vulnerabilities are promptly addressed.

- **Example**: Regularly apply updates from Microsoft that fix known bugs and close security loopholes.

2. **Use of Strong Passwords and Encryption**:

- **Explanation**: Protect databases with strong, complex passwords and encrypt data to prevent unauthorized access.

- **Example**: Enable encryption in Access by using the built-in 'Encrypt with Password' feature and choose a password that combines letters, numbers, and special characters.

3. **Implementation of User Access Controls**:

- **Explanation**: Define and enforce user roles and permissions to ensure users can only access data necessary for their roles.

- **Example**: Restrict editing capabilities to administrators, while granting read-only access to other users.

4. **Regular Backups**:

- **Explanation**: Perform regular backups to prevent data loss and ensure data can be recovered in the event of corruption or other disasters.

- **Example**: Schedule daily or weekly backups, depending on the frequency of data updates, and store backups in a secure, off-site location.

5. **Audit Trails**:

- **Explanation**: Implement audit trails to track and log all access and changes to the database, providing a record that can be used to detect unauthorized activity or inconsistencies.

- **Example**: Use Access's built-in tracking features or third-party tools to log who accessed what data and when.

6. **Secure Data Transmission**:

- **Explanation**: Ensure that data transmitted to and from the database is protected using secure methods like VPNs or SSL/TLS.

- **Example**: Encrypt connections to remote databases with SSL to prevent data interception during transmission.

7. **Antivirus and Anti-malware Protection**:

- **Explanation**: Protect the system running Microsoft Access with updated antivirus and anti-malware software to prevent malware from compromising database security.

- **Example**: Install and regularly update a reputable antivirus program to scan files and protect against malware infections.

Visual Diagram: Access Database Security Workflow

```
+-----------------------------------------------+
|           Database Security Workflow          |
|-----------------------------------------------|
| [Install Updates & Patches]                   |
|     ↓                                         |
| [Configure Encryption & Passwords]            |
|     ↓                                         |
| [Set User Roles & Permissions]                |
|     ↓                                         |
| [Perform Regular Backups]                     |
|     ↓                                         |
| [Enable Audit Trails]                         |
|     ↓                                         |
| [Secure Data Transmissions]                   |
|     ↓                                         |
| [Maintain Antivirus Protection]               |
+-----------------------------------------------+
```

Description:

This flowchart provides an overview of the essential steps involved in securing a Microsoft Access database, highlighting the systematic approach to comprehensive data security.

Following best practices for database security in Microsoft Access is essential for protecting sensitive information from unauthorized access, data loss, and corruption. By implementing strong passwords, encryption, user access controls, and other security measures, organizations can ensure the integrity and confidentiality of their data. Regular updates, backups, and vigilant monitoring are key components of a robust security strategy that adapts to evolving threats and maintains the reliability of database systems.

Conclusion

Security in Microsoft Access is a critical component of database management, especially in environments where data sensitivity is a concern. By effectively implementing Access's built-in security features, organizations can protect their data from unauthorized access and ensure that users have the appropriate levels of access to perform their roles. These measures not only safeguard information but also help in maintaining data integrity and compliance with data protection regulations.

Part IV: Deploying as a Standalone Program

Chapter 10 - Compiling the Database into an Executable

Introduction to Database Compilation into an Executable

Compiling a Microsoft Access database into an executable file is a process designed to package the database and its associated application components into a standalone program. This approach can enhance security, simplify distribution, and provide a professional user experience by allowing users to interact with the database without needing a full installation of Microsoft Access on their machines.

Benefits of Compiling an Access Database into an Executable

1. **Enhanced Security**: Compiling the database into an executable restricts users from modifying the design of forms, reports, and underlying code, which protects the integrity of the database application.

2. **Ease of Distribution**: Distributing a single executable file makes it easier to deploy and update the application across multiple user environments.

3. **User Experience**: Users interact with a clean, controlled application interface, which can be customized to only expose necessary functionalities, enhancing usability and reducing training requirements.

4. **Reduced Dependency**: An executable can run on systems without a full version of Microsoft Access, as long as they have the Access Runtime environment installed, which is available for free.

Process of Compiling an Access Database into an Executable

1. **Develop and Test the Database:**

- Ensure that your Access database is fully developed and rigorously tested. Include all necessary forms, queries, reports, and VBA code.

2. **Create an ACCDE File:**

- Convert your Access database (.accdb) into an ACCDE file. This file format locks down the design elements and VBA code, preventing users from seeing or modifying the source code.

- To create an ACCDE file, open your ACCDB file in Access, go to **File** > **Save As** > **Make ACCDE** and choose a location to save the file.

3. **Package the Solution**:

- Use the Access Deployment Wizard or a similar tool to package the ACCDE file into an installation package. This package will include the Access Runtime environment, allowing the executable to run on computers without Access installed.

- Configure the installation package to include all necessary components, such as additional DLLs, third-party utilities, or other resources needed by the database.

4. **Test the Packaged Application**:

- Before widespread deployment, thoroughly test the packaged application in various environments to ensure it functions as intended. This includes testing all user interactions, data processing, and error handling.

5. **Deploy the Executable**:

- Distribute the executable package to users. Provide installation instructions and support resources to help users get started with the application.

Example: Compiling a Sales Management Database

Scenario: A company uses a sales management database developed in Access and wants to compile it into an executable to distribute to its sales force, who do not have Microsoft Access installed on their computers.

Steps:

1. **Finalize Database**: The developer finalizes all forms, reports, and modules within the ACCDB file.

2. **Create ACCDE**: The database is converted into an ACCDE file to lock down the code and design elements.

3. **Package with Runtime**: Using the Access Deployment Wizard, the ACCDE file is packaged with the Access Runtime environment and necessary supporting files.

4. **Deploy and Support**: The package is distributed to the sales team, and support is provided to assist with installation and troubleshooting.

Visual Diagram: Process of Compiling an Access Database

```
+------------------------------------------------+
|        Compiling Access Database to EXE        |
|------------------------------------------------|
| [Develop & Test Database]                      |
|     ↓                                          |
| [Convert to ACCDE File]                        |
|     ↓                                          |
| [Package with Access Runtime]                  |
|     ↓                                          |
| [Test Packaged Application]                    |
|     ↓                                          |
| [Deploy to Users]                              |
+------------------------------------------------+
```

Description:

This flowchart details the steps from development to deployment involved in compiling an Access database into an executable file, emphasizing the transformation from an ACCDB file to a packaged EXE with runtime.

Preparing Your Database for Distribution:

When preparing a Microsoft Access database for distribution as an executable, it's crucial to ensure that the database is secure, efficient, and user-friendly. This process involves optimizing the database's performance, securing sensitive data, and creating a streamlined user interface that facilitates easy navigation and operation by end-users.

Key Steps in Preparing Your Database for Distribution:

<u>**Optimize Database Performance**</u>:

When preparing a Microsoft Access database for compilation into an executable and subsequent distribution, one of the primary concerns is ensuring optimal performance. This involves refining the database to enhance its speed, efficiency, and reliability under various operational conditions.

Importance of Database Performance Optimization

Optimizing the performance of your Access database is crucial for providing a smooth user experience, minimizing resource consumption, and ensuring that the application can handle the expected load without slowdowns or crashes.

Key Strategies for Optimizing Access Database Performance

1. **Optimize Queries**:

- **Explanation**: Queries are often the heart of a database application. Optimizing these can significantly improve overall performance.

- **Example**: Use query execution plans to identify bottlenecks. Simplify complex queries, eliminate unnecessary subqueries, and ensure that all joins are necessary and efficient.

2. **Use Indexes Wisely**:

- **Explanation**: Indexes can drastically improve the speed of data retrieval operations but can also slow down data insertion, update, and deletion if used excessively.

- **Example**: Create indexes on fields that are frequently used in search criteria or join operations. Avoid indexing fields that undergo frequent changes.

3. **Compact and Repair Database**:

- **Explanation**: Access databases can develop bloat from temporary and deleted objects, which can slow down performance over time.

- **Example**: Regularly use the Compact and Repair Database tool to reduce file size and enhance performance, especially before converting the database into an executable format.

4. **Split the Database**:

- **Explanation**: Splitting a database into a front-end and back-end can improve performance, especially in networked environments.

- **Example**: Keep the user interface, forms, and logic in the front-end locally on user machines, while the back-end with the data tables resides on a server.

5. **Limit the Use of VBA**:

- **Explanation**: While VBA is powerful, it can slow down operations if not used judiciously.

- **Example**: Avoid using VBA for tasks that can be managed through SQL or Access built-in functions, and ensure VBA code is optimized and compiled.

6. **Test Performance Scenarios**:

- **Explanation**: Testing how the database performs under different scenarios can help identify areas for improvement.

- **Example**: Simulate multi-user environments and data-intensive operations to see how the database holds up and adjust settings or design accordingly.

Visual Example: Performance Optimization Process

Flowchart:

```
+------------------------------------------------------------+
| Database Performance Optimization Flow                     |
|------------------------------------------------------------|
| [Identify Slow Queries and Operations]                     |
|      ↓                                                      |
| [Optimize Queries and Use Indexes]                         |
|      ↓                                                      |
| [Compact and Repair Database Regularly]                    |
|      ↓                                                      |
| [Split Database for Improved Load Handling]                |
|      ↓                                                      |
| [Optimize and Minimize VBA Scripts]                        |
|      ↓                                                      |
| [Test with Realistic Performance Scenarios]                |
+------------------------------------------------------------+
```

Description:

This flowchart outlines a systematic approach to optimizing the performance of an Access database, highlighting essential steps from identifying slow components to implementing improvements and testing.

Optimizing the performance of a Microsoft Access database before compiling it into an executable and distributing it is crucial for ensuring that the application runs efficiently across all user environments. By addressing potential performance issues through strategic query optimization, wise use of indexes, regular maintenance, and thoughtful design decisions, developers can create a robust, reliable, and user-friendly database application.

<u>**Secure Sensitive Data**</u>:

When preparing a Microsoft Access database for distribution, especially when compiling it into an executable, securing sensitive data is paramount. This process involves implementing measures to protect data from unauthorized access, manipulation, and breaches, ensuring that the integrity and confidentiality of the data are maintained.

Importance of Data Security in Distribution

Securing sensitive data is crucial not only to comply with privacy laws and regulations but also to maintain trust with users and stakeholders. It protects the organization from potential data breaches that could lead to financial loss, legal consequences, and damage to reputation.

Strategies for Securing Sensitive Data in Access

1. **Implement Strong Encryption**:

- **Explanation**: Encrypting the database file ensures that data is unreadable to anyone who does not have the decryption key or password.

- **Example**: Use Access's built-in encryption feature to encrypt the database before distribution, ensuring that all data stored within is ciphered.

2. **Convert to ACCDE Format**:

- **Explanation**: Converting an Access database (ACCDB) to an ACCDE format locks down the forms, reports, and modules, preventing users from altering the design or viewing the source code.

- **Example**: Convert the database to ACCDE format after final development and testing to secure the VBA code and layout designs.

3. **Use Strong Passwords**:

- **Explanation**: Passwords are the first line of defense against unauthorized access.

- **Example**: Set a strong, complex password for opening the ACCDE file and advise users on secure password management practices.

4. **Limit User Permissions**:

- **Explanation**: Define user roles and permissions to control what data can be accessed or modified by different users within the application.

- **Example**: Allow only administrative users to access sensitive reports or data management features, while other users have limited access based on their operational needs.

5. **Regular Security Audits and Updates**:

- **Explanation**: Continuously monitor and update the security measures implemented in the database to adapt to new threats or changes in compliance requirements.

- **Example**: Periodically review and update the database's encryption and access controls as part of routine maintenance.

6. **Data Access Auditing**:

- **Explanation**: Implement auditing to track access and changes to sensitive data, helping to identify and respond to unauthorized activities quickly.

- **Example**: Use Access's built-in auditing tools to log when data is accessed or changed, by whom, and record any unauthorized access attempts.

Visual Diagram: Securing Sensitive Data in Microsoft Access

Flowchart:

```
+-----------------------------------------------------+
|                                                     |
| Securing Sensitive Data for Database Distribution   |
|-----------------------------------------------------|
|                                                     |
| [Encrypt Database]                                  |
|         ↓                                           |
| [Convert Database to ACCDE Format]                  |
|         ↓                                           |
| [Set Strong User Passwords]                         |
|         ↓                                           |
| [Define and Implement User Permissions]             |
|         ↓                                           |
| [Conduct Regular Security Audits]                   |
|         ↓                                           |
| [Enable Data Access Auditing]                       |
|                                                     |
+-----------------------------------------------------+
```

Description:

This flowchart provides a step-by-step visual representation of the key actions required to secure sensitive data in an Access database. It highlights the comprehensive approach from encryption to auditing.

Securing sensitive data is a critical component of preparing an Access database for distribution as an executable. By implementing strong encryption, converting to ACCDE format, using robust passwords, managing user permissions, and establishing regular audits and access logging, developers can ensure that the database is secure and compliant with relevant data protection standards. These measures not only protect the data but also reinforce the integrity and reliability of the database application as it is distributed and used across various environments.

Simplify the User Interface:

When preparing a Microsoft Access database for distribution, particularly when compiling it into an executable, simplifying the user interface (UI) is essential. A streamlined and intuitive UI enhances user experience, reduces training requirements, and minimizes user errors. This process involves designing the UI to be clean, efficient, and easy to navigate, ensuring that users can perform their tasks effectively without unnecessary complexity.

Importance of a Simplified User Interface

1. **Enhanced Usability**:

- **Explanation**: A simplified UI helps users navigate the application more easily, making it more accessible to users with varying levels of technical skill.

- **Example**: Reducing clutter on forms and reports, and clearly labeling controls and sections to guide users through their workflows smoothly.

2. **Increased Productivity**:

- **Explanation**: By minimizing the complexity of the UI, users can complete tasks more quickly and with less confusion, leading to increased overall productivity.

- **Example**: Designing forms with logical flow and grouping related fields together can speed up data entry and reduce errors.

3. **Reduced Support Costs**:

- **Explanation**: A straightforward and intuitive UI reduces the frequency of user errors and the need for extensive support and training.

- **Example**: A well-designed dashboard that provides immediate access to the most commonly used features can significantly decrease the number of support calls.

Strategies for Simplifying the User Interface

1. **Streamline Navigation**:

- **Explanation**: Organize navigation elements logically and consistently to make it easy for users to find what they need.

- **Example**: Use a navigation form that includes buttons for common tasks like entering new records, generating reports, or querying data, clearly labeled with icons and text.

2. **Optimize Forms and Reports**:

- **Explanation**: Design forms and reports to be clear and simple, displaying only necessary information and controls.

- **Example**: Eliminate rarely used fields from main forms and provide options to access them through expandable sections or separate forms.

3. **Use Tooltips and Help Prompts**:

- **Explanation**: Include tooltips and context-sensitive help prompts to guide users through complex areas or to explain the purpose of specific controls.

- **Example**: Add tooltips to icons and buttons to explain their action when hovered over, reducing the need for external documentation.

4. **Consistent UI Design**:

- **Explanation**: Apply consistent design elements across the database, such as colors, fonts, and control styles, which can help reinforce the user's understanding of the UI.

- **Example**: Use a uniform color scheme that aligns with your organization's branding and standardized fonts that are easy to read.

5. Focus on User Experience (UX) Testing:

- **Explanation**: Conduct user experience testing with real users to identify areas of confusion and opportunities for simplification.

- **Example**: Set up a test scenario for users to complete specific tasks, and observe where they encounter difficulties or delays.

Visual Example: UI Simplification Process

Flowchart:

```
+-----------------------------------------------------+
|      Process of Simplifying UI in Access Database   |
|-----------------------------------------------------|
| [Streamline Navigation]                             |
|      ↓                                              |
| [Optimize Forms & Reports]                          |
|      ↓                                              |
| [Implement Tooltips and Help Prompts]               |
|      ↓                                              |
| [Apply Consistent UI Design]                        |
|      ↓                                              |
| [Conduct UX Testing & Revise]                       |
+-----------------------------------------------------+
```

Description:

This flowchart outlines a systematic approach to simplifying the user interface in a Microsoft Access database. It highlights essential steps from streamlining navigation to conducting user testing and making necessary revisions.

Simplifying the user interface is a crucial step in preparing an Access database for distribution as an executable. It involves enhancing usability, ensuring consistency in design, and reducing the need for extensive user training and support. Through careful design and testing, developers can create a user-friendly interface that facilitates efficient and error-free interaction, leading to a more successful and widely adopted application.

Incorporate Error Handling:

Incorporating robust error handling is a crucial step when preparing a Microsoft Access database for distribution as an executable. Effective error handling ensures that the application operates smoothly and remains user-friendly even when unexpected conditions or errors occur. It also prevents the application from crashing and provides useful feedback to users, helping them understand what went wrong and how to proceed.

Importance of Error Handling

1. **Enhanced Stability and Reliability**:

- **Explanation**: Proper error handling helps maintain application stability by catching exceptions and handling them gracefully without crashing.

- **Example**: Catching data input errors and preventing them from causing a system failure.

2. **Improved User Experience**:

- **Explanation**: Providing clear and informative error messages helps users understand issues and how to resolve them or when to contact support.

- **Example**: Instead of generic error messages, display context-specific guidance that can help the user correct data entry mistakes.

3. **Maintenance and Troubleshooting**:

- **Explanation**: Well-implemented error handling can log errors and their contexts, aiding developers in diagnosing and fixing underlying problems.

- **Example**: Logging detailed error information to a file or a database table for later analysis by the development team.

Strategies for Incorporating Error Handling

1. **Use VBA Error Trapping**:

- **Explanation**: In VBA, utilize error trapping structures like **On Error GoTo** to capture and handle errors methodically.

- **Example**: Create a centralized error handler routine in VBA that logs errors and shows friendly messages to users.

2. **Validate Data Inputs**:

- **Explanation**: Prevent common data input errors by validating data before processing it.

- **Example**: Check for null values, data type mismatches, and range constraints on user forms before submission.

3. **Handle Database Operations Carefully**:

- **Explanation**: Ensure that database operations such as opening connections, running queries, and updating records are performed safely.

- **Example**: Use error handling when performing SQL transactions to rollback changes in case of failures.

4. **Implement Global Error Handler**:

- **Explanation**: Design a global error handling mechanism for unhandled errors that logs the error details and notifies the user appropriately.

- **Example**: Create a module dedicated to capturing unhandled exceptions, logging them, and notifying the system administrators.

5. **Regularly Test Error Scenarios**:

- **Explanation**: Test how the application handles different error scenarios during the development phase to ensure all potential issues are gracefully managed.

- **Example**: Simulate common error conditions, such as database connectivity issues or file access permissions, to validate error handling effectiveness.

Visual Diagram: Error Handling Framework in Access

Flowchart:

```
+-----------------------------------------------------+
|        Access Database Error Handling Framework      |
|-----------------------------------------------------|
| [Start]                                              |
|     ↓                                                |
| [Input Validation at Form Level]                     |
|     ↓                                                |
| [VBA Error Trapping in Code]                         |
|     ↓                                                |
| [Global Error Handler for Uncaught Exceptions]       |
|     ↓                                                |
| [Log Error Details]                                  |
|     ↓                                                |
| [User Notification and Guidance]                     |
|     ↓                                                |
| [End]                                                |
+-----------------------------------------------------+
```

Description:

This flowchart illustrates the comprehensive approach to error handling within an Access database. It shows the process from input validation through to user notification and logging, highlighting the layers of error management involved.

Incorporating sophisticated error handling in a Microsoft Access database prepared for distribution as an executable is essential for ensuring the application is robust, reliable, and user-friendly. By anticipating and managing potential errors, developers can prevent disruptions and provide a seamless experience for end-users, thereby enhancing the overall quality and effectiveness of the application.

<u>Final Testing:</u>

Final testing is a critical phase in preparing a Microsoft Access database for distribution as an executable. This stage ensures that the database application operates as intended, is free from bugs, and provides a smooth user experience. It involves conducting comprehensive tests to validate every aspect of the application, from functionality and usability to performance and security.

Importance of Final Testing

1. **Ensure Functionality:**

- **Explanation**: Verifying that all functions of the database work correctly and as expected.

- **Example**: Testing all queries, forms, reports, and custom code to ensure they perform their intended tasks without errors.

2. **Verify User Experience**:

- **Explanation**: Ensuring the interface is intuitive and the navigation is easy for the end-users.

- **Example**: User testing sessions to gather feedback on the UI/UX and making necessary adjustments based on user input.

3. **Assess Performance**:

- **Explanation**: Checking the database's performance under various loads to ensure it can handle the expected volume of data and number of users.

- **Example**: Stress testing by simulating multiple users accessing the database simultaneously to observe how the system manages high-load situations.

4. **Security Validation**:

- **Explanation**: Confirming that all security measures, including encryption and user permissions, are functioning correctly to protect data integrity and privacy.

- **Example**: Penetration testing to try and breach the database's security setup and identify any vulnerabilities.

Strategies for Effective Final Testing

1. **Develop a Comprehensive Test Plan**:

- **Explanation**: Create a detailed plan that covers all aspects of the application, including functional, usability, performance, and security testing.

- **Example**: A test plan that specifies different scenarios for each function of the application, detailing expected outcomes and criteria for passing.

2. **Use Automated and Manual Testing Methods**:

- **Explanation**: Employ both automated tools and manual testing techniques to cover all testing aspects thoroughly.

- **Example**: Automated scripts to test standard operations and manual testing for scenarios that require human judgment, such as usability.

3. **Involve End-Users in Testing**:

- **Explanation**: Include actual or representative users in the testing process to obtain feedback on how the database performs in real-world scenarios.

- **Example**: Conducting beta testing with a select group of end-users to identify any practical issues not previously detected during internal testing.

4. **Iterate Based on Feedback**:

- **Explanation**: Use the feedback obtained from all testing phases to make iterative improvements to the database.

- **Example**: Adjusting user interfaces, streamlining operations, or enhancing security features based on test results and user suggestions.

Visual Diagram: Final Testing Process for Database Distribution

Flowchart:

```
+-------------------------------------------------------+
|               Final Testing Process Flowchart         |
|-------------------------------------------------------|
| [Develop Test Plan]                                   |
|      ↓                                                |
| [Conduct Functional Testing]                          |
|      ↓                                                |
| [Perform Usability Testing with Users]                |
|      ↓                                                |
| [Execute Performance Testing]                         |
|      ↓                                                |
| [Validate Security Measures]                          |
|      ↓                                                |
| [Collect Feedback and Iterate]                        |
|      ↓                                                |
| [Approve Final Release]                               |
+-------------------------------------------------------+
```

Description:

This flowchart details the structured approach to final testing in the distribution of an Access database executable. It emphasizes the importance of various testing types and the iterative process based on feedback.

Final testing is an indispensable stage in the distribution process of a Microsoft Access database as an executable. It ensures that the application not only meets the design and functional specifications but also provides a secure, efficient, and user-friendly experience. By rigorously testing the database and iteratively improving it based on comprehensive feedback, developers can significantly increase the reliability and success of the distributed application.

Create Documentation and Help Resources:

As you prepare a Microsoft Access database for distribution as an executable, creating comprehensive documentation and help resources is vital. These materials not only guide the end-users through using the application efficiently but also reduce the reliance on direct support, thereby enhancing user satisfaction and minimizing support costs.

Importance of Documentation and Help Resources

1. **User Guidance**:

- **Explanation**: Detailed documentation provides users with clear instructions on how to use the database effectively and troubleshoot common issues.

- **Example**: A user manual that includes step-by-step guides for common tasks such as entering data, generating reports, and querying the database.

2. **Quick Problem Resolution**:

- **Explanation**: Well-organized help resources enable users to resolve issues quickly without needing to contact support.

- **Example**: A FAQ section that addresses common user questions and problems, providing immediate solutions.

3. **Training Support**:

- **Explanation**: Documentation can serve as a training resource for new users, facilitating easier onboarding and lessening the training burden.

- **Example**: Training modules or video tutorials that can be accessed independently by new users to learn the system at their own pace.

4. **Legal and Compliance Information**:

- **Explanation**: Some documentation may be required to ensure compliance with regulations or to provide legal disclaimers and usage guidelines.

- **Example**: Compliance statements or privacy notices included within help files or user manuals.

Strategies for Creating Effective Documentation and Help Resources

1. **Identify Key User Tasks**:

- **Explanation**: Determine the tasks users will perform most frequently and focus documentation efforts on these areas.

- **Example**: Analyze user behavior patterns or consult with stakeholders to prioritize documentation topics.

2. **Use Clear, Concise Language**:

- **Explanation**: Write documentation in simple, jargon-free language to ensure it is accessible to users with varying levels of technical expertise.

- **Example**: Use plain English, avoid technical terms, or provide a glossary for terms that cannot be simplified.

3. **Incorporate Visual Aids**:

- **Explanation**: Visual aids such as screenshots, diagrams, and flowcharts can help users understand complex processes more easily.

- **Example**: Include annotated screenshots in the user manual to illustrate steps for completing tasks in the UI.

4. **Maintain and Update Documentation**:

- **Explanation**: Keep documentation up to date with software updates and changes to ensure continued relevance and accuracy.

- **Example**: Regularly review and revise help files to incorporate new features or changes following software updates.

5. **Provide Multiple Formats**:

- **Explanation**: Offer documentation in various formats to cater to different user preferences and situations.

- **Example**: Make documentation available in PDF format for easy printing, HTML for online access, and interactive help integrated within the application.

Visual Diagram: Documentation Creation Process

Flowchart:

```
+-------------------------------------------------------+
|                                                       |
|        Documentation Creation Process Flowchart       |
|-------------------------------------------------------|
| [Identify Key User Tasks]                             |
|     ↓                                                 |
| [Write Clear, Concise Content]                        |
|     ↓                                                 |
| [Incorporate Visual Aids]                             |
|     ↓                                                 |
| [Format and Organize Documents]                       |
|     ↓                                                 |
| [Review and Revise]                                   |
|     ↓                                                 |
| [Publish in Multiple Formats]                         |
+-------------------------------------------------------+
```

Description:

This flowchart outlines the steps involved in creating effective documentation and help resources, from identifying key tasks to publishing in multiple formats, highlighting the structured approach to ensuring quality and accessibility.

Creating detailed and accessible documentation and help resources is a crucial part of distributing a Microsoft Access database as an executable. Effective documentation not only empowers users but also enhances their overall experience by providing essential support resources. By following structured strategies for content creation and presentation, developers can ensure that users receive all the information they need to successfully navigate and utilize the database application.

Example: Distributing a Sales Tracking Database

Scenario: A sales tracking database is developed in Access and needs to be compiled and distributed as an executable to a sales team.

Steps to Prepare for Distribution:

1. **Optimization**: Index all tables on fields that are frequently searched and used in joins. Refactor complex queries to speed up report generation.

2. **Security**: Convert the database to ACCDE format, encrypt it, and ensure that only relevant parts of the database are accessible to prevent data leakage.

3. **User Interface**: Design a user-friendly interface with custom menus that provide quick access to common tasks like entering new sales data or generating weekly reports.

4. **Error Handling**: Include comprehensive error handling within the application to manage and log errors, providing users with clear information on how to resolve issues.

5. **Testing**: Run a series of tests to ensure the application is stable and behaves as expected under typical usage conditions.

6. **Documentation**: Prepare a detailed user manual that includes troubleshooting information and a FAQ section for end-users.

Visual Diagram: Preparing for Distribution

```
+---------------------------------------------------------+
|        Steps to Prepare Access Database for Distribution |
|---------------------------------------------------------|
| [Optimize Performance]                                  |
|      ↓                                                  |
| [Secure Data & Convert to ACCDE]                        |
|      ↓                                                  |
| [Simplify User Interface]                               |
|      ↓                                                  |
| [Implement Error Handling]                              |
|      ↓                                                  |
| [Conduct Final Testing]                                 |
|      ↓                                                  |
| [Create User Documentation]                             |
+---------------------------------------------------------+
```

Description:

This flowchart outlines the sequential steps involved in preparing an Access database for distribution as an executable. Each step focuses on ensuring that the database is secure, efficient, and user-friendly.

Preparing a Microsoft Access database for distribution as an executable involves several crucial steps, from optimizing performance and securing data to simplifying the user interface and creating comprehensive documentation. These preparations ensure that the database not only meets the operational needs of the users but also maintains high standards of security and usability, facilitating a smooth and effective deployment.

Using Access Developer Extensions

The Access Developer Extensions are a set of tools provided by Microsoft that facilitate the packaging and deployment of Access databases. These tools are particularly useful when preparing a database for distribution as an executable, streamlining the process and ensuring a professional setup experience for end-users.

Overview of Access Developer Extensions

Access Developer Extensions typically include utilities like the Package Solution Wizard, which helps developers create a Windows Installer (MSI) package for their Access applications. This package can include the

Access database itself, any associated files, the Access Runtime, and custom installation options.

Benefits of Using Access Developer Extensions

1.   **Streamlined Packaging Process**:

- **Explanation**: Simplifies the conversion of an Access database into a distributable package that includes all necessary components.

- **Example**: Automatically includes dependencies such as additional libraries and the Access Runtime environment.

2.   **Customizable Installer Options**:

- **Explanation**: Allows developers to customize the installation process, including where files are installed, which shortcuts are created, and how updates are managed.

- **Example**: Configuring the installer to add a desktop shortcut for the database application or to check for updates upon startup.

3.   **Consistent Deployment**:

- **Explanation**: Ensures that the database application is installed consistently across multiple user environments, reducing installation errors and compatibility issues.

- **Example**: Ensuring that all users have the same database version and file structure regardless of their individual system configurations.

How to Use Access Developer Extensions

1.   **Download and Install the Extensions**:

- Access Developer Extensions may need to be downloaded separately or might be included in your Office or Access setup. Ensure they are installed and integrated into your Access environment.

2.   **Prepare Your Database**:

- Before using the Package Solution Wizard, finalize your Access database application, ensuring all forms, reports, and modules are complete and functioning as intended.

3. **Launch the Package Solution Wizard:**

- From within Access, navigate to the 'Database Tools' tab and select the 'Package Solution' wizard from the options available.

4. **Configure the Installer:**

- Use the wizard to set up your installer. This includes defining installation paths, selecting which files to include, configuring shortcuts, and setting other options like agreeing to license terms or specifying required user settings.

5. **Test the Installer:**

- Once the package is created, test the installer on different machines and operating systems to ensure it works correctly. This is crucial to identify and fix any issues before widespread distribution.

Visual Diagram: Using Access Developer Extensions

Flowchart:

```
+----------------------------------------------------------+
|  Using Access Developer Extensions Process Flow          |
|----------------------------------------------------------|
| [Install Developer Extensions]                           |
|     ↓                                                    |
| [Prepare Database Application]                           |
|     ↓                                                    |
| [Launch Package Solution Wizard]                         |
|     ↓                                                    |
| [Configure Installation Settings]                        |
|     ↓                                                    |
| [Build Installer Package]                                |
|     ↓                                                    |
| [Test Installer on Different Systems]                    |
+----------------------------------------------------------+
```

Description:

This flowchart visually represents the steps involved in using the Access Developer Extensions to compile a database into an executable. It emphasizes the streamlined process from installation of the extensions to testing the final installer package.

Using Access Developer Extensions significantly enhances the process of compiling and distributing Microsoft Access databases as executables. These tools facilitate a professional, consistent deployment process, ensuring that end-users receive a seamless installation experience. By leveraging these extensions, developers can confidently package their Access applications, including all necessary components for a successful deployment.

Creating an Executable File:

Creating an executable file from a Microsoft Access database involves packaging the database application along with all necessary components so that it can be installed and run independently of the Microsoft Access IDE. This process enhances the accessibility and security of the application, making it suitable for a broad distribution to users who may not have Microsoft Access installed.

Benefits of Creating an Executable File

1. **Enhanced Security**: Compiling the database into an executable file can help protect the underlying source code from being accessed or modified, securing your intellectual property and sensitive data.

2. **Simplified Distribution**: An executable file allows for easier distribution and installation of the application across multiple environments without requiring each end-user to have Microsoft Access installed.

3. **Improved User Experience**: Users interact with a more streamlined and controlled application, without the complexities and potential distractions of the full Access environment.

Key Steps in Creating an Executable File

1. **Finalize the Access Database**:

- Ensure that all forms, reports, queries, and code within the database are complete and thoroughly tested.

2. **Convert to an ACCDE File**:

- Convert the Access database (.accdb) into an ACCDE file. This step locks down the VBA code and design changes, making your application more secure.

3. **Package the Application**:

- Utilize the Microsoft Access Developer Extensions or a third-party installer package tool to create an executable. This tool will package the ACCDE file and any required dependencies, such as the Access Runtime, into a single installer.

4. **Customize the Installer**:

- Configure the installer settings, including installation paths, shortcuts, and user agreements. This customization ensures that the executable installs all necessary files in the correct locations and creates appropriate shortcuts for the application.

5. **Test the Executable**:

- Thoroughly test the executable in different environments to ensure compatibility and functionality. This testing should mimic real-world usage as closely as possible to capture any issues before widespread deployment.

6. **Deploy the Executable**:

- Distribute the final executable file to users. Provide detailed installation instructions and support resources to ensure a smooth transition for users.

Example: Sales Management Application

Scenario: A developer has created a sales management application in Microsoft Access and needs to distribute it to a sales team that does not have Access installed on their computers.

Steps:

1. **ACCDE Conversion**: The developer converts the fully tested .accdb file into an ACCDE format, securing the code and layout.

2. **Packaging**: Using the Access Developer Extensions, the developer packages the ACCDE file with the Access Runtime environment into an installer.

3. **Customization and Testing**: The installer is customized to include necessary user prompts and tested across different operating systems to ensure functionality.

4. **Deployment**: The executable is distributed to the sales team, with installation support provided to ensure each member can install and run the application independently.

Visual Diagram: Creating an Executable File

Flowchart:

```
+----------------------------------------------------+
|        Process of Creating an Executable File      |
|----------------------------------------------------|
| [Finalize Database]                                |
|     ↓                                              |
| [Convert Database to ACCDE]                        |
|     ↓                                              |
| [Package Application with Runtime]                 |
|     ↓                                              |
| [Customize Installer]                              |
|     ↓                                              |
| [Test Executable]                                  |
|     ↓                                              |
| [Deploy to Users]                                  |
+----------------------------------------------------+
```

Description:

This flowchart illustrates the sequence of actions from finalizing the database to deploying the executable file, highlighting the comprehensive approach required to ensure a successful application distribution.

Creating an executable file from a Microsoft Access database is an essential process for distributing a secure, standalone application. By following the outlined steps and leveraging available tools, developers can ensure their application is accessible, secure, and provides a consistent user experience across multiple environments. This not only enhances user satisfaction but also protects the application from unauthorized access and modifications.

Conclusion

Compiling a Microsoft Access database into an executable file is a powerful way to secure, simplify, and enhance the distribution of a database application. By following a structured process and utilizing tools like the Access Deployment Wizard, developers can ensure that their applications are accessible and usable even in environments without the full version of Access installed. This method not only protects the database from unauthorized changes but also significantly improves the end-user experience.

Chapter 11 - Installation and Distribution

The installation and distribution process for Microsoft Access applications is crucial for ensuring that end-users can easily access and utilize the software. This process involves packaging the application properly, deploying it across various environments, and managing updates and support. A smooth installation process enhances user satisfaction and adoption rates, making it a critical phase in the lifecycle of an application.

Key Considerations for Installation and Distribution

1. **Packaging the Application**:

- **Explanation**: The application must be packaged in a way that ensures all necessary components are included for proper functioning.

- **Example**: Using the Microsoft Access Developer Extensions to package the application with the Access Runtime environment ensures users without Access can still run the application.

2. **Creating an Installer**:

- **Explanation**: An installer simplifies the process of setting up the application on user machines by automating steps like file copying and registry settings.

- **Example**: Tools like Inno Setup or InstallShield can be used to create professional-grade installers that include custom setup options, such as selecting installation paths and creating desktop shortcuts.

3. **Ensuring Compatibility**:

- **Explanation**: The application should be tested on all supported operating systems and configurations to ensure compatibility.

- **Example**: Running compatibility tests on different versions of Windows where the application will be installed, adjusting as necessary to fix any issues that arise.

4. **Providing Clear Installation Instructions**:

- **Explanation**: Proper documentation and instructions guide users through the installation process, reducing the likelihood of errors and support calls.

- **Example**: Detailed step-by-step guides or video tutorials can help users correctly install the application without technical assistance.

5. **Managing Updates and Patches**:

- **Explanation**: After distribution, applications may require updates or patches to add features, fix bugs, or address security vulnerabilities.

- **Example**: Implementing an update mechanism within the application that checks for and installs updates automatically or notifies users of available updates.

Strategies for Effective Distribution

1. **Use of Cloud Services**:

- **Explanation**: Distributing software through cloud platforms can streamline the process and allow for instant updates.

- **Example**: Using services like Microsoft OneDrive or Dropbox to host the installer, ensuring users always download the latest version.

2. **Setting Up User Training Sessions**:

- **Explanation**: Training sessions help users understand how to use the application effectively, reducing initial resistance and improving user engagement.

- **Example**: Organizing live webinars or creating on-demand training videos that cover key features and workflows of the application.

3. **Offering Technical Support**:

- **Explanation**: Providing reliable and accessible technical support is essential for resolving user issues quickly, maintaining satisfaction, and retaining users.

- **Example**: Setting up a dedicated support hotline, email support, or an online chat system where users can seek help.

Visual Diagram: Installation and Distribution Process

Flowchart:

```
+------------------------------------------------------+
|        Installation and Distribution Process         |
|------------------------------------------------------|
| [Package Application]                                 |
|      ↓                                                |
| [Create and Test Installer]                           |
|      ↓                                                |
| [Deploy via Online Platforms]                         |
|      ↓                                                |
| [Provide Installation Instructions]                   |
|      ↓                                                |
| [Conduct User Training]                               |
|      ↓                                                |
| [Manage Updates and Support]                          |
+------------------------------------------------------+
```

Description:

This flowchart outlines the comprehensive steps involved in the installation and distribution of an Access application, emphasizing the importance of each phase from packaging to ongoing support.

Packaging Your Database Application:

Packaging a Microsoft Access database application involves preparing it for distribution by encapsulating all necessary components into a single, distributable installer. This process ensures that end-users receive everything they need to install and run the application on their systems, regardless of their existing software environment.

Objectives of Effective Packaging:

<u>Ensuring Completeness</u>:

When packaging a Microsoft Access database application for distribution, one of the fundamental objectives is ensuring completeness. This means that the package must contain every component necessary for the application to function correctly after installation. This objective is critical to prevent issues related to missing dependencies or incomplete installations that could hinder the application's performance and user satisfaction.

Objectives of Ensuring Completeness

1. **Prevent Installation Errors**: By including all necessary files, you minimize the risk of installation errors that can occur when dependencies are missing.

2. **Facilitate Independent Operation**: Ensuring that the application package is complete allows it to operate independently of external resources or additional installations, providing a better user experience.

3. **Streamline User Setup**: A complete package simplifies the setup process for users, allowing for a quick and hassle-free installation.

Key Components to Include in a Complete Package

1. **Database Files**:

- Include the primary Access database file (ACCDB or ACCDE) and any external linked databases necessary for the application to function.

2. **Runtime Software**:

- If targeting users who do not have Microsoft Access installed, include the Access Runtime environment to allow the full functionality of the Access application without requiring a full version of Access.

3. **External Libraries and Controls**:

- Ensure that any third-party ActiveX controls, DLLs, or other libraries required by the application are included in the package. This is crucial for maintaining the functionality of custom features or interfaces.

4. **Configuration Files and Resources**:

- Include all configuration files, such as INI files or XML files, used by the application. Also, include resources like images, icons, or other multimedia files used within the application's interface.

5. **Documentation and Help Files**:

- Provide comprehensive user manuals, installation guides, and help files. These documents should be easy to access and read, ideally available from within the application itself.

6. **License and Legal Information**:

- Include all necessary licensing information, terms and conditions, and any other legal documentation required for the user to legally use the software.

Example: Packaging a Human Resources Management System

Scenario: A software developer has created a Human Resources Management System in Microsoft Access, intended for use in small to medium-sized businesses without Access installed.

Packaging Steps:

1. **Compile to ACCDE**: The database is compiled into an ACCDE format to ensure source code protection and prevent modifications.

2. **Include Runtime and Libraries**: The Access Runtime is added to the package, along with any external libraries used for PDF generation and data visualization.

3. **Add Resources**: All images and templates used in reporting are included in the package to ensure the reports function correctly.

4. **Documentation**: User guides on how to use the system, FAQs, and troubleshooting tips are included.

5. **Legal Documents**: Licensing agreements and privacy policy documents are bundled with the installation.

Visual Diagram: Ensuring Completeness in Packaging

Flowchart:

```
+-------------------------------------------------------+
|                                                       |
|        Ensuring Completeness in Package Setup         |
|                                                       |
|-------------------------------------------------------|
|                                                       |
| [Compile Database to ACCDE]                           |
|     ↓                                                 |
| [Include Access Runtime & Dependencies]               |
|     ↓                                                 |
| [Add Configuration Files & Resources]                 |
|     ↓                                                 |
| [Incorporate Documentation & Help Files]              |
|     ↓                                                 |
| [Bundle License & Legal Information]                  |
|                                                       |
+-------------------------------------------------------+
```

Description:

This flowchart illustrates the detailed steps involved in packaging a database application to ensure completeness, highlighting the inclusion of all necessary components for a fully functional setup.

Ensuring completeness in the packaging of a Microsoft Access database application is crucial for a successful distribution and installation. It guarantees that the application operates as intended right from the first launch, enhancing user satisfaction and minimizing the need for additional support or troubleshooting. By meticulously including every required component, developers can provide a seamless and professional experience for end-users.

<u>**Facilitating Easy Installation**</u>:

When packaging a Microsoft Access database application for distribution, a key objective is to facilitate easy installation. This involves creating a package that allows end-users to install the application smoothly and without technical difficulties. An easy installation process is crucial for user adoption and satisfaction, particularly for those who may not have advanced technical skills.

Objectives of Facilitating Easy Installation

1. **Reduce User Frustration**: A straightforward and intuitive installation process minimizes user frustration and reduces the likelihood of errors during installation, which can deter users from continuing to use the application.

2. **Minimize Support Calls**: By simplifying the installation process, organizations can significantly reduce the number of support calls and inquiries, freeing up resources for other tasks.

3. **Increase Adoption Rates**: An easy installation process enhances the overall user experience, leading to higher adoption rates and positive user feedback.

Strategies for Ensuring Easy Installation

1. **Automated Installation Scripts**:

- **Explanation**: Use automated scripts that handle all aspects of the installation process, including file copying, registry entries, and setting configurations.

- **Example**: Tools like Inno Setup or InstallShield can be used to create scripts that automatically install the necessary files in the correct directories, register any components, and configure settings without user intervention.

2. **Clear, Step-by-Step Instructions**:

- **Explanation**: Provide clear, concise instructions for the installation process. Instructions should be easy to follow and cater to non-technical users.

- **Example**: Include a printed guide within the package or a digital guide accessible from the installer, detailing each step of the installation process with accompanying screenshots.

3. **Customizable Installation Options**:

- **Explanation**: Allow users to customize certain aspects of the installation to suit their preferences or system requirements, without making the process complex.

- **Example**: Offer options to select installation paths, choose components to install, or decide on shortcut creation through a simple interface during the setup.

4. **Built-in Troubleshooting and Error Handling**:

- **Explanation**: Incorporate troubleshooting steps and error handling directly into the installation script to address common issues that might arise during the installation.

- **Example**: The installer can automatically detect and rectify common issues like insufficient permissions or incompatible system settings, providing solutions or clear error messages.

5. **Testing Across Various Environments**:

- **Explanation**: Ensure the installer works seamlessly across different operating systems and configurations by conducting thorough testing.

- **Example**: Test the installation process on different versions of Windows, with various system settings and user permissions, to ensure compatibility and ease of installation.

Example: Deploying a Retail Management System

Scenario: A software company has developed a retail management system using Microsoft Access and needs to deploy it to multiple retail stores, each with varying levels of IT infrastructure.

Packaging Steps:

1. **Create an Installer**: The company uses InstallShield to create a robust installer that handles all aspects of the installation automatically.

2. **User-Friendly Interface**: The installer includes a graphical interface that guides the user through the process with simple options and clear instructions.

3. **Error Handling Mechanisms**: The installer is equipped to handle common installation errors, such as checking for disk space and permissions before proceeding.

4. **Comprehensive Testing**: Before deployment, the installation package is tested in environments similar to those of the retail stores to ensure it installs without issues.

Visual Diagram: Simplifying the Installation Process

Flowchart:

```
+----------------------------------------------------------+
|            Simplifying the Installation Process          |
|----------------------------------------------------------|
| [Create Automated Installation Script]                   |
|     ↓                                                    |
| [Provide Step-by-Step Instructions]                      |
|     ↓                                                    |
| [Offer Customizable Installation Options]                |
|     ↓                                                    |
| [Incorporate Troubleshooting and Error Handling]         |
|     ↓                                                    |
| [Test Installer Across Environments]                     |
+----------------------------------------------------------+
```

Description:

This flowchart details the steps involved in creating a user-friendly installation process for a database application, emphasizing the importance of automation, clear instructions, customization, error handling, and thorough testing.

Facilitating easy installation is essential for ensuring that end-users can smoothly and successfully deploy Microsoft Access database applications. By implementing automated scripts, providing clear instructions, offering customizable options, handling errors effectively, and conducting comprehensive testing, developers can enhance the installation experience and encourage widespread adoption of their application.

Maintaining Application Integrity:

When distributing a Microsoft Access database application, ensuring the integrity of the application throughout the installation process is crucial. Maintaining application integrity involves safeguarding the application against corruption, unauthorized modifications, and ensuring that it functions as intended on the user's system. This goal is essential for preserving the reliability and trustworthiness of the software.

Objectives of Maintaining Application Integrity

1. **Prevent Corruption**: Ensure that the application and its data are not corrupted during the download, installation, or runtime processes.

2. **Guard Against Tampering**: Protect the application from unauthorized changes that could compromise its functionality or security.

3. **Consistent Performance Across All Installations**: Ensure that the application performs consistently, regardless of the user's system configurations or environments.

Strategies for Ensuring Application Integrity

1. **Digital Signatures**:

- **Explanation**: Use digital signatures to verify the authenticity of the application and ensure that it has not been altered since it was packaged.

- **Example**: Sign the application executable and other critical files with a digital certificate issued by a trusted certificate authority. This process allows users to verify the source and integrity of the software during installation.

2. **Checksums and Hashes**:

- **Explanation**: Employ checksums or cryptographic hashes to verify that files have not been corrupted during download or transfer.

- **Example**: Calculate a hash of the installer package before distribution and provide it on the download page. Users can then verify the hash after downloading to ensure the file is intact and unaltered.

3. **Secure Packaging Tools**:

- **Explanation**: Use reliable and secure tools for creating the installation package to prevent the inclusion of vulnerabilities or malicious code.

- **Example**: Utilize industry-standard packaging tools like Inno Setup or Advanced Installer that are known for their security features and regular updates.

4. **Test for Integrity**:

- **Explanation**: Conduct extensive testing to ensure the application installs correctly under various scenarios and that all components function as expected after installation.

- **Example**: Test installations on clean machines, machines with different versions of required dependencies, and systems with unusual configurations to ensure consistent performance.

5. **Robust Installation Scripts**:

- **Explanation**: Develop installation scripts that handle unexpected conditions gracefully, ensuring that partial installations or errors do not leave the application in an unstable state.

- **Example**: Scripts that can roll back to the initial state if an installation fails, removing any partially installed components.

Example: Deploying a Financial Reporting Tool

Scenario: A company has developed a financial reporting tool in Microsoft Access that needs to be deployed across various corporate environments, each with stringent security requirements.

Packaging Steps:

1. **Digital Signing**: The final executable and all associated libraries are digitally signed to ensure authenticity and integrity.

2. **Checksum Verification**: A SHA-256 hash of the installation package is provided for users to verify after download.

3. **Use of Secure Packaging Tool**: The package is created using Advanced Installer, which includes options for encryption and secure bootstrapping.

4. **Comprehensive Testing**: The installation process is tested in diverse environments to ensure it handles all expected and unexpected scenarios correctly.

5. **Script Robustness**: The installer script includes comprehensive error handling and rollback capabilities to maintain system stability.

Visual Diagram: Maintaining Application Integrity

Flowchart:

```
+-----------------------------------------------------+
|   Maintaining Application Integrity in Packaging    |
|-----------------------------------------------------|
| [Digital Sign Application Files]                    |
|     ↓                                               |
| [Generate and Verify Checksums]                     |
|     ↓                                               |
| [Use Secure Packaging Tools]                        |
|     ↓                                               |
| [Conduct Integrity Testing]                         |
|     ↓                                               |
| [Ensure Robust Installation Scripts]                |
+-----------------------------------------------------+
```

Description:

This flowchart outlines the key steps involved in ensuring the integrity of a packaged database application, from digital signing to the development of robust installation scripts.

Maintaining application integrity during the packaging and distribution of a Microsoft Access database application is paramount for ensuring that the software remains secure, reliable, and performs consistently across all user environments. By implementing comprehensive security measures such as digital signatures, checksums, and using secure packaging tools, developers can safeguard their applications against corruption and unauthorized modifications, thereby enhancing user trust and satisfaction.

Key Steps in Packaging a Database Application

1. **Compile the Database**:

- Convert your Access database into an ACCDE file, which locks down the code and design to prevent tampering and simplifies the distribution of a secure file.

2. **Include Necessary Components**:

- Ensure that all necessary components, such as the Access Runtime for users who do not have Microsoft Access installed, are included. This might also include any third-party controls, libraries, or other dependencies.

3. **Create an Installation Script**:

- Develop an installation script using tools like Inno Setup, InstallShield, or Microsoft's own Packaging Solution Wizard, part of the Developer Extensions. This script defines how the application and its components are installed on a user's system.

4. **Define Installation Paths**:

- Set default installation paths in the script while giving users the option to choose alternative paths. This helps in accommodating users' preferences or system requirements.

5. **Incorporate License Agreements and Documentation**:

- Include any necessary license agreements that must be accepted during installation, as well as user guides or help files that assist in using the application.

6. **Test the Installer**:

- Before distribution, thoroughly test the installer on various systems to ensure it installs the application correctly across different environments. This testing should cover various scenarios, including installations on systems with different versions of Windows and varying levels of user privileges.

Example: Sales Management System

Scenario: A developer has created a sales management system in Access, which is to be used across various independent retail locations without Access installed on their computers.

Packaging Steps:

1. **ACCDE Conversion**: The database is converted into an ACCDE file, ensuring that forms and code are secure and unmodifiable.

2. **Runtime Inclusion**: The Access Runtime is included in the package, allowing users without Microsoft Access to run the application.

3. **Installer Creation**: An installer is created using InstallShield, which lays out the steps for installation, including where files are stored and how they are configured.

4. **Documentation**: User manuals and troubleshooting guides are packaged into the installer.

5. **Installation Testing**: The complete installation process is tested in a controlled environment to ensure it works seamlessly.

Visual Diagram: Packaging Process

Flowchart:

```
+-----------------------------------------------------------+
|          Database Application Packaging                    |
|-----------------------------------------------------------|
| [Compile Database to ACCDE]                               |
|     ↓                                                      |
| [Include Access Runtime & Dependencies]                   |
|     ↓                                                      |
| [Create Installation Script]                              |
|     ↓                                                      |
| [Set Installation Paths & Include Documentation]          |
|     ↓                                                      |
| [Test Installer]                                          |
|     ↓                                                      |
| [Distribute to Users]                                     |
+-----------------------------------------------------------+
```

Description:

This flowchart visually outlines the process of packaging a Microsoft Access database application, highlighting each step from compilation to distribution.

Packaging your database application effectively is crucial for a successful installation and user experience. By following a structured approach to compile, include necessary components, and test the installation process, developers can ensure that their applications are easily and securely distributed and installed across varied user environments.

Creating Installation Setups:

Creating an effective installation setup for Microsoft Access applications involves designing a package that not only delivers the application to the user's computer but also ensures it functions correctly once installed. This process is crucial for providing a smooth user experience and maintaining the application's reliability across various environments.

Objectives of Effective Installation Setups

1. **Seamless User Experience**: The setup process should be straightforward, minimizing the need for user input and reducing the potential for installation errors.

2. **Compatibility Assurance**: Ensure the setup is compatible with different operating systems and configurations where the application will be used.

3. **Error Handling and Recovery**: Incorporate robust error handling in the setup process to manage installation failures and provide options for recovery.

Key Components of Installation Setups

1. **Installer Software**:

- **Explanation**: Use reliable installer software to create a professional and efficient installation experience.

- **Example**: Popular tools like Inno Setup or InstallShield offer extensive customization options and robust support for different system configurations.

2. **Configuration Files**:

- **Explanation**: Include configuration files that can be customized during installation to match the user's environment and preferences.

- **Example**: XML or INI files that users can edit during installation to set application parameters such as database paths or user settings.

3. **Pre-requisites and Dependencies**:

- **Explanation**: Automatically check for and install any necessary prerequisites such as the Access Runtime, .NET frameworks, or other libraries.

- **Example**: The installer checks if the correct version of Access Runtime is installed and, if not, installs it before setting up the main application.

4. **Customizable Installation Options**:

- **Explanation**: Allow users to customize their installation experience by choosing which components to install, where to install them, and whether to create shortcuts.

- **Example**: Users can select to install only certain features of the application, choose the installation directory, or decide whether to create a desktop shortcut.

5. **Automated Installation Scripts**:

- **Explanation**: Use scripts to automate the installation process, making it faster and reducing user error.

- **Example**: Batch or PowerShell scripts that run automatically to set up the application, configure settings, and verify the installation.

Steps to Create an Installation Setup

1. **Design the Installation Flow**:

- Plan the steps that the user will go through during the installation, including any options for customization and input required from the user.

2. **Develop Installation Scripts**:

- Write scripts using the chosen installer software to manage file copying, directory creation, registry entries, and error logging.

3. **Test Across Multiple Environments**:

- Test the installer in various configurations to ensure compatibility and identify any potential issues in different user environments.

4. **Incorporate User Feedback**:

- Gather feedback from beta testers or initial users to refine the installation process, making it more intuitive and robust.

5. **Finalize and Distribute**:

- After thorough testing and refinement, finalize the installer package for distribution, ensuring all components are up to date and function as expected.

Visual Example: Installation Setup Process Flowchart

Flowchart:

```
+------------------------------------------------------------+
|              Installation Setup Process Flow               |
|------------------------------------------------------------|
| [Design Installation Flow]                                 |
|      ↓                                                     |
| [Develop Installation Scripts]                             |
|      ↓                                                     |
| [Test Installer in Multiple Environments]                  |
|      ↓                                                     |
| [Incorporate User Feedback]                                |
|      ↓                                                     |
| [Finalize and Distribute Installer]                        |
+------------------------------------------------------------+
```

Description:

This flowchart outlines the process of creating an installation setup for a Microsoft Access application, from design and development through testing and final distribution.

Creating an installation setup for a Microsoft Access database application is a critical process that ensures the software is easily and correctly installed across various user environments. By using sophisticated installer software, testing extensively, and incorporating user feedback, developers can create a seamless installation experience that enhances user satisfaction and supports the successful deployment of the application.

Distributing Your Standalone Program:

Distributing a standalone program, especially one developed using Microsoft Access, involves several crucial steps to ensure that the end product reaches the users effectively and functions as intended on their systems. This phase is critical for the success of the software as it impacts user adoption, satisfaction, and overall experience.

Objectives of Effective Software Distribution

1. **Broad Accessibility**: Make the software easily accessible to potential users, regardless of their geographical location or technical expertise.

2. **Reliable Delivery**: Ensure the delivery mechanism is reliable and capable of handling high download volumes without failure.

3. **User Support**: Provide adequate support resources to assist users during and after installation.

Key Strategies for Distributing a Standalone Program

1. **Choosing the Right Distribution Channels**:

- **Explanation**: Select appropriate channels that target your intended audience effectively.

- **Example**: For business applications, distribution might be through enterprise IT departments, while consumer apps might be best served through online download portals or email distribution lists.

2. **Creating a Secure Downloadable Package**:

- **Explanation**: Ensure the package is secure and intact, free from tampering or corruption during download.

- **Example**: Use checksums or digital signatures to verify the integrity of the download, allowing users to confirm the authenticity of the software before installation.

3. **Providing Clear Installation Instructions**:

- **Explanation**: Offer straightforward, step-by-step installation guides to assist users through the setup process.

- **Example**: Detailed PDF documents or online tutorials that walk users through the installation process, highlighting common issues and their solutions.

4. **Implementing an Auto-Update Feature**:

- **Explanation**: Incorporate a mechanism within the software that checks for and installs updates automatically.

- **Example**: An update utility that periodically checks a server for new updates and prompts the user to install any available patches or new versions.

5. **Offering Technical Support**:

- **Explanation**: Provide robust technical support to resolve any issues that users encounter during or after installation.

- **Example**: A dedicated support hotline, email support, or an interactive web portal where users can submit support tickets.

Example: Distributing a Retail Management Software

Scenario: A developer has created a retail management software in Microsoft Access designed for small to medium-sized retail stores. The software needs to be distributed to multiple locations across the country.

Distribution Steps:

1. **Online Hosting**: Host the software on a reliable cloud platform that allows users to download the installer directly.

2. **Secure Packaging**: Package the software with a digital signature to ensure integrity and prevent tampering.

3. **Download Instructions**: Provide comprehensive download and installation instructions on the website and include FAQs for troubleshooting common issues.

4. **Auto-Update Setup**: Implement an auto-update feature within the software to ensure that all users have the latest version and security patches.

5. **Customer Support**: Establish a multi-channel support system, including phone, email, and live chat options for user inquiries and troubleshooting.

Visual Diagram: Software Distribution Process

Flowchart:

```
+-----------------------------------------------------+
|            Software Distribution Process            |
|-----------------------------------------------------|
| [Select Distribution Channels]                      |
|     ↓                                               |
| [Secure and Package Software]                       |
|     ↓                                               |
| [Provide Download and Installation Instructions]    |
|     ↓                                               |
| [Implement Auto-Update Feature]                     |
|     ↓                                               |
| [Set Up Technical Support System]                   |
+-----------------------------------------------------+
```

Description:

This flowchart details the process involved in distributing a standalone Microsoft Access program, highlighting steps from selecting distribution channels to setting up a support system.

Distributing your standalone program effectively is as crucial as the development itself. By carefully selecting distribution channels, securing the downloadable package, providing clear installation instructions, ensuring easy update capabilities, and offering comprehensive technical support, developers can maximize the accessibility and usability of their software, thereby enhancing user satisfaction and adoption rates.

Conclusion

Effective installation and distribution are critical to the success of Microsoft Access applications in diverse user environments. By focusing on creating reliable installers, ensuring compatibility, providing detailed instructions, and supporting users post-installation, developers can facilitate a smooth deployment process that enhances user acceptance and overall satisfaction with the application.

Chapter 12 - Maintaining and Updating Your Application

Maintaining and updating a software application, especially one developed in Microsoft Access, is crucial for its long-term success and usability. Regular updates ensure the application remains compatible with new technologies, addresses security vulnerabilities, and meets evolving user needs.

Objectives of Regular Application Maintenance and Updates

Enhance Security:

Security enhancement is a critical objective in the regular maintenance and updating of software applications, especially for those developed in environments like Microsoft Access. As technology evolves and new vulnerabilities are discovered, keeping software secure demands ongoing attention and proactive measures.

Importance of Security Enhancement in Application Updates

Security is crucial not only to protect sensitive data but also to maintain user trust and comply with legal and regulatory standards. Failure to adequately secure an application can lead to data breaches, financial loss, and damage to the organization's reputation.

Objectives of Security Enhancement

1. **Protect Data**: Ensure that all user and organizational data within the application is safeguarded against unauthorized access and leaks.

2. **Prevent Attacks**: Mitigate potential vectors for attacks such as SQL injections, cross-site scripting (XSS), and other common exploits.

3. **Comply with Regulations**: Adhere to industry regulations and standards that mandate certain levels of security, such as GDPR, HIPAA, or PCI DSS.

Key Strategies for Enhancing Security Through Updates

1. **Patch Known Vulnerabilities**:

- **Explanation**: Regularly update the application to patch vulnerabilities that could be exploited by hackers.

- **Example**: If a security flaw is discovered in the way the application handles database queries, an update would include a fix to prevent potential SQL injection attacks.

2. **Update Dependency Libraries**:

- **Explanation**: Keep all third-party libraries and dependencies used by the application up to date with their latest secure versions.

- **Example**: Libraries such as ODBC drivers or other external modules that interact with Access should be regularly updated to their most secure versions to protect against vulnerabilities found in older releases.

3. **Implement Stronger Encryption**:

- **Explanation**: As encryption standards evolve, updating cryptographic methods to more robust and secure options is necessary.

- **Example**: Upgrading the encryption of stored data from older, weaker standards like DES to more secure standards such as AES-256.

4. **Enhance Authentication Mechanisms**:

- **Explanation**: Strengthen the authentication processes to prevent unauthorized access.

- **Example**: Introducing multi-factor authentication (MFA) where users must provide two or more verification factors to gain access to the application.

5. **Regular Security Audits**:

- **Explanation**: Conduct regular security audits and penetration testing to identify and address new vulnerabilities.

- **Example**: Hiring external security experts to perform an annual penetration test and using their findings to guide security enhancements in the next update.

Example: Securing a Financial Management Software

Scenario: A company has developed a financial management software using Microsoft Access and needs to ensure the highest security standards to protect sensitive financial data.

Security Update Steps:

1. **Vulnerability Assessment**: Conduct a thorough assessment of the application to identify potential security weaknesses.

2. **Patch and Update**: Release a security update that patches identified vulnerabilities and updates all outdated dependency libraries.

3. **Upgrade Encryption**: Implement the latest encryption standards for data at rest and in transit within the application.

4. **Security Training**: Provide training sessions for users on the new security features and best practices for data security.

5. **Continuous Monitoring**: Establish ongoing monitoring for unusual access patterns or potential security breaches.

Visual Diagram: Enhancing Security Update Process

Flowchart:

```
+----------------------------------------------------------+
|                                                          |
|     Enhancing Security in Application Updates            |
|                                                          |
|----------------------------------------------------------|
|                                                          |
| [Conduct Vulnerability Assessment]                       |
|                                                          |
|     ↓                                                    |
|                                                          |
| [Patch Vulnerabilities & Update Libraries]               |
|                                                          |
|     ↓                                                    |
|                                                          |
| [Implement Stronger Encryption]                          |
|                                                          |
|     ↓                                                    |
|                                                          |
| [Enhance Authentication Mechanisms]                      |
|                                                          |
|     ↓                                                    |
|                                                          |
| [Perform Regular Security Audits]                        |
|                                                          |
+----------------------------------------------------------+
```

Description:

This flowchart illustrates a structured approach to enhancing security in software updates, highlighting essential steps from vulnerability assessment to regular audits.

Enhancing security through regular application maintenance and updates is essential for protecting sensitive data, maintaining user trust, and ensuring compliance with regulatory standards. By systematically addressing vulnerabilities, updating dependencies, and strengthening security measures, developers can safeguard their applications against emerging threats.

Improve Functionality:

Regular maintenance and updates are not just about fixing bugs or patching security vulnerabilities; they also provide an opportunity to enhance the functionality of an application. This continual improvement is essential to meet evolving user needs, incorporate new technologies, and stay competitive in the market.

Objectives of Functional Enhancements

1. **Enhance User Experience**: Streamline existing features to make them more user-friendly and efficient.

2. **Add New Features**: Introduce new functionalities that meet the latest user demands or business requirements.

3. **Optimize Performance**: Improve the speed and efficiency of the application to handle larger datasets or complex operations more effectively.

Key Strategies for Enhancing Functionality Through Updates

1. **Gather User Feedback**:

- **Explanation**: Continuously collect and analyze user feedback to identify areas for improvement or new features that users are requesting.

- **Example**: Implementing an in-app feedback tool that allows users to easily submit suggestions or complaints.

2. **Implement Feature Requests**:

- **Explanation**: Prioritize and implement new features based on user demand and strategic business objectives.

- **Example**: Adding a new reporting dashboard that users have frequently requested to provide more detailed insights into their data.

3. **Refactor and Optimize Code**:

- **Explanation**: Regularly refactor code to improve readability, reduce complexity, and enhance performance.

- **Example**: Rewriting inefficient SQL queries within the application to speed up data retrieval processes.

4. **Update UI/UX Design**:

- **Explanation**: Update the user interface and user experience designs to align with modern standards and enhance usability.

- **Example**: Redesigning the application's navigation to make it more intuitive and align with current UI design trends.

5. **Integrate with New Technologies**:

- **Explanation**: Incorporate new technologies or platforms that can extend the application's capabilities or integrate with other tools.

- **Example**: Adding support for integrating with popular cloud storage options like Google Drive or Dropbox for data backups.

Example: Enhancing a Customer Relationship Management (CRM) Tool

Scenario: A software company has developed a CRM tool in Microsoft Access and plans to update it to better serve its growing user base and incorporate new industry practices.

Functional Enhancement Steps:

1. **User Surveys and Feedback Analysis**: Conduct surveys and analyze user feedback to identify the most requested features and pain points.

2. **Feature Development**: Develop and integrate new features such as automated email marketing tools and enhanced customer segmentation functionalities.

3. **UI/UX Redesign**: Undertake a redesign of the application's interface to make it more modern and easier to use, focusing on simplifying complex workflows.

4. **Performance Optimization**: Optimize existing functionalities for better performance, such as improving the speed of contact searches and data processing.

5. **Beta Testing and Rollout**: Beta test the updates with a select group of users before rolling out the update to all customers to ensure the new functionalities work as expected.

Visual Diagram: Process of Enhancing Functionality

Flowchart:

```
+-------------------------------------------------+
| Process of Enhancing Application Functionality  |
|-------------------------------------------------|
| [Collect User Feedback]                         |
|     ↓                                           |
| [Analyze Feedback for Feature Requests]         |
|     ↓                                           |
| [Develop and Integrate New Features]            |
|     ↓                                           |
| [Update UI/UX Designs]                          |
|     ↓                                           |
| [Optimize Performance of Existing Features]     |
|     ↓                                           |
| [Beta Testing and Gradual Rollout]              |
+-------------------------------------------------+
```

Description:

This flowchart illustrates the systematic approach to enhancing the functionality of a software application, emphasizing continuous improvement from user feedback to the rollout of new features and optimizations.

Improving the functionality of an application through regular updates is crucial for maintaining user satisfaction, adapting to changes in the market, and leveraging new technological advancements. By actively engaging with users, prioritizing their needs, and continuously enhancing the application, developers can ensure their software remains relevant, powerful, and efficient.

Fix Bugs:

Bug fixing is an essential component of maintaining and updating software applications. Addressing software bugs not only resolves functional and performance issues but also improves user satisfaction and trust in the application. Regular updates that include bug fixes help maintain the application's reliability and prevent minor issues from escalating into major disruptions.

Objectives of Regular Bug Fixes

1. **Enhance Stability**: Correcting bugs increases the overall stability of the application, reducing crashes and unexpected behavior.

2. **Improve Usability**: By fixing bugs that affect user interactions, the overall usability of the application improves, making it more intuitive and efficient for users.

3. **Maintain Security**: Some bugs can create security vulnerabilities; fixing these is crucial for maintaining the security integrity of the application.

4. **Ensure Data Integrity**: Bugs that affect data handling and storage can lead to data loss or corruption; addressing these issues is critical to ensuring data integrity.

Key Strategies for Effective Bug Fixing

1. **Establish a Robust Reporting System**:

- **Explanation**: Implement systems that allow users to easily report bugs, providing developers with clear and actionable information.

- **Example**: An integrated bug reporting tool within the application that users can use to report issues directly, including automatic capture of error logs and system state.

2. **Prioritize Bug Fixes Based on Severity**:

- **Explanation**: Prioritize bugs based on their impact on the application and users, focusing first on those that affect functionality and stability.

- **Example**: Classifying bugs into categories such as 'critical', 'high', 'medium', and 'low' based on their severity and potential impact on users.

3. **Regular Patch Releases**:

- **Explanation**: Schedule regular releases of patches that address known bugs, ensuring users do not have to wait for the next major update for resolutions.

- **Example**: Monthly or quarterly patch updates that include fixes for all critical and high-priority bugs identified since the last update.

4. **Automated Testing**:

- **Explanation**: Use automated testing tools to catch bugs before the software is released or updated. Automation can replicate complex user interactions that might be missed during manual testing.

- **Example**: Implementing continuous integration and continuous deployment (CI/CD) pipelines that include automated regression tests to detect bugs early.

5. **Feedback Loop With Users**:

- **Explanation**: After fixing bugs, maintain a feedback loop with users to ensure that the fixes are effective and do not introduce new issues.

- **Example**: Following up with users who reported specific bugs to confirm that the issue has been resolved to their satisfaction.

Example: Updating a Project Management Application

Scenario: A software company develops a project management tool that users rely on to manage timelines, resources, and budgets. Users report several bugs that cause the application to crash during specific interactions.

Bug Fixing Steps:

1. **Bug Reporting**: Users report crashes through the application's built-in reporting tool, which captures error logs and the actions leading up to the crash.

2. **Bug Triage and Prioritization**: The development team reviews the reports, reproduces the bugs, and prioritizes them based on their severity and impact.

3. **Development of Fixes**: Developers work on fixes for the highest priority bugs, ensuring that solutions do not adversely affect other parts of the application.

4. **Testing and Validation**: The fixes are tested internally and then in a staging environment that mirrors the production system.

5. **Deployment of Patches**: A patch update is released to all users, resolving the reported crashes and improving the application's stability.

Visual Diagram: Bug Fixing Process

Flowchart:

```
+-------------------------------------------------------------+
|                  Bug Fixing Process Flow                    |
|-------------------------------------------------------------|
| [User Reports Bug]                                          |
|      ↓                                                      |
| [Bug Triage and Prioritization]                            |
|      ↓                                                      |
| [Develop Fixes]                                            |
|      ↓                                                      |
| [Test Fixes in Staging]                                    |
|      ↓                                                      |
| [Deploy Patch to Users]                                    |
|      ↓                                                      |
| [Feedback Loop with Users]                                 |
+-------------------------------------------------------------+
```

Description:

This flowchart illustrates the systematic approach to identifying, fixing, and verifying the resolution of bugs within a software application, emphasizing continuous improvement and user involvement.

Regularly fixing bugs is vital for maintaining the functional and operational quality of a software application. By systematically addressing bugs, prioritizing them based on their impact, and continuously engaging with users, developers can ensure their application remains stable, secure, and user-friendly. This approach not only fixes immediate issues but also improves the long-term reliability and reputation of the software.

<u>Ensure Compatibility</u>:

Ensuring compatibility through regular maintenance and updates is crucial for software applications, particularly those like Microsoft Access, which may interact with various operating systems, hardware configurations, and other software applications. This process helps to ensure that the application performs reliably across all supported environments, which is key to maintaining a broad and satisfied user base.

Objectives of Ensuring Compatibility

1. **Broad Usability**: Ensure that the application functions correctly across all supported platforms and devices, providing a consistent user experience.

2. **Prevent Obsolescence**: Keep the application up-to-date with the latest operating systems, software libraries, and technology standards to avoid becoming obsolete.

3. **Reduce Support Queries**: Minimize the number of support queries and issues reported by users related to compatibility problems with new hardware or software environments.

Key Strategies for Ensuring Compatibility

1. **Regular Environment Testing**:

-   **Explanation**: Test the application regularly in different environments, including new operating system versions, new hardware, and alongside other software.

-   **Example**: Using virtual machines or cloud-based testing services to simulate different operating systems like Windows 10 and Windows 11, ensuring the application works seamlessly on all.

2. **Adherence to Standards**:

-   **Explanation**: Follow established coding and development standards that promote compatibility.

-   **Example**: Adhering to SQL standards and best practices in database design to ensure that database queries and structures are compatible with updates in Microsoft Access versions.

3. **Responsive Design Practices**:

-   **Explanation**: Implement design practices that allow the application to function well regardless of the device or screen size, especially for web-based interfaces.

-   **Example**: Using responsive web design techniques if the application has a web component, ensuring it displays correctly on all devices from desktops to smartphones.

4. **Update Dependencies**:

-   **Explanation**: Keep all third-party libraries and dependencies used by the application updated to maintain compatibility with new versions of these libraries.

- **Example**: Regularly updating libraries such as ODBC drivers or .NET frameworks used by the application to the latest stable versions.

5. **Backward Compatibility Checks**:

- **Explanation**: Ensure new updates do not break the application's functionality on older systems that are still supported.

- **Example**: Implementing automated regression testing to check that new updates do not disrupt the application's performance on older versions of Windows that are still in use by a significant portion of users.

Example: Upgrading a Financial Analysis Tool

Scenario: A software development company has created a financial analysis tool in Microsoft Access. As part of their update cycle, they need to ensure that the tool remains compatible with the latest version of Microsoft Excel, as it relies heavily on data imported from Excel spreadsheets.

Compatibility Enhancement Steps:

1. **Testing with New Excel Versions**: Test the application extensively with the latest Excel version to identify any compatibility issues in data exchange and scripting.

2. **Updating Import Scripts**: Modify any import scripts or connections to Excel to utilize the latest features and ensure compatibility with new file formats or security updates.

3. **User Communication and Documentation**: Inform users about the changes and update the documentation to include instructions for using the application with the latest versions of Excel.

4. **Rollback Safeguards**: Provide users with the option to revert to previous versions of the application if they encounter issues with the new version, ensuring continuous accessibility.

Visual Diagram: Compatibility Assurance Process

Flowchart:

```
+----------------------------------------------------------+
|           Compatibility Assurance Process Flow           |
|----------------------------------------------------------|
| [Identify Required Testing Environments]                 |
|      ↓                                                    |
| [Conduct Regular Environment Testing]                    |
|      ↓                                                    |
| [Update Application to Adhere to Standards]              |
|      ↓                                                    |
| [Ensure Responsive Design for Web Components]           |
|      ↓                                                    |
| [Update Dependencies and Perform Regression Tests]|
|      ↓                                                    |
| [Feedback and Iteration]                                 |
+----------------------------------------------------------+
```

Description:

This flowchart details the process for ensuring that an application remains compatible across different environments and technologies, highlighting the importance of regular testing and updates.

Ensuring compatibility in application maintenance is vital for providing a reliable and uniform user experience across all supported platforms and devices. Through thorough testing, adherence to development standards, and careful management of updates, developers can safeguard their applications against compatibility issues that might otherwise alienate users or hinder performance.

Key Strategies for Effective Application Maintenance

1. **Scheduled Updates:**

- **Explanation**: Implement a regular schedule for releasing updates to ensure users can anticipate and plan for changes.

- **Example**: Quarterly updates that introduce enhancements, security patches, and minor bug fixes to ensure stability and security.

2. **User Feedback Loop:**

- **Explanation**: Establish a system for collecting and analyzing user feedback to identify areas for improvement.

- **Example**: Online surveys, user forums, and feedback tools within the application can provide valuable insights into user experiences and pain points.

3. **Automated Update Feature**:

- **Explanation**: Develop an automated update mechanism within the application that seamlessly checks for, downloads, and installs updates without significant user intervention.

- **Example**: A background service that periodically checks for updates and prompts the user when an update is available, providing options to install immediately or at a later time.

4. **Beta Testing of Updates**:

- **Explanation**: Before a full-scale rollout, release the update to a selected group of users for beta testing.

- **Example**: Offering a beta version of the update to users who opt-in for early access can help identify any critical issues before the update is widely released.

5. **Support and Documentation**:

- **Explanation**: Provide comprehensive support and updated documentation alongside new updates to assist users in understanding and utilizing new features.

- **Example**: Update user manuals, release notes, and online help resources concurrently with the software update to ensure users have access to the latest information.

Example: Updating a Project Management Tool

Scenario: A software development company has released a project management tool built in Microsoft Access. To maintain its relevance and utility, the company plans routine updates and maintenance.

Maintenance Steps:

1. **Gather User Feedback**: Utilize in-app feedback tools to collect user suggestions and complaints.

2. **Plan Updates**: Based on the feedback, prioritize new features and bug fixes for the next update.

3. **Develop and Test**: Implement the changes in a development environment and conduct thorough testing, including a beta release phase.

4. **Rollout Updates**: Use the application's automated update system to distribute the update to all users.

5. **Provide Support**: Offer detailed release notes and host webinars to explain new features and changes.

Visual Diagram: Update Process Flowchart

Flowchart:

```
+----------------------------------------------------------+
|          Application Update Process Flowchart            |
|----------------------------------------------------------|
| [Collect User Feedback]                                  |
|      ↓                                                    |
| [Analyze Feedback and Plan Updates]                      |
|      ↓                                                    |
| [Develop and Beta Test Updates]                          |
|      ↓                                                    |
| [Automate and Roll Out Updates]                          |
|      ↓                                                    |
| [Update Documentation and Provide Support]               |
+----------------------------------------------------------+
```

Description:

This flowchart details the process of maintaining and updating an application, from collecting user feedback to rolling out updates and providing support.

Strategies For Updating Your Application:

Effective strategies for updating applications are crucial for ensuring that software continues to meet user needs, maintain security, and integrate technological advancements. This involves not only the technical execution of updates but also strategic planning to minimize disruption and maximize the benefits of each update.

Key Strategies for Updating Applications

1. **Incremental Updates**:

- **Explanation**: Rather than large, infrequent updates, adopt a strategy of smaller, more frequent updates to reduce risk and improve adaptability.

- **Example**: Deploying monthly updates that address immediate user feedback, security patches, and minor feature enhancements. This approach can reduce the impact of each update, making it easier for users to adapt to changes.

2. **Feature Flags**:

- **Explanation**: Use feature flags to roll out new features selectively. This allows developers to test new functionalities with specific user segments before wide release.

- **Example**: Introducing a new data visualization tool within the application that is initially only available to a small group of users. Feedback can be gathered and adjustments made before rolling it out to all users.

3. **Automated Testing**:

- **Explanation**: Automate the testing process to ensure that updates do not introduce new bugs or regressions.

- **Example**: Implementing continuous integration and continuous deployment (CI/CD) pipelines that automatically run a suite of tests whenever updates are made to the codebase.

4. **User Communication and Support**:

- **Explanation**: Clearly communicate upcoming updates and changes to users. Provide robust support to help users adapt to these changes.

- **Example**: Sending out release notes ahead of updates and hosting webinars or training sessions to walk users through major changes.

5. **Rollback Capabilities**:

- **Explanation**: Ensure that there is always a plan to revert to previous versions in case an update fails or negatively impacts users significantly.

- **Example**: Maintaining version control and backups that allow quick rollback to previous stable versions if a new update causes critical issues.

6. **Monitoring and Feedback Collection**:

- **Explanation**: After deploying updates, actively monitor the application's performance and gather user feedback to assess the impact of the changes.

- **Example**: Using application performance monitoring tools to track how well the application performs post-update and setting up user surveys to collect feedback on the new features.

Example: Updating a Project Management Software

Scenario: A software company develops project management tools and needs to update its application to include new collaboration features and improve existing task management functionalities.

Update Steps:

1. **Plan and Develop**: The new features are developed and initially tested in a development environment.

2. **Automated Testing**: Changes are pushed through an automated testing pipeline to catch any issues before deployment.

3. **Incremental Deployment**: The update is rolled out to a select group of users initially, with monitoring tools tracking the performance and any arising issues.

4. **Feedback Collection**: Early adopters are surveyed to provide feedback on the new functionalities and report any bugs.

5. **Full Deployment**: Once the features are verified to be stable and useful, they are rolled out to the entire user base.

Visual Diagram: Update Strategy Flowchart

Flowchart:

```
+-------------------------------------------------------+
|            Application Update Strategy                |
|-------------------------------------------------------|
| [Plan and Develop Updates]                            |
|    ↓                                                  |
| [Automated Testing and Validation]                    |
|    ↓                                                  |
| [Incremental Deployment with Feature Flags]           |
|    ↓                                                  |
| [Monitor Performance and Collect Feedback]            |
|    ↓                                                  |
| [Full Deployment or Rollback if Needed]               |
+-------------------------------------------------------+
```

Description:

This flowchart illustrates a systematic approach to updating an application, highlighting the importance of planning, testing, phased deployment, and feedback integration.

Strategically updating your application is essential for maintaining its relevance and functionality. By implementing incremental updates, using feature flags, ensuring robust testing, communicating with users, and preparing for possible rollbacks, developers can effectively manage updates to enhance the application's value and user satisfaction.

Troubleshooting Common Issues:

Troubleshooting is a critical component of maintaining and updating applications. It involves diagnosing and resolving issues that users encounter, which can range from minor glitches to major functionality failures. Effective troubleshooting ensures that the application remains reliable and efficient, maintaining user satisfaction and operational continuity.

Objectives of Troubleshooting in Application Maintenance:

<u>Rapid Issue Resolution</u>:

Rapid issue resolution is a critical aspect of troubleshooting in application maintenance. It focuses on quickly identifying, diagnosing, and fixing issues that users encounter, minimizing downtime and ensuring a seamless user experience. Prompt resolution of problems is essential for maintaining user trust and satisfaction, particularly in competitive software markets.

Objectives of Rapid Issue Resolution

1. **Minimize Disruption**: Quickly resolve issues to reduce the impact on user productivity and operations.

2. **Maintain High User Satisfaction**: Ensure users remain satisfied by demonstrating responsiveness and competence in handling problems.

3. **Prevent Escalation**: Address issues promptly before they can escalate into more significant problems or affect more users.

Key Strategies for Rapid Issue Resolution

1. **Automated Error Detection**:

- **Explanation**: Implement systems that automatically detect and report errors as they occur, speeding up the initial identification process.

- **Example**: Integrating monitoring tools like Sentry or New Relic that instantly alert developers to errors and provide stack traces and context for faster diagnosis.

2. **Efficient Issue Reporting Tools**:

- **Explanation**: Provide users with easy-to-use tools for reporting issues, ensuring that the development team receives all necessary information to begin troubleshooting immediately.

- **Example**: A feature within the application that allows users to report bugs directly from the interface, automatically including screenshots, error codes, and device information.

3. **Prioritization of Issues**:

- **Explanation**: Use a system to classify and prioritize issues based on their severity and impact on the user experience.

- **Example**: Developing a triage system where issues affecting critical functionalities, like data loss or system crashes, are addressed first.

4. **Knowledge Base and FAQs**:

- **Explanation**: Maintain a detailed knowledge base and frequently asked questions (FAQs) section that can help users self-resolve common issues quickly.

- **Example**: An online portal accessible through the application that provides step-by-step troubleshooting guides and solutions to common problems.

5. **Streamlined Communication Channels**:

- **Explanation**: Establish clear and direct communication channels between users and the support team to facilitate rapid issue resolution.

- **Example**: Implementing live chat support within the application that connects users directly with technical support personnel.

Example: Rapid Resolution in a Document Management System

Scenario: A software company develops a document management system used by law firms. A critical bug occurs that prevents users from saving documents, causing significant disruption.

Rapid Resolution Steps:

1. **Immediate Error Detection**: The system automatically detects the error and alerts the development team via their monitoring system.

2. **User Issue Reporting**: Affected users report the issue through the app, providing additional details and logs.

3. **Priority Handling**: Given the severity of the issue, it is immediately classified as high priority.

4. **Quick Diagnosis and Fix**: Developers quickly isolate the bug, related to a recent update, and deploy a hotfix within a few hours.

5. **Communication and Feedback**: The support team informs all affected users about the resolution, and closely monitors the situation to ensure the fix is effective.

Visual Diagram: Rapid Issue Resolution Flowchart

Flowchart:

```
+------------------------------------------------------+
|            Rapid Issue Resolution Process            |
|------------------------------------------------------|
| [Automated Error Detection & Alert]                  |
|     ↓                                                |
| [User Reports Issue with Detailed Information]       |
|     ↓                                                |
| [Immediate Issue Prioritization]                     |
|     ↓                                                |
| [Quick Diagnosis and Deployment of Fix]             |
|     ↓                                                |
| [Communication with Users & Feedback Collection]    |
+------------------------------------------------------+
```

Description:

This flowchart outlines the process of rapidly resolving issues within an application, highlighting the importance of automated systems, effective user reporting mechanisms, and prioritized handling.

Rapid issue resolution is vital for maintaining operational continuity, user satisfaction, and the overall reliability of software applications. By implementing advanced monitoring tools, efficient reporting systems, and effective communication strategies, developers can ensure that issues are addressed swiftly and efficiently, enhancing user trust and the application's stability.

<u>**Enhance User Experience**</u>:

Effective troubleshooting isn't just about fixing problems—it's also a critical process for enhancing the overall user experience. By addressing issues that disrupt user interaction and functionality, developers can create a smoother, more enjoyable user experience that fosters loyalty and promotes long-term engagement with the application.

Objectives of Enhancing User Experience Through Troubleshooting

1. **Improve Application Usability**: Address issues that hinder usability and streamline interactions to make the application more intuitive and easier to use.

2. **Reduce User Frustration**: Quickly resolve problems that cause user frustration, thereby increasing satisfaction and reducing churn.

3. **Build User Confidence**: Demonstrate a commitment to quality and responsiveness, bolstering user confidence in the product and the team behind it.

Key Strategies for Enhancing User Experience Through Troubleshooting

1. **User-Centric Issue Handling**:

- **Explanation**: Prioritize troubleshooting efforts based on the impact on the user, focusing on issues that directly affect user interactions and satisfaction.

- **Example**: Rapidly addressing a bug that causes a mobile app to crash on login, a critical touchpoint for user engagement.

2. **Proactive Problem Solving**:

- **Explanation**: Anticipate potential user issues based on patterns and feedback, and address them before they affect a broader user base.

- **Example**: Implementing performance improvements for features that users report as slow or unresponsive, even before identifying a specific bug.

3. **Clear and Empathetic Communication**:

- **Explanation**: Communicate openly with users about issues and the steps being taken to resolve them, using language that conveys understanding and empathy.

- **Example**: Sending personalized emails or in-app messages explaining the problem, what is being done to fix it, and expected timelines.

4. **Continuous Feedback Loop**:

- **Explanation**: Establish a feedback loop with users to continuously gather insights on their experience and how it can be improved.

- **Example**: Regularly updating a feedback form within the app that users can easily access to report issues or suggest improvements.

5. **Usability Testing Post-Troubleshooting**:

- **Explanation**: Conduct usability testing after troubleshooting to ensure that the solutions not only resolve the issues but also contribute to a better user experience.

- **Example**: Setting up user testing sessions to observe how changes made to solve a problem affect the way users interact with the application.

Example: Enhancing User Experience in an E-Commerce Platform

Scenario: An e-commerce platform experiences intermittent issues with its checkout process that cause delays and errors during payment, leading to user dissatisfaction and abandoned carts.

Troubleshooting Steps:

1. **Immediate User Support**: Provide immediate assistance to affected users through live chat support, helping them complete their purchases and collecting information about the issue.

2. **Rapid Issue Identification and Resolution**: Quickly identify the underlying cause of the checkout issues, which are traced to a recent update in the payment gateway integration.

3. **Enhanced Communication and Compensation**: Communicate with impacted users, explaining the issue and the steps taken to resolve it, and offer compensation such as discounts on future purchases to restore goodwill.

4. **Post-Fix Usability Testing**: After fixing the issue, conduct usability testing to ensure the checkout process is smoother than before and to identify any further improvements needed.

5. **Feedback and Monitoring**: Implement a system to monitor the checkout process for further issues and actively seek user feedback to ensure the solution's effectiveness.

Visual Diagram: Enhancing User Experience Through Troubleshooting

Flowchart:

```
+-------------------------------------------------------+
| Enhancing User Experience Through Troubleshooting |
|-------------------------------------------------------|
| [Identify and Prioritize User-Centric Issues]      |
|     ↓                                              |
| [Proactively Solve Problems & Improve Performance]|
|     ↓                                              |
| [Communicate Clearly and Empathetically]           |
|     ↓                                              |
| [Implement Continuous User Feedback Loop]          |
|     ↓                                              |
| [Conduct Usability Testing & Monitor Results]      |
+-------------------------------------------------------+
```

Description:

This flowchart details the process of enhancing the user experience through targeted troubleshooting efforts, highlighting the importance of user-centric issue resolution, proactive problem solving, and ongoing user engagement.

Enhancing the user experience through troubleshooting is a dynamic and essential strategy for maintaining the health and appeal of any software application. By focusing on user needs, communicating effectively, and continuously seeking to improve, developers can significantly enhance user satisfaction and strengthen their product's market position.

<u>Improve Product Quality</u>:

Improving product quality through troubleshooting is essential in software maintenance. This process involves identifying, analyzing, and resolving issues that can affect the performance, functionality, and user experience of an application. Effective troubleshooting not only resolves immediate problems but also contributes to the overall enhancement of the product by ensuring that it meets high standards of quality and reliability.

Objectives of Improving Product Quality Through Troubleshooting

1. **Enhance Reliability**: Identify and fix bugs to reduce crashes and other disruptive behaviors, increasing the application's stability.

2. **Optimize Performance**: Address performance bottlenecks identified during troubleshooting to enhance the speed and efficiency of the application.

3. **Refine Features**: Use insights from troubleshooting to refine and improve the functionality and usability of features.

4. **Standardize Processes**: Establish and standardize troubleshooting procedures to maintain a consistent approach to quality improvement.

Key Strategies for Enhancing Product Quality

1. **Systematic Error Logging**:

- **Explanation**: Implement comprehensive error logging to capture detailed information about issues as they occur, facilitating quicker and more effective troubleshooting.

- **Example**: Integrating an automated logging system that records user actions, system events, and error details at the time of occurrence to help developers trace the root cause of issues.

2. **Root Cause Analysis**:

- **Explanation**: Conduct thorough analyses to understand the underlying causes of issues, rather than just addressing their symptoms.

- **Example**: Using techniques like the Five Whys to drill down into an issue—such as a recurring application crash—to uncover deeper systemic problems, such as memory leaks or inefficient database queries.

3. **Iterative Testing and Refinement**:

- **Explanation**: Implement a cycle of testing, feedback, and refinement to continuously improve the application's quality.

- **Example**: After fixing a bug, conducting a series of regression and performance tests to ensure that the fix works and does not adversely affect other parts of the application.

4. **User Feedback Integration**:

- **Explanation**: Regularly incorporate user feedback into the troubleshooting process to ensure that the application meets user expectations and needs.

- **Example**: Setting up a user feedback portal that allows users to report issues and suggest improvements, which are then prioritized and addressed in product updates.

5. **Quality Assurance Best Practices**:

- **Explanation**: Adhere to industry best practices for quality assurance during the troubleshooting and update processes.

- **Example**: Implementing standardized QA procedures such as peer reviews, code audits, and pre-release beta testing phases to ensure high quality before updates are rolled out.

Example: Troubleshooting in a Business Analytics Tool

Scenario: A company develops a complex business analytics tool that has been experiencing intermittent data synchronization issues, affecting the accuracy of reports.

Troubleshooting Steps:

1. **Error Logging and Monitoring**: Enhance the application's logging capabilities to capture detailed information during data sync operations.

2. **Root Cause Analysis**: Analyze the logs to identify patterns or specific conditions under which synchronization failures occur.

3. **Implement Fixes and Optimize**: Develop fixes for the identified issues and optimize data handling procedures to prevent future occurrences.

4. **User Testing and Feedback**: Release the fixed version to a select group of users and collect detailed feedback on the changes.

5. **Final Quality Assurance**: Conduct extensive quality assurance testing before rolling out the update to all users to ensure the problem is comprehensively resolved.

Visual Diagram: Quality Improvement Through Troubleshooting

Flowchart:

```
+-------------------------------------------------+
|   Quality Improvement Through Troubleshooting    |
|-------------------------------------------------|
| [Systematic Error Logging]                      |
|     ↓                                           |
| [Conduct Root Cause Analysis]                   |
|     ↓                                           |
| [Iterative Testing & Refinement]                |
|     ↓                                           |
| [Integrate User Feedback]                       |
|     ↓                                           |
| [Implement QA Best Practices]                   |
+-------------------------------------------------+
```

Description:

This flowchart illustrates the structured approach to improving product quality through effective troubleshooting, highlighting key activities from logging errors to implementing quality assurance best practices.

Improving product quality through troubleshooting is a dynamic and essential aspect of software maintenance. By focusing on comprehensive error logging, thorough root cause analysis, iterative testing, and user feedback integration, developers can enhance the stability, performance, and usability of their applications. This systematic approach not only addresses immediate issues but also contributes to the long-term improvement and success of the product.

Key Strategies for Effective Troubleshooting

1. **Establish a Clear Reporting Mechanism**:

- **Explanation**: Provide users with an easy and clear way to report issues, including necessary details like the error messages received, actions leading up to the issue, and the environment in which the issue occurred.

- **Example**: An integrated error reporting tool within the application that automatically captures and sends error logs and user actions to the support team.

2. **Prioritize Issues Based on Severity and Impact**:

- **Explanation**: Classify issues based on their severity and the impact they have on user operations to prioritize troubleshooting efforts.

- **Example**: High-priority issues such as data loss or application crashes are addressed immediately, while lower-priority cosmetic issues are scheduled for regular maintenance updates.

3. **Use a Systematic Diagnostic Approach**:

- **Explanation**: Apply a structured approach to diagnosing issues, starting from verifying the problem, isolating the cause, and testing solutions.

- **Example**: Using the "divide and conquer" method to isolate the components involved in the issue and systematically testing each component to identify the fault.

4. **Maintain a Knowledge Base**:

- **Explanation**: Develop and continuously update a knowledge base with information on known issues, their symptoms, and steps for resolution.

- **Example**: A searchable online database accessible to both support staff and users that includes troubleshooting guides, FAQ sections, and community-driven solutions.

5. **Regular Training for Support Staff**:

- **Explanation**: Ensure that support staff are well-trained and familiar with the latest application features and common issues.

- **Example**: Regular training sessions and workshops to keep the support team updated on new functionalities and troubleshooting procedures.

Example: Troubleshooting a Customer Relationship Management (CRM) Application

Scenario: A software company has developed a CRM application that is experiencing recurring issues with its email integration feature, causing emails to fail to send.

Troubleshooting Steps:

1. **Issue Reporting**: Users report the issue through the application, which logs the error and captures details about the system state and user actions.

2. **Initial Assessment**: The support team replicates the problem based on the logs and identifies it as a priority issue due to its impact on communications.

3. **Diagnosis and Isolation**: The team tests the email module in isolation and discovers a compatibility issue with the latest email server update.

4. **Resolution and Testing**: The development team implements a fix to ensure compatibility with the email server, which is then tested internally before being rolled out.

5. **Feedback and Monitoring**: After the fix is deployed, the support team monitors the situation and follows up with users to ensure the resolution is effective.

Visual Diagram: Troubleshooting Process Flowchart

Flowchart:

```
+----------------------------------------------------+
|            Troubleshooting Process Flow            |
|----------------------------------------------------|
| [Issue Reporting by Users]                         |
|    ↓                                               |
| [Initial Assessment and Priority Setting]          |
|    ↓                                               |
| [Diagnosis and Isolation of Issue]                 |
|    ↓                                               |
| [Development of Fix and Internal Testing]          |
|    ↓                                               |
| [Deployment of Solution and User Feedback]         |
+----------------------------------------------------+
```

Description:

This flowchart outlines a structured process for troubleshooting issues within an application, from initial reporting to resolution and user feedback.

Effective troubleshooting is essential for maintaining the health and functionality of any software application. By establishing clear mechanisms for issue reporting, prioritizing problems, employing systematic diagnostic methods, maintaining a comprehensive knowledge base, and ensuring that support staff are well-trained, developers can quickly and efficiently resolve issues, thereby improving the user experience and enhancing the overall product quality.

Gathering User Feedback:

Gathering user feedback is an essential part of maintaining and updating software applications. This process involves actively collecting insights from users about their experiences, preferences, and issues encountered while using the application. By systematically integrating this feedback into the development process, teams can make informed improvements that enhance functionality, usability, and user satisfaction.

Objectives of Gathering User Feedback

<u>Understand User Needs</u>:

Understanding user needs is a fundamental objective when gathering feedback during the maintenance and updating of software applications. This process involves actively listening to users to grasp their requirements, preferences, and the challenges they face while using the application. By accurately identifying these needs, developers can tailor updates and improvements to enhance user satisfaction and ensure the application serves its intended purpose effectively.

Objectives of Understanding User Needs

1. **Tailor Features to User Requirements**: Customize the application's features to better align with what users actually need, rather than what developers assume they need.

2. **Prioritize Development Efforts**: Focus development resources on areas that will bring the most value to users, improving efficiency and effectiveness.

3. **Enhance User Engagement**: Make the application more engaging by ensuring it responds directly to user feedback and adapts to their changing requirements.

4. **Increase User Satisfaction**: Improve overall user satisfaction by showing users that their input directly influences the application's development.

Key Strategies for Understanding User Needs

1. **Segmented User Surveys:**

- **Explanation**: Conduct targeted surveys that reach different segments of the user base to understand specific needs and preferences.

- **Example**: Deploying separate surveys to new users, power users, and sporadic users to capture the full range of experiences and expectations.

2. **User Behavior Analytics**:

- **Explanation**: Utilize tools to analyze how users interact with the application, identifying which features are used most and which may be causing frustration.

- **Example**: Implementing analytics to track click-through rates, feature usage patterns, and dropout rates on complex workflows within the application.

3. **Direct User Interviews**:

- **Explanation**: Engage with users directly through interviews to dive deep into their experiences, gaining insights that are not always visible through quantitative data.

- **Example**: Conducting monthly video calls with a rotating group of users to discuss their ongoing experiences and gather qualitative feedback.

4. **Feedback Widgets within the Application**:

- **Explanation**: Integrate feedback mechanisms directly into the application, making it easy for users to provide feedback at the moment of interaction.

- **Example**: Embedding a simple "Rate this feature" widget with an optional comment box on key features within the application.

5. **Community Forums and User Groups**:

- **Explanation**: Foster active user communities where users can discuss their experiences, offer solutions, and provide feedback in a more informal setting.

- **Example**: Setting up dedicated forums or user groups on platforms like Discord or LinkedIn where users can share tips, tricks, and feedback.

Example: Enhancing a Photo Editing Software

Scenario: A software company develops a photo editing tool and wants to better understand the needs of amateur photographers to make the tool more user-friendly.

Steps to Understand User Needs:

1. **Segmented Surveys**: Send out surveys specifically designed for amateur photographers who use the application, focusing on their workflows and pain points.

2. **Behavioral Analytics**: Analyze usage data to see which editing features are most used by amateurs versus professional photographers.

3. **Direct Interviews**: Invite amateur photographers to participate in detailed interviews to discuss what features they find most useful and what additional tools they desire.

4. **Community Engagement**: Create a community forum for amateur photographers to share their work, discuss features, and provide feedback on the tool.

5. **Iterative Updates**: Based on the collected data and feedback, iteratively update the software to refine existing tools, add new features requested by users, and improve the overall ease of use.

Identify Pain Points:

In the context of software maintenance and updates, identifying pain points through user feedback is crucial. Pain points are specific problems that users encounter while interacting with an application, which can range from minor usability issues to major functional obstacles. Understanding these issues allows development teams to prioritize fixes and enhancements that directly improve user experience and application performance.

Objectives of Identifying Pain Points

1. **Enhance User Satisfaction**: Directly address the issues that frustrate users or hinder their productivity, thereby improving their overall satisfaction with the application.

2. **Increase Adoption and Retention**: By resolving pain points, make the application more attractive to new users and increase the likelihood of existing users continuing to use the software.

3. **Streamline User Interactions**: Remove obstacles and inefficiencies in the application's workflow, making interactions more intuitive and less time-consuming.

4. **Boost Application Performance**: Improve the application's performance by fixing issues that cause slowdowns, crashes, or other disruptions.

Key Strategies for Identifying Pain Points

1. **In-App Feedback Tools:**

- **Explanation**: Incorporate tools within the application that allow users to easily report issues as they occur.

- **Example**: A feedback button or shortcut that users can access to quickly describe a problem or frustration, possibly accompanied by automatic screenshots or logs of recent activity.

2. **User Surveys:**

- **Explanation**: Regularly conduct surveys that ask targeted questions about users' experiences and specifically probe for areas of dissatisfaction.

- **Example**: Surveys that include questions like "What is the most frustrating part of using the application?" or "Which tasks take longer than you expect?"

3. **Usability Testing Sessions:**

- **Explanation**: Organize sessions where users perform typical tasks while observers (either in-person or remotely) note where they encounter difficulties or express frustration.

- **Example**: Setting up controlled testing environments where users are asked to complete specific workflows, while moderators record where users struggle or ask for help.

4. **Analytics and Log Analysis:**

- **Explanation**: Use analytical tools to track where users frequently abandon tasks, repeat actions unnecessarily, or generate error logs.

- **Example**: Analyzing usage data to identify features with high dropout rates or functions that trigger error reports more than others.

5. **Social Media and Forum Monitoring:**

- **Explanation**: Monitor social media platforms and user forums for discussions about the application, paying special attention to common complaints or issues users post about.

- **Example**: Regularly scanning Twitter, Reddit, and specialized tech forums where users might discuss their challenges and frustrations with the application.

Example: Streamlining a Project Management Tool

Scenario: A project management software company notices from user feedback that clients find the task assignment process cumbersome and error-prone.

Steps to Identify and Resolve Pain Points:

1. **Feedback Collection**: Utilize in-app feedback tools to gather specific complaints about the task assignment feature.

2. **Detailed Surveys**: Send out surveys asking for detailed feedback on the task management process, seeking clarity on common pain points.

3. **Observational Usability Testing**: Conduct usability testing sessions focused on the task management features to observe difficulties users face in real-time.

4. **Data Analysis**: Review product analytics to identify patterns or trends in how users interact with the task assignment features, particularly looking for high rates of modifications or corrections.

5. **Iterative Improvements**: Based on findings, redesign the task assignment interface to simplify the process, and then roll out changes in a controlled beta to measure impact before a full release.

Validate New Features:

Validating new features through user feedback is a crucial part of the software development cycle, especially when maintaining and updating applications. This process involves assessing how new functionalities perform in real-world scenarios, ensuring they meet user expectations, and align with their needs. Effective validation can significantly enhance product adoption and user satisfaction.

Objectives of Validating New Features

1. **Ensure Relevance**: Confirm that new features address actual user needs and fit into their workflows.

2. **Assess Usability**: Evaluate whether the features are intuitive and easy to use from the user's perspective.

3. **Identify Improvements**: Gather insights that could lead to refinements and enhancements before wider release.

4. **Mitigate Risk**: Reduce the risk of feature failure by catching potential issues early in the development process.

Key Strategies for Validating New Features

1. **Beta Testing Programs**:

- **Explanation**: Invite a select group of users to try out new features before a full rollout. This group should represent a cross-section of your user base.

- **Example**: Launching a beta version of a new project management tool within the application to existing users who volunteer for early access and are likely to provide constructive feedback.

2. **A/B Testing**:

- **Explanation**: Compare two versions of a feature to see which one performs better in terms of user engagement and satisfaction.

- **Example**: For a new user dashboard design, randomly show half of the users the new dashboard and the other half the old one, and analyze which version has better usability metrics.

3. **Feedback Surveys Post-Feature Release**:

- **Explanation**: Conduct surveys specifically designed to gather feedback on new features after users have had a chance to use them.

- **Example**: Sending out a survey asking targeted questions about the user experience with the new dashboard, including ease of use, problems encountered, and overall satisfaction.

4. **Usage Analytics**:

- **Explanation**: Utilize software analytics to track how often and how effectively the new features are being used.

- **Example**: Monitoring backend data to see how frequently users engage with the new feature and tracking any common drop-off points that might indicate usability issues.

5. **In-App Feedback Tools**:

- **Explanation**: Implement tools that allow users to easily provide feedback while using the new features, without needing to exit the application.

- **Example**: Adding a "Feedback" button within the new feature that users can click to report bugs, suggest improvements, or offer other types of feedback directly.

Example: Introducing a Collaborative Editing Feature in a Document Management System

Scenario: A software company introduces a collaborative editing feature to its document management system, allowing multiple users to edit documents simultaneously.

Steps to Validate the Feature:

1. **Beta Testing**: The feature is rolled out to a group of key enterprise customers who have requested this functionality in the past.

2. **Feedback Collection**: After a month of usage, detailed feedback is collected through in-app surveys focusing on the functionality and usability of the feature.

3. **Performance Monitoring**: Analytics are used to monitor how the feature is being used, identifying any performance issues or bugs.

4. **Iterative Improvements**: Based on the feedback and analytics, the feature is refined to fix reported bugs and improve the interface.

5. **Full Rollout**: After multiple iterations and positive validation from the initial user group, the feature is fully rolled out to all users.

Drive Product Development:

Incorporating user feedback into the product development cycle is vital for aligning software updates and enhancements with actual user needs and market demands. This approach ensures that the application evolves in a direction that enhances its value to users, addresses their challenges, and integrates innovative solutions that improve their experience.

Objectives of Driving Product Development Through User Feedback

1. **Align Features with User Needs**: Ensure that new features and improvements directly address the needs and preferences of users.

2. **Prioritize Development Resources**: Efficiently allocate development resources to areas that will provide the most significant benefit to users.

3. **Innovate Responsively**: Adapt and innovate based on real-time insights from users, staying ahead of market trends and competitive pressures.

4. **Increase Market Relevance**: Continuously refine the application to meet changing market conditions and user expectations, maintaining its relevance and appeal.

Key Strategies for Driving Product Development Through User Feedback

1. **Continuous Feedback Collection**:

- **Explanation**: Implement ongoing mechanisms to collect feedback, ensuring a steady stream of insights into user needs and preferences.

- **Example**: Setting up automated in-app surveys that trigger based on specific user interactions, and maintaining open channels like feedback forms and support emails.

2. **Feature Voting Systems**:

- **Explanation**: Allow users to vote on potential new features or improvements, helping to prioritize development based on user interest.

- **Example**: An online portal where users can submit feature ideas and vote on existing proposals, with the development team committing to review the most popular suggestions.

3. **Data-Driven Decision Making**:

- **Explanation**: Utilize analytics to support feedback, analyzing how users interact with the application to identify patterns and trends that can inform development.

- **Example**: Using advanced analytics tools to track feature usage rates, user engagement metrics, and dropout points to identify areas for improvement.

4. **User-Centric Design Workshops**:

- **Explanation**: Conduct workshops that include both users and developers, focusing on co-creating solutions to address user-identified problems and needs.

- **Example**: Regularly scheduled workshops where users and developers brainstorm improvements and prototype new features together in a collaborative environment.

5. **Iterative Development and Testing**:

- **Explanation**: Employ an agile development methodology that incorporates user feedback at every stage, allowing for rapid iteration and adaptation of features before final rollout.

- **Example**: Using sprint-based development cycles where user feedback from the previous release informs the priorities and tasks of the upcoming sprint.

Example: Enhancing a Mobile Health App

Scenario: A development team for a mobile health application wants to enhance its functionality to better support user wellness goals based on recent user feedback.

Product Development Steps:

1. **Feedback Collection**: Utilize in-app prompts to gather feedback from users about desired features, such as meal tracking or meditation reminders.

2. **Feature Prioritization**: Implement a feature voting system on the community forum to determine which new features users most desire.

3. **Prototyping New Features**: Conduct design workshops with selected users to prototype the top-voted features, such as an integrated diet planner.

4. **Agile Development Cycles**: Develop and test the new features in short sprints, releasing early versions to beta testers for rapid feedback and iteration.

5. **Full Deployment**: Once features are refined and well-received in testing, roll them out to the full user base, continuing to monitor usage and satisfaction.

Key Strategies for Effective Feedback Gathering

1. **Incorporate Feedback Mechanisms**:

- **Explanation**: Embed various feedback mechanisms within the application to facilitate easy feedback submission.

- **Example**: Implement features like in-app surveys, feedback buttons, and popup questionnaires that prompt users to provide feedback at different stages of their interaction with the application.

2. **Utilize Social Media and Online Forums**:

- **Explanation**: Engage with users on social media platforms and online forums where they are already discussing the product.

- **Example**: Monitor and participate in discussions on platforms like Twitter, Reddit, and specialized forums related to the software's niche to gather informal feedback and user sentiments.

3. **Conduct User Interviews and Focus Groups**:

- **Explanation**: Organize in-depth sessions with users to collect detailed feedback and explore new ideas or features.

- **Example**: Schedule regular video calls or in-person meetings with a diverse group of users to discuss their experiences and gather qualitative insights.

4. **Analyze Usage Data**:

- **Explanation**: Collect and analyze data on how users interact with the application to identify usage patterns and potential areas for improvement.

- **Example**: Use analytics tools to track which features are most and least used, how users navigate through the application, and where they encounter issues.

5. **Regularly Update and Iterate**:

- **Explanation**: Establish a continuous improvement cycle based on user feedback to regularly update the application and address the needs identified.

- **Example**: Implement a development cycle that incorporates feedback into every release, ensuring that the application evolves in response to user needs.

Example: Enhancing a Learning Management System (LMS)

Scenario: A company has developed an LMS used by educational institutions. Feedback indicates that users find the course creation process complex and cumbersome.

Improvement Steps:

1. **Feedback Collection**: Deploy an in-app survey targeting educators to gather detailed feedback on their experiences with the course creation features.

2. **Data Analysis**: Analyze the feedback to identify common themes and specific functionalities that cause user difficulties.

3. **Feature Redesign**: Based on the analysis, redesign the course creation workflow to be more intuitive and user-friendly.

4. **User Testing**: Invite a group of educators to test the new design and provide feedback on its effectiveness.

5. **Implementation and Monitoring**: Roll out the improved feature to all users and continue to monitor its impact through user feedback and usage analytics.

Visual Diagram: Feedback Gathering and Improvement Cycle

Flowchart:

```
+--------------------------------------------------------+
|   Feedback Gathering and Improvement Cycle       |
|--------------------------------------------------------|
| [Incorporate Feedback Mechanisms]                |
|     ↓                                            |
| [Collect Feedback via Social Media & Forums]     |
|     ↓                                            |
| [Conduct User Interviews & Focus Groups]         |
|     ↓                                            |
| [Analyze Usage Data & Feedback]                  |
|     ↓                                            |
| [Update & Iterate Based on Feedback]             |
+--------------------------------------------------------+
```

Description:

This flowchart outlines the structured process of gathering user feedback and integrating it into product improvements, highlighting the cyclic nature of feedback and updates.

Gathering user feedback is vital for the continuous improvement of any application. By implementing diverse feedback mechanisms, engaging with users across different platforms, and integrating insights into development processes, teams can ensure their application meets and exceeds user expectations, thereby fostering loyalty and driving long-term success.

Conclusion

Regular maintenance and timely updates are essential to the lifecycle of any software application. By implementing structured update processes, engaging with users, and providing necessary support, developers can ensure their applications remain secure, functional, and aligned with user needs. This approach not only improves the application but also enhances user satisfaction and trust in the product.

Part V: Case Studies and Real-World Applications

Chapter 13 - Case Studies

Case studies are an invaluable resource in software development, providing detailed insights into the practical applications, challenges, and successes of software projects. They serve as an educational tool and a source of inspiration, illustrating how theoretical concepts are applied in real-world scenarios. By examining case studies, developers, stakeholders, and users can better understand the potential impact of software solutions and learn from the experiences of others.

Objectives of Using Case Studies

1. **Showcase Success Stories**: Highlight successful implementations and the specific benefits achieved through software solutions.

2. **Analyze Challenges and Solutions**: Provide an in-depth look at the challenges faced during development and how they were overcome.

3. **Drive Innovation and Improvement**: Encourage innovation by sharing insights and lessons learned that can be applied to future projects.

4. **Enhance Credibility and Trust**: Build credibility and trust with potential clients and partners by demonstrating proven capabilities and results.

Key Elements of Effective Case Studies

1. **Background Information**:

   - **Explanation**: Set the stage by providing context about the project, including the client's industry, initial challenges, and project goals.

   - **Example**: A case study on a custom CRM software developed for a retail chain, detailing the client's need for better customer data management and personalized marketing.

2. **Solution Overview**:

- **Explanation**: Describe the solution that was implemented, focusing on specific technologies, methodologies, and innovative approaches used.

- **Example**: Explaining the development of the CRM system using cloud-based technologies, integration of AI for data analytics, and mobile app development for on-the-go access by sales personnel.

3. **Challenges and Resolutions**:

   - **Explanation**: Discuss any significant challenges that arose during the project and how they were resolved.

   - **Example**: Detailing challenges such as data migration issues, user adoption hurdles, and custom feature requests, along with strategies used to address them.

4. **Results and Impact**:

   - **Explanation**: Highlight the outcomes of the project, including both qualitative and quantitative results.

   - **Example**: Showcasing improvements in customer retention rates, increased sales, enhanced employee productivity, and feedback from the client and end-users.

5. **Lessons Learned**:

   - **Explanation**: Reflect on the project to extract valuable lessons that can inform future projects.

   - **Example**: Insights gained regarding best practices for user training, the importance of early and continuous stakeholder engagement, and tips for effective project management.

Example Case Study: Development of a Health Tracking Application

Scenario: A software company was tasked with developing a health tracking application for a healthcare provider aiming to improve patient engagement and health monitoring.

Structure of the Case Study:

- **Background**: The healthcare provider's need for digital tools to enhance patient engagement and streamline health data tracking.

- **Solution**: A mobile application that allows patients to monitor various health metrics, set reminders for medication, and communicate directly with healthcare providers.

- **Challenges**: Integrating real-time health data from various medical devices, ensuring data privacy and security, and fostering user adoption among a predominantly elderly patient base.

- **Results**: Significant improvements in patient engagement metrics, a reduction in missed appointments, and positive feedback from patients and medical staff.

- **Lessons Learned**: The importance of involving end-users in the design process, challenges in managing data security, and strategies for effective cross-platform integration.

Real-World Applications of Access Databases:

Microsoft Access is a powerful tool for creating and managing databases, and its real-world applications are diverse, ranging from small businesses to large organizations. These case studies illustrate how different sectors utilize Access databases to streamline operations, enhance data management, and improve decision-making processes.

Objectives of Using Access Databases in Real-World Applications

1. **Efficient Data Management**: Leverage Access to organize and manage data efficiently, making it easier to store, retrieve, and use information.

2. **Cost-Effective Solutions**: Utilize Access as a cost-effective solution for database management, especially suitable for small to medium-sized enterprises.

3. **Customizable Functionality**: Take advantage of the customizable nature of Access to tailor database solutions to specific business needs.

4. **Integration Capabilities**: Use Access's ability to integrate with other Microsoft products and various data sources to enhance functionality and user experience.

Key Real-World Applications

1. **Small Business Inventory Management:**

- **Example**: A small retail business uses an Access database to manage its inventory, track sales, and reorder products. The database helps the business monitor sales trends, manage stock levels, and generate reports for financial analysis.

- **Impact**: Improved inventory accuracy, reduced overstock, and enhanced ability to respond to sales trends.

2. **Educational Institutions: Student and Course Management**:

- **Example**: A community college utilizes an Access database to manage student records, course registrations, and grading systems. The system allows for easy access to student performance and administrative reporting.

- **Impact**: Streamlined student management processes, enhanced data accuracy, and simplified access to educational insights for teachers and administrators.

3. **Non-Profit Organization Donor Management**:

- **Example**: A non-profit organization implements an Access database to track donor contributions, manage fundraising events, and maintain contact information. This system simplifies the process of generating donor reports and analyzing fundraising efforts.

- **Impact**: Increased efficiency in managing donor relationships, improved fundraising outcomes, and enhanced reporting capabilities for compliance and transparency.

4. **Healthcare Patient Records Management**:

- **Example**: A small clinic uses an Access database to keep detailed records of patient visits, treatments, and medical histories. The system integrates with billing and allows the clinic to maintain secure, easily accessible patient records.

- **Impact**: Improved patient care through better data management, reduced paperwork, and quicker access to patient histories.

5. **Manufacturing Process Tracking**:

- **Example**: A manufacturing company uses Access to track production processes, inventory of raw materials, and maintenance schedules. The database facilitates real-time monitoring of production lines and maintenance alerts.

- **Impact**: Enhanced production efficiency, reduced downtime, and better resource management.

Lessons Learned from Successful Access Projects:

Learning from successful Microsoft Access projects is invaluable for developers and organizations aiming to optimize their database solutions. By analyzing what has worked well in various contexts, teams can replicate success and avoid common pitfalls. This section delves into the critical lessons gleaned from various successful Access projects across different industries and applications.

Objectives of Analyzing Lessons from Access Projects

1. **Enhance Project Efficiency**: Understand strategies that lead to time and cost savings during the project lifecycle.

2. **Improve Design and Functionality**: Identify best practices in database design and user interface to enhance functionality and user experience.

3. **Strengthen Data Integrity and Security**: Learn methods to ensure data integrity and secure sensitive information effectively.

4. **Facilitate User Adoption and Training**: Recognize techniques that aid in smoother user adoption and effective training programs.

Key Lessons Learned from Successful Access Projects

1. **Thorough Planning and Requirements Gathering**:

   - **Explanation**: The foundation of a successful Access project lies in thoroughly understanding the user needs and business processes before beginning the design.

   - **Example**: A manufacturing company spent considerable time upfront gathering detailed requirements from all end-users, which led to a highly customized and well-received inventory management system.

2. **Scalability and Future-Proofing**:

   - **Explanation**: Designing the database with scalability in mind ensures that the system can handle increased data volume and user load without performance degradation.

- **Example**: A retail chain developed their Access database to accommodate future expansions, including new store locations and increased product lines, avoiding costly overhauls later.

3. **Simplifying User Interface**:

   - **Explanation**: A simple, intuitive user interface enhances user adoption and reduces training time.

   - **Example**: A healthcare provider redesigned their patient records system with a focus on minimizing screen transitions and input steps, significantly reducing user errors and increasing staff satisfaction.

4. **Robust Testing and Validation**:

   - **Explanation**: Rigorous testing, including user acceptance testing, is critical to ensure the system meets all specified requirements and is free of bugs.

   - **Example**: A financial services firm implemented a multi-stage testing protocol that involved end-users at every phase to capture and rectify issues before full-scale deployment.

5. **Regular Maintenance and Updates**:

   - **Explanation**: Establishing a routine for regular maintenance and updates ensures the longevity and relevance of the database system.

   - **Example**: An educational institution set up a semi-annual review of their student management system to update features, apply patches, and make improvements based on feedback.

6. **Effective Training and Support**:

   - **Explanation**: Providing comprehensive training and ongoing support is essential for ensuring users are comfortable and proficient with the system.

   - **Example**: A corporate training company developed a series of tutorial videos and quick-reference guides to support users transitioning to a new project tracking system.

Visual Diagram: Implementing Lessons from Successful Projects

Flowchart:

```
+----------------------------------------------------+
| Implementing Lessons from Successful Projects      |
|----------------------------------------------------|
| [Plan and Gather Requirements]                     |
|      ↓                                             |
| [Design for Scalability and Future Needs]          |
|      ↓                                             |
| [Develop Intuitive User Interfaces]                |
|      ↓                                             |
| [Conduct Comprehensive Testing]                    |
|      ↓                                             |
| [Schedule Regular Maintenance]                     |
|      ↓                                             |
| [Provide Effective Training and Support]           |
+----------------------------------------------------+
```

Description:

This flowchart outlines the process of implementing lessons learned from successful Access projects, emphasizing a structured approach from planning to support.

The lessons learned from successful Microsoft Access projects provide valuable insights that can significantly improve the success rate of future projects. By understanding and implementing these lessons, organizations can enhance the effectiveness, usability, and longevity of their Access databases, ensuring they continue to meet evolving business needs and user expectations effectively.

Conclusion

Case studies are a powerful tool in software development, offering tangible examples of how software projects are conceived, implemented, and refined. They not only highlight successes but also openly discuss challenges, providing a holistic view that benefits developers, clients, and the industry at large. Through detailed documentation and analysis, case studies help pave the way for better practices, innovative solutions, and improved project outcomes.

Chapter 14 - Appendix

Glossary of terms:

In software development and database management, understanding specific terminology is crucial for professionals to communicate effectively and grasp the technical aspects of projects and documentation. This appendix provides a glossary of key terms frequently used in the context of database development, particularly with Microsoft Access, enhancing clarity and aiding in the comprehension of related materials.

Objectives of the Glossary

1. **Standardize Terminology**: Ensure consistent use of terms across documents and communications to prevent misunderstandings.

2. **Enhance Understanding**: Help new users, stakeholders, and non-technical readers understand technical content more easily.

3. **Support Training and Learning**: Serve as a learning tool for training new employees or educating clients about the technical aspects of a project.

Key Terms and Definitions

- **Database**: A structured set of data held in a computer, especially one that is accessible in various ways.

- **Microsoft Access**: A database management system from Microsoft that combines the relational Microsoft Jet Database Engine with a graphical user interface and software-development tools.

- **Query**: A request for data or information from a database table or combination of tables. This data may be generated as results returned by Structured Query Language (SQL).

- **Form**: In database context, a form is a window or screen that contains numerous fields, or spaces to enter data. Forms are used to enter, modify, and view records.

- **Report**: A formatted and organized presentation of data, extracted from a database and presented in a readable format.

- **Macro**: A macro in Microsoft Access is a tool that allows you to automate tasks and add functionality to your forms, reports, and controls.

- **Module**: A collection of declarations, statements, and procedures that are stored together as a unit. Modules can contain executable code and declarations of variables, constants, and other procedure declarations.

- **Primary Key**: A field in a table which uniquely identifies each row/record in that database table.

- **Foreign Key**: A field (or collection of fields) in one table that uniquely identifies a row of another table or the same table. In simpler terms, the foreign key is defined in a second table, but it refers to the primary key or a unique key in the first table.

- **Normalization**: The process of organizing data in a database. This includes creating tables and establishing relationships between those tables according to rules designed both to protect the data and to make the database more flexible by eliminating redundancy and inconsistent dependency.

- **SQL (Structured Query Language)**: A standard programming language specifically designed for managing data held in a relational database management system, or for stream processing in a relational data stream management system.

Example Use Case in a Glossary Entry

Term: Relational Database

- **Definition**: A database structured to recognize relations among stored items of information according to a relational model of data. Common relational database management systems (RDBMS) include Microsoft Access, SQL Server, and Oracle.

- **Example**: In a retail business management system, a relational database could link data from the inventory, sales, and employee information, allowing comprehensive data analysis and reporting.

The glossary of terms serves as an essential resource for anyone involved in database projects, particularly those new to Microsoft Access or database management in general. By defining these terms clearly, the glossary not only aids in enhancing communication and understanding but also supports educational initiatives and ensures consistency across project documentation and development efforts.

Further Resources for Learning:

In the ever-evolving field of software development and database management, continuous learning is crucial. This appendix provides a curated list of resources for individuals seeking to expand their knowledge and skills in areas related to Microsoft Access, database design, and general software development. These resources are intended to support a wide range of learners, from beginners to advanced users.

Objectives of Providing Learning Resources

1. **Enhance Skill Development**: Equip learners with the tools and knowledge necessary to advance their technical skills and professional competencies.

2. **Support Continuous Education**: Provide avenues for ongoing learning to help professionals keep up with new technologies and methodologies.

3. **Encourage Self-Paced Learning**: Offer resources that allow individuals to learn at their own pace, adapting their learning to fit their schedules and needs.

4. **Foster Professional Growth**: Aid in the professional growth of learners by providing access to a variety of educational materials and community resources.

Categories of Learning Resources

1. **Online Courses**:

   - **Platforms**: Coursera, Udemy, LinkedIn Learning, and Khan Academy.

   - **Examples**: Courses like "Mastering Microsoft Access" on Udemy or "Database Management Essentials" on Coursera provide structured learning paths from beginner to advanced levels.

2. **Books and eBooks**:

   - **Recommendations**: "Access 2019 Bible" by Michael Alexander and Richard Kusleika, "Microsoft Access 2019 Programming by Example" by Julitta Korol.

   - **Use**: These books serve as comprehensive guides for both fundamental concepts and advanced techniques in Microsoft Access.

3. **Video Tutorials**:

   - **Platforms**: YouTube, Vimeo, and specialized educational websites like Lynda.com.

   - **Examples**: Video series such as "Access Database Design & Programming" which offer visual and practical examples to enhance understanding.

4. **Forums and Community Groups**:

   - **Recommendations**: Microsoft Access forums on Microsoft Tech Community, Stack Overflow, and Access-programmers.co.uk.

   - **Use**: These forums are invaluable for troubleshooting, advice, and sharing experiences with other community members.

5. **Documentation and Online Manuals**:

   - **Sources**: Official Microsoft Access documentation, W3Schools for SQL, and database theory portals.

   - **Examples**: Microsoft's own resources are particularly useful for in-depth technical details and updates on new features.

6. **Workshops and Webinars**:

   - **Opportunities**: Look for workshops and webinars hosted by tech companies, universities, and professional training organizations.

   - **Benefits**: These live sessions often include Q&A opportunities and can provide the latest industry insights and networking opportunities.

7. **Interactive Learning Tools**:

- **Tools**: Websites like Codecademy and FreeCodeCamp where you can practice SQL and database design interactively.

- **Advantages**: Interactive tools offer hands-on experience and immediate feedback, which is beneficial for mastering practical skills.

Example Use Case in Learning Resources

Scenario: A database administrator looking to upgrade their skills in database security.

- **Recommended Path**: Start with an online course in database security on Coursera, followed by joining a security-focused webinar series, and participate in relevant discussions in security forums.

Conclusion:

The wealth of resources available for learning database management and software development ensures that individuals can find the tools and information they need to succeed. By carefully selecting appropriate materials and actively engaging in the learning process, professionals can continuously develop their skills and adapt to the changing technological landscape.